LINCOLN CHRISTIAN COLLEGE

P9-DFN-151

Case Studies in Missions

Case Studies in Missions

Paul G. and Frances F. Hiebert

BAKER BOOK HOUSE
Grand Rapids, Michigan 49516

No case studies in this book may be copied for class use unless a fee is sent to the publisher. The fee per student per case is $.35. When submitting payment, please list the cases copied and the number of students in the class. Send to

Baker Book House
P.O. Box 6287
Grand Rapids, MI 49516

Copyright 1987 by
Baker Book House

ISBN: 0-8010-4308-5

Library of Congress
Catalog Card Number: 87-70401

Printed in the United States of America

To **Menno** and **Emma Grace Flaming,**
Fran's parents
They helped guide us in the love
and fear of the Lord,
and taught us the importance
of Christian faithfulness.

Contents

Part 3: **Traditional Customs**   81

Part 4: **Sickness and Death**   113

Part 5: **Finances and Bribery**   133

Part 6: **Conversion and Theology**   149

Part 7: **Walls That Divide People**   167

Part 8: **Church-Mission Relationships**   **181**

Part 9: **Loyalty to Church and State**   **209**

Part 10: **Everyday Problems of Missionary Life**   **233**

Preface

Much has been written about Christian missions in recent years. A great deal of the writing has been theoretical. This provides us with extensive discussions of the theology, history, and anthropology of missions. It wrestles with the problems of colonialism, contextualization, and religious pluralism.

Such general discussions are essential, for they provide us with the conceptual frameworks within which we do missions. But they often leave us wondering how we should apply their dictums to everyday life. Are missionaries neocolonialists when they assume positions of leadership in other lands, or when they hire servants to help in the home? Are national leaders selling out their own culture when they ask expatriate missionaries for advice? Is burning of incense at Christian funerals an inappropriate form of contextualization? May Christians beat drums or dance during their worship services? Missionaries now come from churches around the world—not only from the West—and they face many such cross-cultural situations. Like it or not, we live our lives on this level of making decisions in the context of specific historical and cultural situations. And many of our important decisions in this missionary context are made, not after long, careful deliberation, but of necessity on the spur of the moment when action cannot be delayed, or by a series of small decisions, no one of which seems important by itself.

Furthermore, few writers on missions deal with the many ordinary problems of daily living that take so much of the missionaries' time. What kind of houses should they live in? Should they own a car? What kind of clothes should they wear? Where should their children go to school? Should they be paid in local currencies? Should they give tips to government officials, or are these bribes? These are pressing issues that missionaries cannot avoid, and the way they are resolved will have a ripple effect over the whole of their ministries.

In seeking ways to bridge the gap between theory and practice, and to deal with everyday problems, the Harvard Business and Law School pioneered work in the case-study method for those professions and established the Case Study Institute. The success of this method in helping people to deal with real-life situations led the Association of Theological Schools to advocate its use in seminaries. It was at one of the Summer Case Method Institutes sponsored by the ATS that both of us were introduced to the uses of cases as a teaching method. Earlier, when we were missionaries in India, Paul had used the case-research method as developed by E. A. Hoebel and K. N. Llewellyn at the University of Oklahoma. Now we began to see the importance of cases as a classroom tool.

Over the past seven years, we collected cases around the world. Many were written by missionaries and church leaders from different countries, who were studying at the School of World Mission, Fuller Theological Seminary. Others were contributed by students at the Union Biblical Seminary, Pune, India. Still others came from the Haggai Institute in Singapore or from those who ministered in other parts of the world. It is to these writers—both those whose cases have been included and those whose cases were omitted to avoid repetition—that we want to extend our heartfelt thanks. They have made us aware of the tremendous range of problems people face in cross-cultural ministries, and they have freely granted us time to explore details further with them.

We would also like to thank the case writers for the permission they gave us to edit and publish their cases to fit the format recommended by the Case Study Institute. Much of this editing was done by Frances. Names and places have been changed in order to protect those involved. While these cases are based on historical events, their purpose is not to examine specific events, but to deal with problems commonly faced by cross-cultural missionaries and national church leaders in their ministries.

The writers and actors in the cases represent different theological and ethical positions. These do not always reflect our own positions. We present them as they were given to us, as they are representative of the different positions one finds in the church around the world. Because no generally accepted alternative has been found, we continue the traditional use of the male pronoun for God, although we believe that God is neither male or female.

There are many who helped make this project possible to whom we would like to express our appreciation. In a special way we would like to thank the trustees of Fuller Theological Seminary, who granted Paul a sabbatical during which much of the work was completed. Our dear friends Jack Rogers and the late Glenn Barker introduced us to the Case Method Institute, and Jack helped make it possible for Fran to participate. Peter Chao and Mark Chan of Eagles Evangelism in Singapore lent us their computer at a crucial stage in the preparation of the manuscript. Above all, we want to give thanks to God for the privilege of learning from so many of God's people working around the world.

We have a twofold purpose in presenting these cases. First, we hope that local churches will use them in order to learn more about the missionary task. As sending churches—whether in North America, Korea, India, or Africa—become more informed, they can pray and support more meaningfully the task of which they are an integral part.

Second, we believe that these cases can help prepare missionaries and candidates for their ministries. Cases by themselves do not provide an adequate training for missions. Added to biblical and missiological instruction, however, cases can help prepare missionaries for decisions they will face on the field.

We pray that these cases, by informing churches about the missionary task and making the ministries of missionaries and church leaders more effective, may bring glory to Jesus Christ.

Paul and Frances Hiebert
Pasadena, October 1986.

Introduction
Using Case Studies in Missions

There is a wide gulf between the world of biblical times and our modern environment—a gulf that needs to be bridged if we want to make the biblical message relevant to contemporary lives. The Bible is clear about many things: the need for forgiveness and salvation, for love and discipleship, and for living holy lives in a sinful world. But what does this mean in an age of television, genetic engineering, business on Sunday, nuclear weapons, and sexual freedom? What does it mean for Christians living in a world of poverty and injustice? What does it mean in a pluralistic city in which people of many religions must live together side by side? We need a hermeneutical method that can help our understanding of what the Scriptures are saying to us today.

Furthermore, we ourselves live in widely varying cultural settings. Missions, anthropology, the ease of travel, and international communications are making us aware of how different are our perceptions of reality. But what does it mean to make the gospel relevant in these different cultural contexts? What does Scripture have to say to Americans divided by class and plagued by violence and drugs? And what does it mean to be a Christian in an African village where men often have several wives, or in an Indian village divided by a caste system deeply rooted in Hinduism?

Too often we judge Christians in other societies by our own cultural norms. American Christians who avoid alcoholic beverages are shocked that their European brothers and sisters drink beer freely; European Christians are dismayed at the materialism of Americans and their ostentatious display of wealth. Western Christians condemn polygamy in Africa; African Christians cannot understand the increasing acceptance of divorce within the churches in the West and a general disregard for the aged and widowed.

Clearly we need a hermeneutical method that can deal with cultural and historical differences. Too often we evangelicals have been ahistorical and acultural in our understanding and application of the Bible. But how can we deal with these differences and retain theological absolutes?

The Hermeneutical Task

The first requirement of a biblical hermeneutics is the recognition of the authority of the Scriptures and a thorough knowledge of their teachings. The latter involves a careful exegesis of the biblical message within its own historical and cultural contexts. We need to know how God spoke to specific people in the real settings of their lives. What did he say to them? How did he deal with their sinful past or their present waywardness? How did he expect his people to relate to their own societies and to the cultures that surrounded them? And how did he lead them? The Bible is full of evidence of God's interaction with humans in real-life settings. These cases are more than illustrations of how God acts in history. They are definitive statements about the nature of God, of humans, of sin and salvation, and of godly living in an evil world. They are the paradigm by which we must understand our own lives. In hermeneutics, there is no substitute for a thorough knowledge of the Scriptures.

Biblical knowledge alone, however, is not enough. John Stott points out that some evangelicals know their Bibles well, but their preaching is detached from present-day realities (see figure 1). Consequently, their message has little relevance for today. In order to build a hermeneutical bridge between the Bible and our world, we also need a thorough exegesis of our contemporary contexts. To live and minister as Christians in a city setting, we must understand its structures and ways of life. To minister to tribal people, we must know their language and culture.

A knowledge of our world is important, but by itself it is not sufficient to our task. Unfortunately, many preachers today begin and end with the newspaper and their own human experience. If, however, contemporary experience is the sole basis for understanding the gospel, we are left with a theological and ethical relativism in which Christianity becomes a civil religion justifying existing cultural practices.

A biblical hermeneutics must begin with the Scriptures, which stand in judgment on all cultures—affirming that which is good and

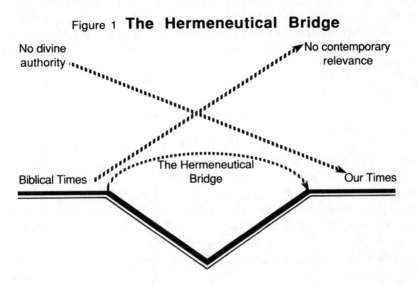

Figure 1 **The Hermeneutical Bridge**

No divine authority / No contemporary relevance / Biblical Times / The Hermeneutical Bridge / Our Times

condemning that which is evil. Such a hermeneutics must continue with a knowledge of these cultures, for only then will we know what is being judged. Finally, the biblical evaluation of each human situation must be communicated to those in that situation so that they may hear and respond. Only then will the hermeneutical task be completed.

But who should build this hermeneutical bridge? Too often we have turned the task over to religious "experts." Consequently, ordinary Christians are not encouraged to think theologically. They are expected to learn and obey the teaching of the experts. They are taught to be followers, not priests, in the church. The result is often a nominal Christianity in which people have little understanding of the doctrines they follow and of how these doctrines apply to their everyday lives. In such situations, church leaders become policemen who enforce their rules on the parishioners.

Central to the Reformation was the doctrine of the priesthood of believers. All Christians are to read and interpret the Bible, and all are called to apply it to their lives. The Reformers believed that the Holy Spirit works not only in trained leaders, but in all who follow Christ. In the sixteenth century, the Anabaptists were the ones who most ardently embraced and applied this doctrine in their emphasis on Christian discipleship.

If, however, everyone interprets the Scriptures individually, where are the theological absolutes and the unity of faith and fellowship? Does this not open the door to theological relativism? What check is there against those who bend Scriptures to fit their own purposes?

First, there are the Scriptures themselves. As Christians we seek to be faithful to the Bible and its teaching. In humility we must recognize that our own understandings of Scriptures are partial and biased, although this does not mean that our understandings are totally subjective. To the extent that we constantly test our theological interpretations against biblical teachings, they become increasingly rooted in the biblical message itself.

Second, we must depend upon the work of the Holy Spirit and trust that the same Holy Spirit is at work in the lives of all believers.

Finally, we must test our interpretations within the community of the church. As C. Norman Kraus points out, the Scriptures find meaning and application only within a "community of interpretation." This community includes not only the body of the church living today, but also the saints who have gone before us. It is within this hermeneutical community that other principles of interpretation take their place.

Case Studies as Community Hermeneutics

How does a church learn to become a hermeneutical community, and how can we help people learn to apply biblical principles to their own lives? One means is the case-study method, by which *a real-life problem is presented to a class or group for discussion.* The cases in this book are based on true experiences in the lives of missionaries and church leaders around the world. Although names and places have been changed to protect the privacy of those involved, the problems presented are very real. Many of them arise with minor variations in different cultures around the world, and they are the kinds of crises of which life itself is made. Since reality is stranger and more complex than fiction, hypothical cases do not ring true.

The central problem in a good case study has no simple solution—no black-or-white answer. If the biblical teaching is clear in the situation, there is no "case." We are simply called to obedience. But in many life situations there are problems with no one right answer—problems in which committed Christians disagree on the solutions. For example, may Christians take other Christians to court? Are they allowed to drink wine, or go to movies, or dance, or use traditional African drums in church, or wear colored spots on their foreheads in India, or place incense sticks and bow before the body of their dead parent in China? Each of these questions has generated a great deal of discussion and disagreement among deeply committed Christians.

In the case-study method, *the solution is worked out by a community of participants.* It is not handed down by some authority figure. The participants must seek to understand the viewpoints of the different actors in the case and the different members of their group. Together they must work towards a biblical solution the group can support.

This process—in which everyone has the right to speak and the responsibility to listen—helps Christians to grow, for it teaches them discernment. Wayne Dye writes that the most effective missionaries are those who teach new converts how to search and apply the Scriptures to their own lives, not those who teach them to obey the missionary.

Finally, in the case-study method as outlined here, the participants are encouraged to *seek a biblical solution to the problem under the guidance of the Holy Spirit*. This ability to apply scriptural principles to everyday life is the heart of Christian discipleship. To learn to do so, as our East African brothers and sisters say, is to learn to "walk in the light."

There is a danger, however, when using the case-study method, as there is in life itself, of relying on pragmatic and secular solutions. All too often in our church and business meetings we begin with a passage of Scripture and prayer and then use secular models to make our decisions. In the end this leads us to theological and ethical relativism.

We Christians must base our decisions on biblical principles and on God's leading. We may disagree about how these apply in any given situation, but we affirm divine absolutes in the very fact of turning to them.

Teaching and Participating in Case Studies

A few comments are needed regarding teaching as it relates to participating in case studies. (See also Appendix B.)

First, the discussion of real-life cases has several goals. Among them are the following:

1. To help people to identify the main issues in a case as well as those of lesser importance related to it.
2. To teach people to listen to and try to understand other people's perspectives and points of view.
3. To encourage people to examine all the possible alternatives for action before they make a decision.
4. To demonstrate the importance of feelings, attitudes, values, and relationships in the decision-making process.
5. To help people to seek God's will in such cases through the study of Scripture, the discernment of God's leading, and the reaching of a consensus decision that emerges out of a body of believers acting as a hermeneutical community, and not out of individual opinion.

Second, the discussion of a case results in a successful learning experience most often when the following requirements are met:

1. All of the participants in the discussion should read the case carefully prior to or at the beginning of the discussion. They should become thoroughly acquainted with all the details.
2. The analysis of the case should progress toward a solution. Generally there are at least four stages in the discussion: (a) the construction of a "time line"—a listing of the order in which the events occurring in the case have taken place; (b) the identification of all the characters in the case, what is known about them, and how they view the situation; (c) the discussion of the major and minor issues involved in choosing a course of action; and (d) the exploration of various solutions, giving particular attention to how we discern the will of God when we make decisions.
3. *All* who are present should voice their ideas and be able to give reasons for them. The leader of the discussion should not allow any one person or group to dominate the session and should encourage those who are shy to participate.
4. Individuals should hold firmly to what they truly believe but be willing to change their opinions on the basis of newly perceived insights or evidence. People should contribute whatever they have in the way of theoretical and experiential knowledge that is relevant to the discussion.
5. Participants should remember to keep a sense of humor in the discussion. This is an indication that we know ourselves to be fallible beings whose wisdom is always partial and never absolute. Humor often serves as the oil that keeps the social processes functioning.
6. The leader should not subtly manipulate the discussion and the decisions so as to achieve his or her own point of view.
7. The leader and the participants must constantly keep in mind the importance of seeking God's guidance in reaching a solution.

Finally, after the problem has been discussed and some resolution reached, it is important for the leader and the participants to disengage themselves from the case, to clear up misunderstandings, and to restore fellowship among themselves. It is easy for participants to become so involved in a case that they lose their objectivity. Accusations may be made and hostile feelings generated that need to be dealt with before the session breaks up. The leader must help the group detach itself from the case and discuss the dynamics of the session. Feelings of hurt, anger, and resentment must be settled, for although in one sense the group is a class dealing vicariously with a real-life situation, in another sense it is a community of believers and should manifest the love, forgiveness, and care for one another in the class situation that should characterize the body of Christ.

Bibliography

Dye, T. Wayne. 1982. *The Bible translations strategy: An analysis of its spiritual impact.* Ph.D. dissertation. Fuller Theological Seminary.

Kraus, C. Norman. 1979. *The authentic witness.* Grand Rapids: Eerdmans.

Swartley, Willard M. 1983. *Slavery, sabbath, war, and women: case issues in biblical interpretation.* Scottdale: Herald Press.

PART 1

Idols and Ancestors

How should Christians relate to idols? The biblical injunctions are clear—we are to worship no other god but God. All idols are to be destroyed. But what exactly are "idols"? Are statues of saints in a church idols? Is the picture of Christ on the wall at home an idol? Is a rock representing a local village spirit an idol? What is "worship," and how does it differ from "respect"?

Questions such as these constantly arise as we go to new cultures with the gospel. They are not new. The early church wrestled with the question of the responsibility of Christians to the Roman emperors, who declared themselves gods. Could Christians simply bow to the emperors to express political allegiance? Or did it always signify worship? And how should the church view Mary and the saints? The Council of Nicaea in A.D. 787 wrestled long with the distinction between worship (latreia) and respect (proskynesis).

We must reject idols, but what should we do with things associated with them, such as incense, drums, dances, kneeling, or raising of hands? Can any of these cultural religious practices be reinterpreted and used in the Christian church?

And what about the corporate nature of most religious activities? People are not just individuals; they exist as part of families and other social groups and as such have responsibilities to those groups. What should a woman do if she is the only Christian convert in a Hindu family? Should she continue to offer food each evening to caste and family gods on behalf of her family members, in order to win them to Christ? Or should she risk divorce and the loss of her children by refusing to do so?

Closely related to the question of idolatry is that of ancestors. How should we treat them? In the West we give relatively little thought to them and have no strong theology on the relationship between the living and the dead. Yet, in missions, no problem has been more wide-spread or more difficult to resolve. The early church faced this issue when Greeks and Romans became Christians. Then the debate centered in part on the use of tombstones, which in Roman culture were associated with the deification of the dead. Since then it has been a central question for the church in China, Japan, Korea, India, Africa, and parts of the Americas. It is a problem wherever new Christians are people who live in tribal and peasant societies where kinship ties are strong.

In societies built on ties of blood, ancestors play an important role as founders of families, lineages, clans, and the tribe itself. They are also seen as important mediators between humans and spirits. In the spirit world, ancestors act on behalf of their descendants, defending them from evil spirits and interceding on their behalf before the gods. On earth, they provide wisdom and guidance to the living.

In such societies the linkage between parent and child is seen as more than biological. It is also social and spiritual. This can be seen in the Old Testament, where the people of Israel referred to Jehovah as the God of Abraham, Isaac, and Jacob—their ancestors; where they told stories of their forefathers; and where the sins of parents brought judgment on their children.

What should missionaries do with beliefs and rituals regarding ancestors? If they simply reject these as "ancestor worship," Christianity is branded as a religion that dishonors parents. Unfortunately, this has happened in many parts of the world. On the other hand, if the missionaries accept these practices uncritically, they open the door for syncretism in the church.

What is needed is a critical evaluation of past practices in the light of Scripture. We first need to distinguish between worship and respect. Not all ancestor veneration is worship—some of it may simply be showing love and appreciation. But what *is* the crucial difference between worship and respect? For example, may Christians in good conscience put flowers on a grave? If so, why not food? And is it wrong to speak to ancestors and ask their help?

What we need is a theology of ancestors. The Bible is clear about honoring our parents, but how do we do so without worshiping them?

In seeking to avoid ancestor worship, are we in danger of failing to show true respect for parents?

Finally, there is the evangelistic question. Dr. Chow Lien-Hwa of Taipei writes, "In Taiwan, more than 90 percent of the Chinese do not want to become Christians because they must give up ancestor practices." This raises critical questions. What are the essential changes that must take place when a person becomes a true follower of Christ? Which of these changes must take place at conversion and which should be handled as a matter of Christian growth?

The cases in this section illustrate some of the ways in which questions related to idols and ancestors arise.

Bibliography

Hsu, Francis L. K. 1948. *Under the ancestors' shadow.* London: Routledge and Kegan Paul.

Hung, Daniel M. 1983. Mission blockade: Ancestor worship. *Evangelical Missions Quarterly* 19:32–40 (January).

Hwang, Bernard. 1977. Ancestor cult today. *Missiology: An International Review* 5:339–365 (July)

Newell, William H., ed. 1976. *Ancestors.* The Hague: Mouton Publishers.

Ro, Bong. 1984. *Consultation on ancestor practices.* Taichung, Taiwan: Asian Theological Association.

Smith, Robert J. 1974. *Ancestor worship in contemporary Japan.* Stanford: Stanford University Press.

1

The Ancestral Feast
Greg Roth

I don't know how to answer your question, Moses," the young missionary began. "I am certain of one thing, though. There are times when we must choose between our traditional cultures and being faithful to Christ."

"That's right, Alan," Moses replied, "but you must realize that Christianity has destroyed much of our culture, causing us to lose our sense of destiny. Now that we have accepted European ways and have seen them fail, we are left with nothing. We must regain what we left behind."

The two friends were relaxing under a tree near a beachfront house along the West African coastline. Moses, a forty-five-year-old Ghanaian, held an established reputation as a language instructor in the capital city. Alan was a young missionary who had studied with him for the past year. They had become close friends. Moses also worked for an insurance company in order to support his wife and three children. Years earlier he had married a second wife, who remained in her village, but after a few years he became convinced that this transgressed his Christian commitment and found a way to release her from their vows.

Moses had suggested that Alan accompany him and his family to his home village to observe the traditional festival that honored the ancestral spirits. He thought it would give the new missionary a deeper understanding of the local culture. Alan agreed to go, but a problem arose when Moses' wife, Grace, refused to attend. She was a committed Christian and insisted that participating in the libation to the ancestors and lesser deities would be sin. Alan debated within himself for

several days before he finally agreed to go. He had studied some anthropology and knew that he would not attach the same meaning to
the festival that the people would. Moreover, this would give him an
opportunity to get slides for his deputation work.

The day of the festival arrived, and Moses brought his children
along in Alan's car. After an hour on the road, they arrived at Ak-
wataman, and immediately went to greet the chief. After the introduc-
tory formalities, the chief sat back on his carved wooden stool and
inquired as to the purpose of their visit. Alan and Moses suggested that
they had come to observe the festival of the ancestors and to learn
about the culture. Looking very pleased, the chief began to talk about
his cultural heritage:

> Akwataman is named after Nii Akwata, my ancestor, who founded
> this village. Before my ancestors settled here, Nii Akwata was a war
> captain who lived over there under the mountains. There came a drought
> that was so severe the people had to move, so my ancestor started for
> water holes. It was a hard time for the village, but Nii found water at this
> river. He dedicated the village here, and because of his discovery and the
> successful job he did as a war captain, they named the village after him.
> It is in honor of him and the subsequent residents of our village, that we
> celebrate this festival today.

Later the elders prepared the ancestral feast. They brought the gin
bottle, used to pour out a libation to the spirits of the ancestors, and
the large pottery bowl used for the meal. They mixed handfuls of
yellow corn dough with palm nut and fish. The chief then began to
dance to the beat of the village drummers, swaying and announcing
that the festival had begun. The villagers gathered behind him as he
poured gin on the ground and called out for the spirits to join the
procession.

At this point Alan became a little uneasy, wondering whether or not
he should participate. But he was distracted by opportunities to pho-
tograph the chief's pouring of the gin on the ground and decided to
follow along. The chief grabbed a handful of sourdough, dipped it into
the soup, and threw it against a wall, calling to the ancestral spirits in
that building to come out. He splattered the yellow mixture freely on
the houses and tossed handfuls into rooms where he recalled people
had died. Then he ran off down the trail to the next set of houses. Moses
and Alan followed the villagers as they danced from house to house,
singing, drumming, and dancing along behind the chief, who proudly
spattered the mixture on each home. One of the villagers who spoke
English explained to Alan that this was a harvest meal, and that the

throwing of the food showed they could scoff at hunger because their crops were abundant.

After the chief had offered food at all of the houses in the village to show the unity of the community in the shared meal, he led the parading throng back to his house, where he once again began to dance and sway under the sacred tree. Suddenly, as if provoked by someone, he fixed his eyes on Daniel, Moses' oldest son, who was sitting with disinterest on a nearby porch, and said, "You brood of vipers! Why do you live in the cities and never return to your home to honor the ancestors? You attend mission schools, claim to be a Christian, and think you are too good for your own culture. What a wicked and perverse generation!" Daniel looked noticeably hurt by the chief's comments.

Later, after the dancing stopped, the young missionary asked the chief if he was against Christianity. The chief responded:

> The pagans are better in telling the truth than the Christians, because the Christians don't have the fear of God. Their God doesn't take action quickly enough to judge them when they lie. Our local gods are quick to show us their power, so when we swear by them we are careful to tell the truth. You know that some of us in this village were trained in Christian schools, and I no longer use the magic of my ancestors. I have never put black powder under my skin, or buried a live goat or cat in the house to gain spiritual power. In the old days, even humans were buried in the house of the chief. But I have seen Christians reject their old culture and refuse to honor their ancestors. All that you have seen us do we do in order to keep our tradition. If we lose our tradition, we have lost everything. The rituals you have seen are not paganism, they are our tradition, or what you call our culture.

As they sat talking, the chief asked Alan if he would join him in a toast to the ancestors as a testimony to those they honored today. Alan looked over at Moses seated nearby, his stomach churning with tension as he considered whether or not he should drink the toast. "Will the young Christians be offended or encouraged if I drink? But would my refusal anger the chief and other pagans in the village and close the door to further evangelism?" he wondered. The glass was passed from hand to hand toward Alan. He began to sweat. What should he do?

2

Grandmother's Funeral
Mamoru B. Ogata

It was almost midnight when the phone rang and Masashi heard about his grandmother's death. "Come quickly," his mother said. "The funeral will be day after tomorrow." Masashi had expected the call, for he had visited his grandmother a week before and seen that she was very frail. Much to Masashi's joy, she had accepted Christ during that visit. He had sat by her bed and told her about the gospel and invited her to believe. Though she was weak, she had nodded her head, and her peaceful smile convinced Masashi that she was a believer. But that had only added to his anxiety about what he would have to do at her funeral, which he knew would be conducted according Buddhist tradition.

During the three-hour train ride to his parents' home the next day, the young seminary student recalled the events that had led up to this moment. He had grown up in a small village with two Shinto shrines and a Buddhist temple. There were no Christians in the area. Masashi's father worked in a nearby chemical factory and in his spare time worked a small farm. He was proud when he had completed his new house, and even more so when he was elected president of the village and made responsible for the village religious activities.

Masashi had gone to Tokyo for his education and had graduated from Waseda University. While there he had heard about Christ through some young people. He had experienced the power of God and the support of a Christian fellowship during some difficult experiences in his life. Masashi had become a disciple of Jesus. Back home, the villagers had commented on the change that had taken place in his life, now that he was a Christian. Later, after he had prayed for his mother when she was ill and she had recovered, she had become sympathetic to his new faith. He had led one of his brothers to Christian faith. They were the only Christians in the village. The other brother had remained skeptical of Christianity.

It was afternoon when Masashi arrived at his father's house. The relatives were already making preparations for a Buddhist funeral. After greeting his parents, he said, "Father, Grandmother became a Christian when I was here a week ago. She should have a Christian funeral." But Masashi's father had refused. He did not want any criticism from the relatives or villagers. Masashi had helped in the funeral arrangements out of respect for the grandmother he had loved dearly, but he knew that he would face a difficult decision when the funeral took place.

The next day the men of Masashi's house association placed the body in the coffin they had made, dug the grave, and prepared the altar for the Buddhist funeral. The women had helped feed and entertain the more than two hundred guests who arrived for the burial.

At the climax of the ceremonies, Masashi stood in line as a member of his family. His father was first, his mother second, and he as the eldest son was third. Behind him was his Christian brother, watching to see what he would do. Each in turn was expected to offer burning incense to the dead. All were watching Masashi as his turn came to venerate his grandmother. As he approached the coffin, Masashi. . . .

3

A Wedding in the People's Republic of China
David Wang

We must help these young people! Their marriage, faith, and future are at stake. I am so glad that God brought you back to China at just this moment to help us!" As Jim Craig listened to the Reverend Ma, his close friend and able colleague, he pondered what to say. Must a Christian dishonor his family by rejecting the age-old tradition of ancestor veneration?

Jim had the highest respect for Reverend Ma, who had suffered much for his faith during the Communist regime. But their relationship went deeper than mutual respect. Both had grown up together in the mission school started by Jim's father, a missionary who had served in Yunnan many years before. In time Jim had succeeded his father, and Ma was his closest friend and colleague. When Jim was expelled from China as a foreigner, he had turned the school over to Mr. and Mrs. Ma. Later he learned that they had been sent to a labor camp because of their "collaboration with American imperialists." They were released in 1979 and a few months later had led Kwok-hu and Lin-kit to faith in Jesus Christ. Because they had no children of their own, the Mas considered these two young people as their own flesh and blood.

Jim first met Kwok-hua and Lin-kit a year later, when he was allowed for the first time to return to China to visit his old friends. It was obvious to Jim that they would make a fine couple. Both loved the Lord dearly, and both worked in the same factory—Kwok-hua as a mechanic and Lin-kit as a teacher in the factory kindergarten. When they

31

applied to their work unit for permission to marry, it was readily granted because of their excellent work records.

One possible problem had been resolved. Although the families of the young couple were from different social backgrounds, they had both agreed to the marriage. Lin-kit's father came from the "worker class." At an early age he had joined the Communist Party, but during the era of the Gang of Four he was removed from office. In 1979 he had been reinstated and assigned an administrative position in a department store. His wife had died when Lin-kit was a child, and he had been both father and mother to her. He had not objected when she became a Christian. He said to Reverend Ma, "My daughter is grown up. She should make her own decisions. If she wants to become a Christian, I will not object. Maybe I should adopt some religion. I am growing old, and I have found that nothing really satisfies me." However, he had warned Lin-kit that her relationship with Kwok-hua might not always be smooth. "Bamboo goes with bamboo, wood goes with wood," he said. "You and Kwok-hua are from different classes, and he has a big family."

Kwok-hua's parents came from high-class families. Before the "Liberation" his father, Chiang Ping, had worked with an American firm, so when the Communists came to power he was recruited to work in the nationalized foreign-trade department. But at the time of Kwok-hua's birth he was arrested as a spy and sentenced to labor camp. He was released in 1978 and reinstated a year later, at which time his position and properties were returned to him. "This is a miracle! Our ancestors have not only protected me and brought our family back together, they have also blessed us with good fortune," he concluded. When Kwok-hua became a Christian, Chaing Ting did not object. "The foreign missionaries did a lot of good when they were in our country. Kwok-hua must, however, continue to carry on the name of the family and uphold the light for the ancestors," he said.

The two families met to arrange the marriage. Because Kwok-hua was his only son, Chiang Ping decided to hold a banquet at the neighborhood committee hall. This was not only to celebrate the wedding but also to recognize the blessings of the ancestors and "wash away the bad luck and welcome in the new fortune." Chiang Ping ordered a new set of ancestor plaques because the old set had been destroyed during the Cultural Revolution. On them were inscribed the names of the family ancestors. Chiang Ping enshrined the plaques on the family altar, and he and his wife began again to venerate them weekly and on important occasions, for they symbolized the living presence of their ancestors. Having grown up under atheistic Communism, neither one of the young couple understood the meaning of "handing over the ancestor plaques," so they went about happily preparing for the wedding. When an elderly Christian woman solved their housing problem by agreeing to let them move into her house, they took it as an endorsement of God's blessings upon their union.

Kwok-hua's relatives from far and near gathered for the banquet, and then his father and uncles explained to him the ritual of turning over the family ancestor plaques. After the wedding the young couple was to visit the bride's father to bid him farewell. Then they would return to Chiang Ping's home, where Lin-kit would become a member of the family clan. The whole family would then offer thanksgiving offerings of rice, fish, chicken, pork, fruit, and rice wine to the ancestors. The couple would be expected to kneel down and offer cups of reverence tea to the ancestors and to Kwok-hua's father and uncles. The plaques would then be moved to the new couple's home, and they would be required to offer food and incense to the plaques regularly. Kwok-hua's mother pointed out, "Our ancestors have been so good to us. None of the family died during the Cultural Revolution. We are happily reunited. Your father has been reinstated and even received his properties back, and you have found this wonderful bride. We are all so grateful to our ancestors and heaven!"

The uncles and relatives were all excited, but Kwok-hua and Lin-kit were shocked! And Kwok-hua's response was even more shocking to the family: "No, father, we cannot do that! We cannot worship the ancestor plaques or kneel to you and the uncles. We are Christians, and we worship only God and Jesus Christ."

The rest of the evening was a disaster. Kwok-hua's father was furious. His mother cried all night. The relatives tried to comfort the parents. Finally one of the uncles said to Kwok-hua, "I have talked with your father. If you don't want to kneel to us, it is all right. Even your father and mother do not insist that you and Lin-kit kneel to them. But we now have our ancestor plaques back. You *must* honor them. You are the firstborn male child of this generation. If you fail to honor our ancestors, none of us can ever face them again. We don't know about your Christian religion. We thought it was something good, but if it teaches you to dishonor your ancestors, it should be condemned. If you do not honor them, you must be excommunicated from our family."

Early the next morning the young couple sought help from Reverend Ma, who called in Jim and explained the whole matter. "Jim, please tell us what to do," he pleaded.

4

Family Gods
Paul G. Hiebert

Marcella looked at the beautiful young woman seated on the mat and at the baby playing with his mother's hair, so innocent of her dilemma. "If only life were that simple!" thought Marcella, knowing that she had to give some answer to this new believer. The answer that came to her from her classroom days was clear. Karnamma should have nothing to do with the worship of her family idols or with other Hindu rituals of her household. But the classroom discussions never dealt with the complexities of real life. Marcella wondered whether she could in good conscience ask Karnamma, a new Christian, to pay a price that she as a missionary had never begun to pay. And did the Bible not teach that a woman had certain responsibilities to her family? But what were those responsibilities when the wife became a Christian and the rest of the family remained Hindu?

Five years before, Marcella had come as a doctor to South India and started a hospital in a small town. Not only had this won her the good will of the Hindus and Muslims of the region, but it also had opened the door for an effective medical and evangelical ministry among them. She had a particular burden for young mothers, so twice a week she went out to hold maternal clinics in remote villages, often staying overnight in some Christian's home. Most of the converts had come from the "untouchable" castes, and much of Marcella's work was among the women of these despised groups. As her reputation spread, however, she began to find the doors open for ministry to women from the higher castes. She was invited into the homes of expectant mothers in the "clean" section of the village, and there learned to love and appreciate the women who had so few opportunities to hear of Christ.

"Lord," she often prayed, "please open the door for the gospel to enter these homes!"

One day Karnamma came quietly when Marcella was at camp, waiting patiently at the door until the missionary noticed her. As a Komati, a member of one of the highest-ranking clean castes, she had risked the anger of her family and friends by coming. She knew that they would beat her when she returned if they found out that she had come to the Christian hut in the "untouchable" hamlet where Marcella was spending the night. After Marcella invited her in, Karnamma sat by the door and in desperation told her story.

Six years before, Karnamma had been married by parental arrangement to Ramayya, a promising young merchant in Peduru. There had been the usual traumas of a young bride who was leaving the loving care of her parents to live with her husband in the household of his father and mother and, in this case, two married brothers. Karnamma had been spared a domineering mother-in-law and jealous sisters-in-law, but as the youngest wife in the house she had to do much of the cleaning and cooking. Everyone was pleased when she became pregnant, but a little disappointed when the child was a girl. "We will make a special offering to Vasavi Kanyaka, so that next time it is certain to be a boy," they said. "At least you have shown yourself to be a mother."

Karnamma enjoyed the added prestige of motherhood, even though she often could not act the role. Her father-in-law and mother-in-law, Krishnayya and Achamma, had the right to play with the child whenever they wished. Besides, she still had to do most of the menial work in the house. First one and then the other of Ramayya's older brothers moved away to large towns where they got good jobs. Both had had the opportunity of going to school. Ramayya remained at home to run the family store.

As Achamma became bedridden with arthritis, Karnamma had to take responsibility for running the household. With this came the obligation to make the evening offerings of food and incense to Vasavi Kanyaka Parameshwari, the goddess of all the Komati (merchants). Different members of the family had the right to choose their own personal gods (*ishta devata*), but all Komati were also expected to worship their caste deity (*kula devata*). Ramayya worshiped Krishna, but Karnamma had chosen Vasavi Kanyaka as her personal deity. Vasavi had been a young Komati virgin who lived centuries before. When the king, who was from another caste, tried to marry her, she committed suicide to avoid the sin of marrying out of caste. She went to heaven and there was the patron of all Komati. Karnamma made a pilgrimage to Vasavi's shrine in the city and promised her special offerings if she granted Karnamma a son. When Karnamma gave birth to a son a year later, all took it as a sign of Vasavi Kanyaka Parameshwari's approval.

Now assisted by two servants, Karnamma had more free time, including time to listen to the family radio. She was surprised one day to hear a Christian preacher whose speech showed that he was a converted Brahmin, the highest of all castes. She had heard about Christianity but assumed that it was a false religion followed only by "untouchables." She listened carefully and, over the next few weeks, became convinced that Jesus Christ is indeed the Lord of high-caste people as well as low. After one of the messages, she knelt by her bed and prayed for salvation. A deep peace filled her life.

Karnamma wondered what it meant to be a Christian. She continued to listen to the radio broadcasts and managed to get a copy of the New Testament. When she shared her experiences with two or three of her closest friends, she found that one of them had also been listening to the broadcast and was interested in the gospel. At first Karnamma continued her duties around the house. But one day, after hearing a sermon on the uniqueness of Christ and the sin of idolatry, she began to question the daily offering of food and incense to Vasavi Kanyaka and the ancestors. Was it not arrogant for the Christians to claim that theirs was the only god? Were there not many gods, all as equally worthy of worship as the Hindus claimed? She could worship Christ, but Karnamma wondered why she must condemn the worship of Vasavi Kanyaka, or Krishna, or any of the other household gods. Moreover, what was she to do as a wife in a Hindu home? Was it wrong for her, as a Christian, to perform the family worship rites? On the other hand, how could she, as wife and head of the household, not do so?

That evening, deeply disturbed by her inner conflict, she refused to make the offerings, claiming to be sick. Her mother-in-law somehow managed to perform the rites. The next night her husband was angry when she again wanted to avoid the ceremonies. He was even more angry when she told him of her new faith in Christ. He said, "I have never stopped you from listening to the radio, even though I knew you were listening to a Christian preacher. After all, you have a right to have your own personal god [ishta devata]. But you are still my wife and a member of our family, so you must continue to offer our family sacrifices to our caste and household deities [kula devata]. Does your new god think that he is the only god? How can he forbid us to worship our own gods?"

Karnamma was silenced by his attack and resumed her duties to the household gods. She rationalized that this was the only way she could win the complete approval of her husband and family, who had already seen and appreciated the changes that had taken place in her life after her conversion. She was also afraid that she would be thrown out of the house and village if she refused to obey her husband. She knew that her parents would not take her in if they found that she had turned against the goddess of all Komati. She saw no way out.

A week later Karnamma heard that the missionary doctor was coming that day for a clinic in the hamlet of "untouchables" outside of town. In the evening she slipped out of the house as if to go to the market, but instead made her way across the fields to the house where Marcella was staying. "What shall I do?" Karnamma asked. "How can I as a Christian offer sacrifices to idols? On the other hand, how can I deny my responsibilities as a wife and mother, and what will happen to me if I don't comply?" Then she sat silent, eagerly awaiting Marcella's answer. Finally Marcella broke the long silence and said. . . .

5

Food Offered to Idols
Simon P. David

Rajasekaran looked across the room at the large picture of the blue-faced god Krishna, heavily garlanded with marigolds and tinsel, and then at the printing-press workers gathered around the small shrine set up before the god. It was Friday, and Rajasekaran realized that he had arrived just at the completion of weekly prayers to Krishna, the patron god of the press. Like many businessmen in this city in South India, the proprietor provided money to purchase coconuts, bananas, and sugar to offer to the deity at the weekly *puja*. He believed that the prosperity of his shop was due to the blessing of the god for his faithful offerings.

As assistant editor of a Christian magazine, it was Rajasekaran's responsibility to work with the press workers in order to make certain that the publication was properly printed on schedule. Today there had been some urgent matters to take care of, so he had come earlier than usual. He had hurried into the room, and Mani, the press foreman, had seen him before he realized that the *puja* ceremonies were still going on.

Over the past months, Mani and the editor had developed a close friendship as they worked together. Rajasekaran hoped someday to win his friend to Christ, but right now Mani was pulling him by the hand toward the group receiving the food that had been offered to Krishna and having *kunkumam* (colored powder) placed as spots on their foreheads to signify that they had been purified by eating the leftovers of the god. Rajasekaran knew that for many Hindus, including Mani, eating the food offered to a god was a sign of goodwill, much like receiving a Christmas present. But he also knew that for orthodox

Hindus, partaking of the food and the *kunkumam* was part of the worship of an idol. Rajasekaran did not want to harm his relationship with Mani, but he also did not want to compromise his Christian witness. He saw Mani hold out the platter of food, and he. . . .

6

The Neighborhood Celebration
Anonymous

Henry Thompson looked at Mrs. Sato, uncertain about what he should say. The year-end celebrations would be held tomorrow, and there was no time to call a church meeting to discuss her problem. Yet she needed an answer before the celebrations. Would her participation in a Shinto ceremony violate her Christian commitment?

Thompson had come to Japan three years earlier. After studying the language, he and his wife had moved to Tokyo to plant a church. They had carefully built friendships with people in their part of the city and started Bible-study groups in their home. It was from these that they had won their first converts, and Mrs. Reiko Sato was one of them. Mrs. Sato had grown in her faith and been baptized six months previously. She was now a staunch member of the small congregation. Even so, Henry knew little about her life in the Japanese setting, except that she was the only Christian in her neighborhood and that she was a widow.

That had changed when Mrs. Sato came to seek his advice. She told him that her neighborhood, like most neighborhoods in Tokyo, had its own association in which everyone was expected to participate. Throughout the year her association raised funds for worthwhile projects and for neighborhood friendship meetings. She explained that it is not so much that everyone is *expected* to attend, but that it is inconceivable for someone not to go, unless they were very ill.

Normally the party was held in some public hall, but this year the association leaders had arranged to hold the celebrations at the local Shinto shrine. They had also decided that a sizable donation to refurbish the shrine would be required from all who attended. When Mrs.

Sato regretfully declined to attend on the grounds that she was a Christian, the leaders, thinking she had misunderstood the invitation, sent several women to her house. Again Mrs. Sato told them she could not participate in the year-end party, and the women left, not quite sure what to do. A few days later the chairman of the neighborhood association came to the door. When he heard that Mrs. Sato was refusing to attend the festivities because she was a Christian, he became angry and demanded, "What is wrong with being a good Japanese? You can be a Christian, but Shinto is our national spirit. If you do not attend, you are rejecting our country!" Mrs. Sato had refused even then, but during the following days the community pressure had become unbearable. Her friends and neighbors began to question her about her loyalties to Japan, and others began to look at her with suspicion. She hated to go out of the house for her daily shopping and errands. It was then that she had come to Henry Thompson for help.

"What shall I do?" she asked. "Is it so wrong to attend the year-end celebrations, just because they are held at the Shinto shrine? And what can I do about the donation?" Henry realized that it was hard for him as a foreigner to understand what it meant to become a Christian in the Japanese setting. Yet, as pastor of the local church, he had to give her an answer. He recalled Paul's exhortation to be all things to all people in order to win them to Christ (1 Cor. 9:19–23). He also recalled Paul's injunction that Christians should not be associated with idols (2 Cor. 6:14–18). Henry thought a moment, and then he said. . . .

PART 2

Women and Men

Anthropologists have identified hostility between women and men as a universal characteristic of human cultures. Each culture develops its own ways of dealing with this inherent antagonism. After all, unless the "war between the sexes" is regulated in some way, the society could not function. One way to deal with it is by rigid role assignments. Women do this; men do that. For example, in Western culture of the last century, society prescribed that women's place is in the home and that men run the country. Another way is for the culture to determine through myth or religion that one sex is superior to the other and therefore is meant to have power and control. With few exceptions in the history of human culture, this superiority has been ascribed to the male.

From a Christian point of view, as understood by the present authors, the antagonism between women and men is a result of the first couple's disobedience to God. Before that, Adam and Eve lived as equals, thrilled by the discovery of their mutual humanity. The war began after the fall.

Mildred Enns Toews describes the initiation of hostilities in graphic and gripping terms: "The actual combat scene between God and man is initiated by the serpent. To obey, or not to obey God, that is the question. All parties are agreed that likeness to God is the bottom line. Shall it be as God intended, a likeness in character by obedience; or as the serpent suggests, a likeness in power by knowledge?" (*Through the Lens of Eden*, unpublished). Adam and Eve decide for power and the die is cast. They rejected the rule of God, and power struggles became the universal and dominant characteristic of human relationships. And, one might add, especially those between women and men. That was the only human relationship on the scene.

Genesis 3 records God's response to human disobedience. The serpent is cursed; the ground is cursed. The man and the woman are not cursed by their gracious Creator but there is a description of how life will be for them after the fall.

It is important to recognize that this is description and not prescription. God created the woman as the man's equal and gave them both the command to culture the earth and to create human culture. God did not intend for men to rule over women, but the biblical record says it will happen. The human choice for power rather than character as the "image of God" ensured that they would struggle against each other in order to exercise an independent authority that belongs to God alone. The history of relationships between women and men from that time until this is a history of men trying to rule over women and of women struggling to find their own avenues to power. Men dominate; women manipulate. The ways that cultures devise to regulate this power struggle often are oppressive and repressive. Both sexes suffer as a result.

Enter Jesus and the Good News of the restored kingdom of God! In Christ, men and women are liberated from the power struggle. They are free to relate as equals—to culture the earth and create social cultures in the way that God originally intended them to do. The only difference is that another mandate has been added to the first. The new people of God have the responsibility to make the Good News known to every culture. That freedom and responsibility should be exercised through the harmonious and mutual relationship between women and men. It is possible only because of the redemptive work of Jesus Christ.

Then why does the struggle continue—even among Christians? Why do we offer cases that deal with male-female relationships and suggest that there are few easy answers to the problems they raise?

One reason is that many Christians have an errant theology of manhood and womanhood. Dr. Arthur Glasser, the missiologist-theologian of the School of World Mission at Fuller Seminary, is well worth hearing on this point. He says that evangelicals since World War II often make the mistake of beginning their theology after the fall and take little account of the fact that there *was* life before the fall. Unless we take account of God's original purpose for humanity, we have an incomplete understanding of the meaning of redemption. That kind of incomplete theology has made it possible for us to split social concern from evangelism. It also allows us to believe that the hierarchy of man over woman resulting from the fall is what God intended. It is blind to the biblical description of the state of equality between women and men in the first two chapters of Genesis. And it has not heard the apostle Paul when he says in Galatians 3:28 that in Christ that state has been restored. Another reason for the continued hostilities is that while the kingdom of God is real in the lives of Christians, we are still awaiting our final liberation from the effects of sin. The old lust for power must be crucified daily. We must seek to image God obediently by taking on God's characteristics instead of trying to usurp God's power.

Some Christian missiologists continue to support oppressive cultural norms for the relationship between women and men in the name of "respect" for all cultures. They do this partly to atone for the sins of Western cultural domination. According to such thinking, missionaries should only help people to change their allegiance to Jesus Christ, instead of whatever else they are worshiping, and disturb the culture as little as possible. They seem to overlook the fact that a change of religious allegiance, after all, is the most fundamental of cultural disturbances.

When it comes to conflicts between the gospel and culture, Christians should give more weight to Scripture than to relativistic social sciences. The Bible teaches us to love and respect all *people*, because they are valued and loved by God so much that God was willing to die for them. But the cultural *structures* that have been devised by people are tragically flawed, including those that regulate the balance of power between men and women. They are the structures of rebellion. The gospel challenges every culture—Western or Eastern—to submit to the rule of God. And the Good News is that whatever must be rejected in human culture is nothing compared to the grandeur of God's original and restored plan for women and men.

The cases in this section deal with a variety of relationships between women and men. Most, however, have to do with marriage and cohabitation. Few problems in missions are so widespread or generate such deeply felt responses as those related to polygamy, common-law marriages, trial marriages, premarital intercourse, and other sexual customs found around the world. In part these responses rest on biblical teaching regarding sexual behavior. In part they rest on the obsession of Western cultures with sex and their tendency to regard sexual offenses as the greatest of sins.

In order to give a Christian answer to these customs, we need to understand the functions they serve within each given society, for if the church seeks to abolish them, it may need to provide alternative ways of dealing with the social problems the customs have addressed.

An example of this need to understand social customs before we change them is polygamy, the practice of marrying more than one wife. This is found in more than one-half of the societies around the world. There are many reasons for its prevalence. A man may take a second wife to have another worker for his fields, to have children if his first wife is barren, to add to his status as an important man in the village, to cement an alliance with another village or tribe, or to guarantee his economic security. Or a man may take a second wife for sexual purposes. In many tribes a husband may not have sexual relations with his wife after she has had a child until that child is weaned— often not until the age of two or three. The people fear that if she bears another baby too soon, both children will suffer for lack of nourishment and die. So a husband may take a second wife rather than go to prostitutes.

One of the most common reasons for polygamy is to handle social crises. What should a young mother do if her husband dies? Who will support her, provide her companionship, meet her sexual needs, father more children, and raise the ones she already has? Western societies are concerned mainly with the first of these needs—namely, providing the widow enough money through insurance, savings, social security, and possibly a job. They do very poorly in meeting her other needs. In many societies the problem is solved by having the dead man's closest male relative—a brother, cousin, or second cousin—marry the widow and raise her children, even though he may already have a wife. It is important that he provide for the widow and the children—that he be a father to the children and companion to the woman, and generate more children to maintain the strength of the tribe. Sexual rights are usually of secondary importance in such situations.

How should a missionary deal with polygamy? In the first place, we need to study the Scriptures to see how they deal with the issue. Is polygamy a sin? On the one hand, elders and leaders are exhorted to have one wife (1 Tim. 3:2, 12), just as they are to have obedient children (1 Tim. 3:4, 12). On the other hand, Abraham, Moses, and David, and other Old Testament leaders had multiple wives. And how does polygamy relate to divorce? If a man with three wives becomes a Christian, should he keep all three, or divorce two of them? Are marriages made before the individuals become Christians true marriages, or must they be remarried after they become Christians? In short, a missionary needs to develop a theology of sex and marriage.

In the second place, we need to study the functions of marriage in the society in which the problem arises. As we have already seen, in most societies marriage is more than the union of two individuals. It serves such important functions as providing for widows and orphans. If we then forbid a man from marrying his relative's widow because he already has a wife, who should take care of her? Who should provide for her economic, social, and sexual needs? Who should father more children and raise those she already has? In changing a culture, it is important to consider not only the changes themselves, but the effects such changes have upon other areas in the society.

In the third place, we need to consider the missiological consequences of various actions. If we ask a convert to put away his second and third wives, how will they, their children, and their relatives respond to the gospel? On the other hand, if polygamists are admitted into the church, where will the church be in its marriage practices fifty or a hundred years from now?

Finally, we need to examine the specific facts of the case at hand. No two human cases are alike. A man who becomes a Christian after he already has three wives is different from a monogamous Christian husband who wants to take two more. The tangles of human lives are too complex to be solved by one or two simple rules.

So far we have discussed only polygamy. Similarly, theological and sociocultural studies must be made of common-law marriage (prevalent in Latin America, since the Catholic Church does not permit divorce), trial marriages (common in the Pacific islands), premarital intercourse, and other sexual customs. Only then will missionaries and young churches be able to bring biblical teachings to bear on the sexual customs of the society in which they live.

Bibliography

Bilezikian, Gilbert. 1985. *Beyond sex roles.* Grand Rapids: Baker Book House.

Filbeck, David. 1973. Abuse in marriage. *Missiology: An International Review* 1:225–235 (April).

Fountain, Oswald C. 1974. Polygyny and the church. *Missiology: An International Review* 4:111–119 (January).

Glahamany, Jean-Baptiste. 1981. Two problems: Bridewealth and polygamy. *African Ecclesiastical Review* 23:104–106 (April).

Hiebert, Frances. 1982. Missionary women as models in the cross-cultural context. *Missiology: An International Review* 10:455–460 (October).

Hillman, Eugene. 1975. *Polygyny reconsidered.* New York: Orbis.

––––––. 1982. The polygamy debate: A progress report. *Missiology* 10:161–170.

Horan, Hubert. 1976. Polygamy comes home to roost. *Missiology: An International Review* 4:443–453 (October).

Iteka, Patrick. 1981. Polygamy and the local church. *African Ecclesiastical Review* 23:106–108.

John, C. B., and Webster E. L., eds. 1985. *The church and women in the Third World*. Philadelphia: Westminster Press.

Kirwen, Michael C. 1979. *African widows*. Maryknoll: Orbis Books.

Malcolm, Kari Torjesen. 1982. *Women at the crossroads*. Downers Grove: Inter-Varsity Press.

Omoregbe, Joseph. 1979 Is polygamy incompatible with Christianity? *African Ecclesiastical Review* 21:363–372 (December).

Reyburn, William D. 1978. Kaka kinship, sex and adultery. *Readings in missionary anthropology*, William Smalley ed. (pp. 241–254). South Pasadena: William Carey Library

Spencer, Aida Besancon. 1985. *Beyond the curse*. Nashville: Thomas Nelson Publishers.

Terrien, Samuel. 1985. *Till the heart sings*. Philadelphia: Fortress Press.

Tippett, Alan R. 1970. Polygamy as a missionary problem: The anthropological issues. *Practical Anthropology* 7:75–79 (March-April).

Trobisch, Walter. 1971. *My wife made me a polygamist*. Downers Grove: Inter-Varsity Press.

———. 1978. Pre-marital relations and Christian marriage in Africa. *Readings in missionary anthropology*, William Smalley ed. (pp. 274–278). South Pasadena: William Carey Library.

Urrutia, Francisco Javier. 1981. Can polygamy be compatible with Christianity? *African Ecclesiastical Review* 23:275–291 (October).

7

The Law of Liberty Versus the Law of Love
Bobbie Pendell

Kneeling numb and exhausted beside her bed in the back bedroom, Nancy knew it was more than the surprise of finding the two men, Mehmet and Zeki, in the house a moment ago that was filling her with such dread. (That meant an implied rule had been broken!) It was also her sore throat, and the weight of deciding whether to leave the House of Ruth under the care of twenty-six-year-old Reyhan, or to close it while she was on the year's furlough slated to begin in just two weeks.

Dismantling their lovely home was the last thing forty-five-year-old Nancy wanted to do. It was her dream-come-true for needy Muslim women in this unevangelized Middle East city, a peaceful base for single women to receive something in Christ's name—used clothing and a cup of hot tea for the "bag ladies" combing the trash outside, a tape library of Bible stories and tracts for cautious distribution, prayer and Bible study, and even live-in discipleship for three of the five single women who had been baptized.

"Lord, help!" she prayed. "I'm so mixed up and angry. Customs *are* changing, but how fast, Lord? Is what my friends advised only eight months ago already outdated? . . . You know I *hate* having to enforce on these young believers the taboos of their own culture; that seems so wrong. Lord, show me if their rebellion is your way of smashing a burdensome rule that shouldn't be. . . . But Lord, is it possible that you're showing me what will happen to your name after I leave if their defiance isn't dealt with?"

Everything had gone so well until now. Nancy had arrived four years before, wanting to establish a home for single women because she believed the gospel would spread quickly among independent and rejected women. The idea had come from her reading about Lydia, the woman at the well, the Magdalene, and the Macedonian slave girl. It was an unexplored concept. Her prayer partners at home caught her vision and had given financially so that she could open the first House of Ruth less than a year after her arrival in the Middle East.

That first year was grueling, but beautiful Mene, a twenty-six-year-old divorcée, committed her life to Christ and moved in with Nancy. She grew strong in the Lord and was thrilled to have a place for sharing Christ with their neighbors, many of whom, like Mene, felt rejected by society due to divorce or separation. All who visited the two learned something of Jesus, usually for the first time, and nobody left without prayers.

When Mene's brother pleaded for her help with his failing business in another city, she left for one year. Nancy moved into a large apartment in a less-conservative neighborhood and continued the House of Ruth. For the past ten months she had roomed with Selma and Reyhan, two recent converts who had taken the step of baptism. Neither of the two had ever lived in such comfortable surroundings, or with Christians, and both gloried in their newfound freedom to minister openly to their friends at work and school. The three women's "family prayer times" had created close ties between them. Nancy was pleased to think she could leave the home under Reyhan's supervision while she was on furlough, although Mene often warned her, "Reyhan can't manage it. She's too stubborn."

The "no-men-unless-accompanied-by-wives" rule for the House of Ruth was a long-standing one. Experienced missionaries had warned: "In this country, single girls should live with their parents if they are unmarried, so be absolutely certain you *never* entertain men or allow the women to do so." Mene had agreed. Although the residents of the House of Ruth had bent the rule occasionally for brief chats with Christian "brothers" (with the front door opened wide, as is the Muslim custom for such emergencies), so far as Nancy knew, no neighbor had ever criticized "the *gavur*" (non-Muslims/ those who leave Islam) or "the foreign lady" ("everyone knows *all* Western women are immoral"). One neighbor had even told another that Nancy's companions were "pure girls." This delighted her, for Nancy wanted to win her neighbors to Christ.

Reyhan thought the rule forbidding male visitors was needless, but both she and Selma had agreed to it before moving in the previous September. When winter cold closed the city's outdoor cafes, however, and there seemed no place to gather after Sunday services, the women and several male converts, including Mehmet and Zeki, insisted that the rule was unnecessary. Mehmet had chided Nancy last fall, saying,

> You misunderstand our people, Nancy. We are not such backward people as you think; this is a modern country. Your neighbors don't care what people do so long as they're polite. Besides, the women only want to entertain us *Christian men*, not Muslims. . . . Once we had to live under the harsh Muslim customs like this, but Jesus has set us free from the law. You urge us to love and trust one another, but you don't really trust us. How can we grow closer if we have no place to meet?

Nancy sympathized and hoped they were correct, but Mene insisted they were wrong. Not knowing what to believe or how to maintain unity without jeopardizing the House of Ruth's fine reputation, Nancy asked three non-Christian friends in the neighborhood how they would view the women's occasional entertaining of men. All three were in their early thirties and were considered "modern," having lived in America in recent years.

The first simply raised his eyebrows, a most emphatic way of saying, "No!"

"I say to hell with this sick society—let them do it, Nancy," fumed the second, a bachelor.

At that outburst, the third, an air-force major, bit his lip in the Muslim gesture that meant "Shame on you!" He added, "Why tell Nancy that? You know someone will call the police. Why, I probably would if they did it more than five times. I may be a modern man, but my wife and the neighbors are not. They'd call your ladies 'prostitutes.' No, Sister, never let those single women entertain men there."

When Nancy, Reyhan, and Selma could not agree on a policy, they agreed to abide by the decision of "the regulars." Since they were aware that, as "firstfruits," what each convert did very much affected the entire body, corporate decisions were encouraged. The decision of the five older members—four missionaries and Mene, who had recently returned from her brother's city—was a firm no. In the end, even Reyhan and Selma joined in to make the vote unanimous.

Winter passed without further incidents, and Nancy assumed the issue was dead. The women matured as a body, thanks to one couple's increased willingness to host the singles and to the added availability of their meeting hall.

Now it was June, and Nancy was hoping to leave everything to Reyhan and Selma while she was on furlough. Then, last night, she was surprised to find Reyhan, Selma, Mehmet, and Zeki praying with an unfamiliar young woman in the living room with the door closed. All five had rushed to explain that the stranger had just confessed her faith in Christ. At this exciting news, Nancy had relaxed and enjoyed their brief visit.

But tonight was different. It began with an argument. "We've decided not to obey that silly rule, Nancy. We have been set free in Christ, and that means free to be ourselves," Reyhan had announced when she learned Nancy's sore throat would keep her at home that evening. "Jesus didn't worry about his neighbors, and neither should we. Besides, if we tell Selma's college friends about your rule, they'll mock Christianity and tell us it's as backward as Islam."

Nancy had pleaded: "But what about 1 Peter 2:12, where we're told to maintain good conduct among the Gentiles, so that when they spread stories about us as *gavur*, they will remember how honorably we live and someday give praise to God? We are warned never to give even the appearance of evil, Reyhan, so that we may win others to Christ. . . ." Reyhan had responded with well-chosen Scriptures of her own. Nothing was resolved, and silence hung heavily over the usually cheery apartment until the doorbell rang several hours later.

Nancy went to the door, and much to her dismay, there stood Mehmet and Zeki. Reyhan and Selma had invited them as guests for dinner! Angry, hurt, and embarrassed, Nancy had reminded all four of the fellowship's decision last fall, but none of them could even remember voting.

Not knowing what to say or do, Nancy had escaped to her bedroom. She wanted to climb into bed and nurse her sore throat and hurt feelings until morning. But the issue about male guests had to be resolved immediately, for with that rested the fate of the House of Ruth. Nancy prayed once more, "Oh, Lord, give us love. . . . Show us how to balance our liberty in you with your demands that we not cause others to stumble. And *please*, Lord, keep us from divisions between nationals and foreigners, young and old." She dried her eyes, opened her bedroom door, and walked down the hall toward the dining room where the four were seated.

8

Pastoral Counseling for an Abused Wife
Frances F. Hiebert

Pastor Samuel put the telephone down with a sigh and returned to the table in his house, where his wife and their guests were happily chatting over the evening meal. The guests, Professor Gordon and his wife, had come for a visit to Singapore from a seminary in America where Pastor Samuel planned to do some graduate work next year. They had met only recently, but already they were all experiencing the warm fellowship of those who are part of the family of God.

His wife, Leela, and their guests stopped talking when they saw the serious expression on Pastor Samuel's face. They looked at him expectantly as he sat down at the table again. He could see the concern on their faces as they waited for him to speak.

"That call was from a woman who has been coming to see me about a very serious personal matter," the pastor told them. "I have prayed about this matter and puzzled over it for many hours, but I still don't know exactly how to advise her. I am going to share this problem with you because I need help. I know you will treat the matter confidentially and, in any case, you are leaving for America soon and will never be involved in it yourselves." Pastor Samuel looked at the older man across the table and added, "You know that I have only been a pastor for about five years, and it seems that there are some questions for which they don't teach the answers in seminary—such as how to help a woman whose husband is abusing her!"

Then Pastor Samuel began to tell them the story of an Indian woman who was part of the large population of Indian immigrants and their families that came to work on the docks in Singapore. Although this woman, Padma, was not a member of his church, she had come to see him because a friend had told her that the Samuels were also originally from Madras.

Padma told Pastor Samuel that she herself was a Christian but had not been practicing her faith very seriously until after she had come to Singapore. She came from a family in Madras that had experienced a great deal of difficulty. Her father had been ill for several years while she was attending a Catholic girls' high school and had died just before her graduation. Padma was forced to take employment as a day laborer in order to help her mother support the family, which included three younger brothers.

At the construction site in Madras where she worked, Padma met a man by the name of Ram who was about eight years older than she. Because her family's circumstances were so desperately difficult, Padma agreed to live with this man if he would help to support her mother and younger brothers. He promised that he would, so Padma became his common-law wife.

Padma was quite distressed when, after a year of living with Ram, he decided to go to Singapore because he had heard that even a dock worker could become a rich man there. Ram wanted Padma to go with him, but she was afraid and reluctant to leave her mother and brothers. Finally, however, she agreed to go on the condition that Ram would go to the Catholic priest with her so they could be legally married. He consented, and they were married three days before leaving Madras.

After they had settled in Singapore, Ram earned much more money than he had in Madras. They had been in Singapore a little more than a year when their first child, a girl, had been born. Padma had to leave her work as a housemaid to care for the child because she had no family to help her, as she would have had at home in Madras. Also, in a very short time after the birth of the first child, Padma found herself pregnant again. When she came to see Pastor Samuel for the first time, it was about two months before the second baby was due to be born.

During the first year they lived in Singapore, Padma told Pastor Samuel, Ram had provided well for them. He was not even too displeased when the child had been born, in spite of the fact that it was a girl. Occasionally he would even allow Padma to send a small money order home to her mother.

It was shortly after she became pregnant the second time that the real trouble started. Padma knew soon after she began to live with Ram that there were other women in his life. Padma mainly ignored this fact because, in her experience, "men are like that." But what was happening now was something much worse. Since they had more money, Ram had begun getting drunk more often. He could be very ugly when he was drunk, so she kept herself out of the way as much as possible.

Padma told Pastor Samuel that during the time of her first pregnancy she had come in contact with some Pentecostal Christians through an Indian friend who rode the same bus Padma took to work every morning. The Christians showed her a lot of love and concern, and she came to depend on them for a place to hide from Ram when he was drinking. These friends showed Padma how to commit her life to Jesus Christ and live in fellowship with him in a way that she had never known before. Her new life in Christ was a great comfort to her when things got rough at home.

Padma tried to show love to Ram because her Christian friends taught her that she should do this even when he was cruel to her. "It is the way Christ wants us to treat others because of his love for us," they had said. One day she even tried to explain to Ram about her new relationship to Jesus. He become very angry and threatened to beat her if she ever talked about it again.

After the first child was born, there was a brief period of happiness for Padma, but it didn't last for long. It was then that Ram began to abuse her physically, especially after he had been drinking.

Then one night Ram brought another woman home with him. He insisted that Padma cook for them, and the other woman spent the night in his bed. Now Padma's life had turned into a living hell. Ram insisted on bringing his women home whenever he pleased, and Padma was obliged to serve them.

Padma turned to the Pentecostal pastor for help. He was very sympathetic. He and his wife gave Padma all the support that they possibly could. When Padma came to their home one night with her face bruised and bleeding, they bathed her wounds and prayed with her until she stopped her sobbing.

Finally, after several more severe beatings, Padma told the Pentecostal pastor that she was thinking of leaving her husband and going back to her mother in Madras. She was afraid of not only the physical violence but also of the venereal disease that was being carried into her home. The pastor told her that while he had great sympathy for her, he could not advise her to leave her husband. A Christian woman should obey her husband and love him, even if he was not a Christian. In that way he might also become a Christian. She should do her best to bear the suffering and trust God to bring about a change in her husband. Padma said that although she wanted Ram to become a Christian more than anything else in the world, she didn't know how she could stand up under his abuse much longer. And what might happen to her child and the baby that was yet to be born?

Another Christian friend then advised Padma to go and talk with Pastor Samuel. By the time she had finished her story, Pastor Samuel's heart was aching for this poor woman, but he was not sure what he should tell her to do. He also hesitated to interfere in the counseling advice being given by a fellow pastor. From then on, however, Pastor Samuel and his wife opened their home to Padma at any time of the day or night. Leela often cared for Padma's child when she was feeling too ill to do it herself.

When Pastor Samuel had answered the phone, Padma was weeping on the other end of the line. "Pastor Samuel," she sobbed, "I don't think I can stand it any longer."

Now Pastor Samuel looked around the table at his wife and their guests. The two women had tears in their eyes, and Professor Gordon had put his arm around his wife's shoulders. "What do you think I should say to Padma?" Pastor Samuel asked.

9

Wife Beating
William A. Benner

The Reverend Solomon Begari, chairman of the Pastor's Disciplinary Committee, looked at the other two members of the committee and said, "We must decide whether Pastor Trombo should be disciplined for beating his wife, and, if so, what that discipline should be. There is no doubt that he beat her, but she disobeys him and embarrasses him in public. The question is, is this something for which we should discipline a husband, particularly a pastor?"

The missionaries who lived by the church had brought the problem before the committee. One afternoon Pastor James Trombo returned home and found his young daughter playing with rat poison, which was scattered on the floor around her. His wife, Paeyam, was nowhere to be seen. He rushed his child to the hospital to have her stomach pumped, just in case she had eaten some of it. When he returned home, he beat his wife after he found out that she had gone to town to buy a dress. She had left their daughter asleep on the floor, expecting to be gone only a short while. Pastor Trombo had scolded his wife several times before this for leaving the child when she was asleep, but Paeyam had taken to ignoring his rebukes and sometimes publicly embarrassed him out of spite.

Immediately after her beating, Paeyam went across the street to the home of Carl and Lynne Hansen, the missionaries in the area. Paeyam had worked for them for several months, ever since their arrival in the South Sea Islands. Carl and Lynne both liked Paeyam and were shocked to see her weeping and bruised. Although Carl had found it hard to work with Pastor Trombo, who seemed to him to be arrogant and authoritarian, he and Lynne had to admit that the pastor's church was flourishing. Beside the many highlanders who attended the church, Pastor Trombo had a real ministry among the coastal people working in the town.

Carl went immediately to talk to Pastor Trombo, but he would not listen to Carl's remonstrance. "This is the custom of our people," he said. The missionaries felt that they could not drop the case, so they reported it to the Pastor's Disciplinary Committee of the Zion Churches of the South Pacific Islands.

Rumors of the beating circulated among the church members, causing various reactions. Some of the older people felt that Paeyam had finally gotten what she deserved and now would probably straighten up if the committee affirmed her husband. After all, wife beating was common in the highlands cultures. Many others who had been raised in the church were concerned. They felt that Pastor Trombo had done wrong and might even have committed a sin, although they were not exactly sure what kind of a sin. The new converts from the coastal people were generally confused. They liked Pastor Trombo and found him to be a good pastor, but they were used to treating their wives with more equality than the highlanders. Their wives were not beaten, except by an occasional drunk husband.

The members of the committee considered all these facts and the possible consequences of various decisions. They realized that if they affirmed Pastor Trombo, many people, including the missionaries and coastal people, would not understand. It would seem to them that the committee was condoning the practice of wife beating. Moreover, it would cause friction between the church leaders and the missionaries.

On the other hand, if the committee decided to discipline Pastor Trombo, it would cause problems with the older highlanders in the congregation and detract from his ministry. The committee's decision would affect the future of the church, Pastor Trombo's ministry, and his relationships in his family. No matter what they did, it seemed as if someone in the church would not understand.

Pastor Solomon Begari looked at the other committee members and said, "As the disciplinary committee of the Zion churches, we must make a final decision in this case. We have talked to Pastor Trombo, to the missionaries, and to our other pastors, and no agreement seems possible. And we cannot put off the decision without seriously hurting the church and the people involved. What should we do?"

10

The Marriage Tangle
Gladwin Jaykar

Do you mean to say that we should accept this application and permit her to be baptized, even though she is living with a man to whom she is not married?" asked Mr. Rao, chairman of the church committee.

"Yes," responded Mr. Bhagat, "but remember she was forced by her parents to marry a Hindu she hated after she and my son were married to each other in spirit and in body. In the sight of God, that Hindu wedding was no marriage. We should marry Umesh and Runa in church and admit them into our fellowship."

"What about the law?" Mr. Rao asked. "Have you thought about the consequences? The court will not recognize their vows to each other as marriage. Until Runa is divorced from Krishna, we cannot marry her to Umesh. And if they continue to live together without marriage, we cannot accept them into the fellowship of the church."

The meeting continued late into the night, with much debate among the committee members. Finally, when no clear consensus was in sight, Mr. Rao announced, "We will meet again tomorrow night to decide the issue. I want each of you to think carefully about whether we should baptize a woman who has been married against her will to a Hindu of her own caste, but who now wants to marry a young man in our church."

The matter was public knowledge in the church. Mr. Bhagat, a Christian convert from the Bhil tribe in South India, was the supervisor in the hostel of the large church high school. Umesh, Mr. Bhagat's oldest son, was in the tenth class, along with students from many different castes, most of whom were not Christians. Two missionaries and an Indian pastor were in charge of the school.

Umesh was admired by all as a good sportsman. While in school he fell in love with Runa, a girl from a high Hindu caste. Her father, Mr. Thakur, was a wealthy farmer, a member of a high "clean" caste, and a leader in the village. When Mr. Thakur heard about the matter, he took Runa out of school and warned Umesh's father to keep his son away from the girl. Mr. Bhagat did not approve of the relationship either, but he thought it would be short-lived.

Then one day the news spread: Umesh had run away with Runa. Mr. Thakur reported the matter to the police and a search was made. "If I find your son, I will kill him," Mr. Thakur said to Umesh's father. "Is this what your Christianity teaches? Be off with your new religion." A few days later Runa was found and brought home. Mr. Bhagat beat Umesh, and the church elders summoned Mr. Bhagat to clear up the matter. But he refused to appear before the church committee.

Little was seen of Runa the following year, but she continued to correspond with Umesh secretly. Shortly thereafter her father arranged a marriage for her to Krishna, a young man from her own caste. Runa was confined to her house until the marriage was performed.

A month after her marriage, Runa managed to slip out of her new home. She went straight to Umesh's house and said to him, "Umesh, I can't live without you. Forgive me, for I was compelled to get married to Krishna. You are my first love and I am still yours. Accept me back, or I will die. Here are my ornaments of pure gold. We have enough money to live at least for a month. Let us leave here and live or die together!" Fortunately for Umesh, his parents were not at home at the time, so he took Runa and fled.

When Runa did not return home that night, her husband and father were alarmed. Asking around, they found out that Runa had been seen going toward Umesh's house. Immediately they went to the police and logged a criminal complaint against Umesh. His parents were interrogated but knew nothing about their son. Finally, in despair, Mr. Thakur said to the police, "I have done everything for my daughter, and now I have lost everything. Leave the couple alone. I am no longer her father."

News spread rapidly through the village, and the chairman of the church committee called an urgent meeting. The committee decided to give Mr. Bhagat an early retirement and to excommunicate his son. There had been disagreement, however, on whether they should excommunicate Mr. Bhagat and his family as well. Mr. Bhagat told the members, "I am a tribal, and the majority of the members in the church are tribals. We will close the church and lock it up if you excommunicate me and my family!" Chairman Rao had decided to defer the decision to a later meeting.

Before the next meeting was scheduled, Mr. Thakur, who had lost his reputation in the village, sold his house and left for the city. Umesh and Runa returned to stay in the house of Umesh's father. Mr. Bhagat then sent an application to the church committee, in which he wrote, "Please baptize Runa and marry her to my son. Is this not a good opportunity to win her for Christ and to help our church grow?"

The application had been supported by a few of the committee members, mainly those who were related to Mr. Bhagat. Other members had disagreed, saying that it was against biblical teachings. One elder stood up and said, "Let Runa be divorced from the husband she was forced to marry against her will, and then let her be married to Umesh." Another said, "We need to give them some teaching, and then we can baptize them." A third said, "If we allow her to stay as she is, the Hindus will come and persecute us. They will say that Christians are abducting their daughters and making them Christians." The debate had gone on and on. Finally Mr. Rao had said, "We are not near a decision. We need to think and pray about the matter seriously. We will meet again tomorrow night."

As Mr. Rao walked home slowly, he could not keep his mind off the problem and how it would impact the church and its reputation in the Hindu village. "How can we allow such things to go on in the church?" he asked himself. "If we are not careful, the matter could divide the church, and bring disgrace to Christianity in the village. But what alternative do we have? If we return her to her Hindu husband, he will either kill her or reject her. Moreover, she will look for every opportunity to return to live with Umesh because they love one another. But they are not married. If we try to marry them, the court will object and imprison us because she is not divorced, and the Hindus will persecute us even more. If we seek a divorce for her, the angry husband may block it out of honor and revenge. What should we do as elders in the church?"

11

Too Many Wives
Paul G. Hiebert

Tom and Sarah Ward looked at the old chief seated on his stool in front of his hut, and at his wives squatting expectantly behind him. They had prayed two years for Amadu's conversion. Now he had summoned them and told them that he and his wives were ready to become Christians and wanted to be baptized into the church. The young missionaries expressed their joy at his decision and told him they would ask for a meeting of the church council the next day to act on his request.

Now, as Tom and Sarah sat under the night sky brilliantly lit with stars, they wrestled with the question of what they should recommend to the church council the next morning. Their decision seemed to depend on a number of entangled issues. Should the church baptize polygamists and their wives? And what about Amadu? He was the chief of the village and a natural leader. Should they recognize this and make him a leader in the church? They knew that even if they did not ordain him as the leading elder in the church, the people would recognize him as such. Did Paul's instructions that a leader have one wife apply only to the apostle's own cultural setting, or did they apply to the church at all times? And what about themselves? Should they as young missionaries take a stand against their mission's policy if they disagreed with it or if it hampered the growth of the church, even though this might lead to their dismissal?

Two years earlier, shortly after they arrived in Africa as American missionaries, the Wards were sent by their mission board and the West Africa Evangelical Church to begin a church in a new tribe in the Ivory Coast. At the outset they went to see Amadu, the local chief of the village where they felt called to work. They asked him for permission to live near the village and talk to his people about Jesus Christ. He welcomed them and gave them a place to build their house. Amadu had listened without comment when they shared with him the Good News of salvation through Jesus Christ. But he showed no opposition when five families and two single men in the village decided to become Christians. The married men were young and had only one wife each, so the Wards had not faced the question of polygamy. Gladly they baptized the converts and organized a new church. Mugbe, one of the married men, was recognized by the other Christians as their leader, so Tom and Sarah spent considerable time teaching him the Scripture and the responsibilities of a church leader. But the church was young, and the converts could not read, so they mainly looked to the missionaries for guidance in their newfound faith.

Now the chief wanted to become a Christian. What should they do? If they accepted him into the church, the door would be wide open for them to reach other families in the village. But what about his wives? At first the question seemed only to be one of polygamy, but the more they discussed the case, the more they realized that there were many other social factors involved.

First, both the West Africa Evangelical Church and the African Evangelical Mission, under which the young missionaries served, had already taken a strong stand against polygamy. In this they agreed with the stand taken by other mission agencies that had begun work in West Africa in the late nineteenth century. At the Lambeth Conference organized by the Anglican Church in 1888, a resolution had been passed that stated:

> It is the opinion of this Conference that persons living in polygamy be not admitted to baptism, but that they be accepted as candidates and kept under Christian instruction until such time as they shall be in a position to accept the law of Christ.
>
> The wives of polygamists may, in the opinon of this Conference, be admitted in some cases to baptism, but it must be left to the local authorities of the church to decide under what circumstances they may be baptized.

The African Evangelical Mission had resolved that the wives of a polygamist could be baptized if they were true converts, because they were usually the involuntary victims of the custom. But the mission would baptize no man who retained more than one wife. A polygamist was encouraged to "free himself" for baptism by putting aside all wives except one; otherwise he must wait until God freed him by the death of all but one of his wives.

The Wards were aware of the fact that some of the African churches, after they became independent from mission control, were beginning to reexamine the question of polygamy. In Tanzania one church had decided:

> An unbeliever who has more than one wife, if converted to Christianity and requiring baptism, may be baptized with his believing wives and children with the permission of the Bishop. (He is not to take any more wives as long as any of his wives are still alive.) And they can be received for communion.

As they discussed the problem, Sarah and Tom talked about the biblical teachings regarding polygamy. Did Paul in 1 Timothy 3 require "one wife" of all Christians, or only of the leaders? And what about the traditional marriages? Were the traditional tribal weddings true marriages that had to be honored? If so, were they not asking the old chief to divorce some of his wives if he had to send them away? Which was worse—polygamy or divorce?

The young missionaries considered the impact of various policies on the growth of the church. On the one hand, if they permitted polygamy among the laity, one of the great barriers to the spread of the gospel in the tribe would be removed. Would this not, however, open the door for sin to enter the church? On the other hand, the church might accept only those who were polygamists *before* their conversion and take a strong stand against Christians' taking more than one wife. But once they accepted polygamists into the church, it would be hard to eliminate polygamy from the church in the long run. In other parts of Africa where polygamists had been admitted into the church, young Christian men under strong pressures from their kinsmen often took second wives, particularly when their first wives were barren. They knew that they would be disciplined; but after a time, if they showed proper repentance, they could be reinstated with their wives because there already were polygamists in the church. Finally, the church might follow the policy practiced by many other churches in Africa and deny church membership to polygamists altogether. But did this not hinder the growth of the church, and was this not condemning new believers for sins they committed before they became Christians? Was monogamy essential for conversion, or could it be handled as a matter of spiritual growth within the church?

Tom and Sarah had also considered the specific case of Amadu. If they asked the old chief to give up all but one of his wives, which one should he keep? The first marriage had been arranged for him by his parents. That wife had borne him no children, so he had married a second who gave him three sons and a daughter. Later his brother had died, leaving him to care for two widows and several children. By tribal custom, he was automatically "married" to the widows. In time these wives had also borne him children. Finally, as a tribal chief, he had taken another wife to add to his prestige and cement relationships between the clans. It was this young wife who now cared for him daily in his old age.

What about the wives and children who were put away so that the chief could be baptized—what would become of them? How would they respond to the gospel? And what about widows? According to the customs of the tribe, widows were automatically married to the nearest kinsman of their deceased husband. If polygamy was prohibited, who would care for them? The church would have to find other ways to provide for widows and their children.

There was also the question of leadership. If the church admitted the old chief into membership, he would automatically become the church leader. Mugbe might remain the official pastor, but everyone, in fact, would look to the old chief for leadership. How did this fit with Paul's teachings about a leader being the husband of one wife?

Finally, Tom and Sarah wondered about their own relationships to the various groups with whom they worked. What about their relationship to the mission? If they believed the mission policy to be wrong, were they obligated as missionaries to enforce it? What about their relationship to the West Africa Evangelical Church? Some of its young leaders were beginning to question the mission policy and were calling for a reexamination of the whole issue. What about their obligations to the church in their village, and to the non-Christian villagers? Were they not responsible under God for opening the door of salvation to these people?

It was late when Tom and Sarah finished their discussion and agreed that tomorrow they would recommend to the church that. . . .

12

Adultery or Polygamy?
Stephen Asonibare

"If a Christian takes a second wife, is it adultery or is it polygamy? Are you ready to decide? And what should we do with Mayele, Ayo, and Uzi?" Elder Mbangu asked the church council. He looked over at Pastor Aina, seated quietly on the bench, and wondered how he, Mayele's father, would vote. Mbangu also thought about the older men in the church who had become Christians after they had married several wives, and about the non-Christians who often accused the Christians of not taking care of their widows.

The policy of the church was clear. Members found to be in adultery were to be censured and held under church discipline until they repented and broke the relationship. Those who were polygamists were to be rebuked, and not admitted to the fellowship of the Lord's Table until they publicly took a stand against polygamy as an accepted practice. The local church believed that although the Bible teaches that polygamy is not ideal for Christians, it does not teach that polygamists who follow Christ are condemned to hell for marrying more than one wife. The congregation had taken this stand, in part, out of consideration for new converts who had married several wives before their conversions. However, until now they had not had to face the question of what to do when a Christian took a second wife.

The facts of the case were also clear. Mayele was the second son in Pastor Aina's family. Mayele's older brother, Oji, had little education and held an ordinary laborer's job. He married Ayo, a Muslim who converted to Christianity in order to marry Oji. She became a good wife and mother of three children and was a faithful member in the church.

Pastor Aina arranged for Mayele to go to school. After completing high school, Mayele found a good job. He met Nsimba in church and the two were soon very much in love with each other. No one was surprised when they announced their engagement. Within a year, they planned to be married.

Then Oji was killed in a tragic automobile accident, leaving his wife and three children with no means of support. Pastor Aina tried hard to help her, but he still had four unmarried children at home, and his salary was small. Ayo could not return to her parents, for they had disowned her when she became a Christian. Nor could she find a job to support herself and the children. Moreover, the children were too young to be left alone.

One day Pastor Aina called Mayele for a talk. He told his son that he and his wife had thought much about the family that Oji had left behind. They had come to the conclusion that the best thing for the family was for Mayele to assume his traditional responsibility as a brother by marrying Ayo. This was their tribal way of caring for widows and orphans. It would be heartless to send Ayo and her children back to her parents' home. Furthermore, Ayo had proven herself to be a woman of integrity and a good wife, and no one knew what Nsimba would be like after marriage. Finally, Pastor Aina and his family would be spared the heavy costs of a bride-price and the elaborate wedding appropriate for Mayele's marriage to Nsimba. A simple service would suffice if Mayele married Ayo instead.

Mayele told his father he wanted to think about the matter and would let him know the next day. He knew that it was not going to be easy to convince Nsimba to break off their engagement. When he talked to her, he tried to make her realize that what had happened to Ayo could happen to Nsimba herself, and that there had to be some way to care for widows and orphans. In the end Nsimba told Mayele to do what he believed right.

After much agonizing thought, Mayele agreed to carry out his father's wishes and abide by the customs of his tribe. After a simple church wedding, Ayo and her children moved into Mayele's house. At first, things seemed to work out well for the couple. Ayo gave birth to two daughters, which gave the couple a family of five.

But then outsiders began to notice that something had gone wrong between the two. Mayele worried that his earning power could not cope with the responsibility of caring for so big a family. He longed for more education, but he did not know how to get it and care for the family at the same time. Moreover, it troubled him that Ayo had only given him girls. He had no son.

Nsimba learned of the growing estrangement. Still unmarried, she began sending messages to Mayele and eventually visited him in his office. Each time they were together, she reminded him of their promise some years before to give their lives to each other. Mayele was caught between his discontent at home and his love for Nsimba.

When Mayele consulted his young friends, they told him he should live his own life. They assured him a brighter future awaited him if he furthered his education. He could marry Nsimba after he graduated from the university. After all, his marriage to Ayo had been forced on him. This advice disturbed Mayele, for he felt it was wrong. Nevertheless, in the end, he sent Ayo back to the village and took Nsimba home as a wife.

Matters came to a head when Nsimba became pregnant. The church council called a meeting to deal with the issue. Mayele argued that he had married Ayo at the urging of the elders to fulfill his traditional role as a brother, but that he was already engaged to Nsimba before his brother's death. He pointed out that their denomination regarded such engagements as "native marriages." They saw wedding rituals in the church as simply giving church recognition to such marriages, not as the official weddings. He and Nsimba were therefore husband and wife before Oji died. Furthermore, he had not divorced Ayo, and would continue to support her as best he could. Consequently, he should be treated as a polygamist.

Some of the elders pointed out, however, that Mayele and Nsimba had never had a church wedding. Moreover, Mayele had sent Ayo back to the village even though he had not officially divorced her. He was therefore guilty of adultery and should be required to send Nsimba away and take Ayo back into his home.

Others felt that the church was partly to blame for the dilemma, for the elders had put pressure on Mayele to take responsibility for Ayo. This custom worked well when a man was allowed to have more than one wife, but since the church took a strong stand on monogamous marriages, they would have to find other ways to care for widows. But how? In any case, according to their tribal custom, Mayele's engagement to Nsimba was tantamount to marriage, so Mayele should be treated as a polygamist and not as an adulterer. He should take Ayo back and try to keep peace in his home. The real problem was the fact that he became a polygamist *after* he was a Christian, and the church had no policy to deal with such cases.

After a prolonged discussion, Elder Mbangu looked at the council and asked, "Are you ready to make a decision in this case? If so, what should we do with Mayele and Nsimba—what must they do to be restored to fellowship in the church? And who should take care of Ayo and her family?"

13

The Christian Polygamist
Samuel Nkulila

Bishop Yohana had just concluded a two-week crusade in the city of Moshi, Tanzania, and 350 persons had committed their lives to Jesus in the last evening alone. One of those was a man by the name of Musa. Because of the conversion of this man, the pastor and committee of one of the smaller churches in the city had a rather large problem—Musa had too many wives.

Musa was a man of some means. He owned 200 cows, a big farm, and had 10,000 shillings in the bank. His farm lay a few miles from the edge of the city where the small church was located. Musa had a friend in the city who belonged to the church, and he had attended services several times with his friend. They had some long discussions about the Christian faith. On one occasion his friend had introduced him to the pastor of the church.

On the morning after his conversion, Musa knocked on the door of the pastor. After greeting him, Musa told him with unmistakable joy that he had become a Christian. A slight shadow came over his face, however, when he confided to the pastor that he now had a problem that he didn't have before his conversion.

"Pastor," he said, "I praise God for saving me from sin. But according to your teaching, I am supposed to have only one wife. I have seven wives and twenty-five children! What shall I do?"

The pastor was taken aback. In his rather small and poor congregation, they had not yet faced this dilemma. With little time to consider, the pastor fell back on the missionary teaching in the Bible Institute where he had received his training. "Of course, the Bible, which is God's Holy Word, demands that you remain with your first wife only. The rest can go. If you stay with them, you will be committing adultery. Also, if you stay with them, you cannot take Holy Communion in the church. So, go quickly. Get yourself organized. Keep the first wife with her five children and send the others and their twenty children away."

The new convert went away from the pastor's home with a heavy heart. "What kind of religion is this?" he asked himself. "When one person is saved, does it mean that others must be lost? I thought that coming to Jesus was supposed to take away my burdens. Now it seems that a much heavier one has fallen on me."

The next day, Musa decided to travel by bus some hundred miles from his home to see Bishop Yohana. He explained his situation to the bishop, who listened thoughtfully and was very sympathetic. He asked Musa if he truly would follow Jesus if something could be done to care for his seven wives and twenty-five children.

"Of course, Bishop," Musa replied. "That is all I request."

"Go home now, Musa," the bishop said kindly but firmly. "I am going to discuss your case with the church committee next week, and we shall let you know what has been decided."

The following week, Bishop Yohana called the committee together. It was the first time they had faced the issue of polygamy in their congregation. It was quite a challenge to them, and they talked for hours.

The bishop said, "Gentlemen, the crucial issue here is the welfare of the family. If Musa keeps only his first wife and her children, who will care for the other six wives and their children? Since Musa is well able to care for them all, can we not find a more humane approach to the problem?"

One of the deacons said, "Musa can do one thing. He can build another house, where he will live with his first wife, at least one mile from the grouped houses of the former family. He can still be responsible for seeing that his other wives and children are getting food, clothes, and medical care. But he should not sleep in their houses anymore."

Musa's friend, who was also on the committee, lamented, "This is inhuman. Musa's family has been together for over twenty years, and now, simply because he has become a Christian, must the family fall apart?"

But another committee member shouted angrily, "That is how the Way is—a hard and lonely journey. We are to forsake all else if we want to follow Jesus."

The meeting was a tough one. Scripture after Scripture was quoted on both sides of the issue. One side quoted Scriptures to support the idea that Musa should have nothing to do with any except his first wife. The other side quoted Scriptures about Christian love and compassion for all people. To them, there was also an issue of fairness and justice. They maintained that Musa was a rich man, and he had an obligation to support his whole family. Musa, they pointed out, was fully prepared to do this.

The bishop went home without the case having been settled, but the church committee dedicated itself to a week of prayer and Bible study. At the end of the week they came to a conclusion. The commitee decided that Musa could not continue in polygamy and still have fellowship with their church, for that would be a stumbling block to the whole community. They would allow him, however, to visit his former wives and their twenty children. He should also support them financially and see that their needs were met.

Musa seemed quite relieved by their decision, and expressed his agreement. He began attending Sunday school, and after six months he was baptized.

Another six months went by. Then one Sunday afternoon at the close of the service, there was a meeting of the church elders. Musa interrupted the meeting with these words, "Forgive me, Elders, but I want to inform you that my third wife, Wandi, has been blessed with a baby girl. Now, praise God, we have twenty-six children!"

A dead silence greeted Musa's words. Obviously Musa had not followed their advice. Now how should they deal with him? They would have to confront him the following Sunday, but what should they say?

Postscript

When the elders met the following Sunday, they decided on a different approach. They would tell Musa that he could stay with his wives, trusting that the Holy Spirit would speak to the "illegitimate" wives and convict them to leave Musa. In this way, it was hoped that those who felt free to go should do so, and eventually, the "true" wife would remain.

Musa's friend left the meeting still wondering if they could not have found a better solution.

14

Love Him or Leave Him?
Evelyn Jensen

Marilyn looked at the woman who sat dejected and forlorn on the chair beside her. Marilyn had come to Quito as a missionary four years before to work among the women of that city. She had heard many tales of suffering and despair, but somehow over the years it had not become easier for her to bear the burdens of these women with them. She had learned to know Luz in the church only a few months back and had rejoiced at the woman's spiritual growth. Now Luz, on the verge of tears, had come for help. She told Marilyn that her *conviviente* (common-law spouse) had refused to marry her. When she raised the question, he had shouted in anger: "No, I will not marry you. There is no reason for us to be married. And besides, *Yo soy muy hombre!* [I am a real man!]." He slammed the door on his way out to the corner bar to spend the evening with his buddies. Now Luz was pleading with Marilyn to tell her what to do.

As they sat together, Luz told Marilyn about her life. She had been born in a village about a hundred miles from the large city of Quito. Her parents had not been rich, but they had provided well for the material needs of their family. They had been devout Catholics, especially her mother, who regularly attended mass and supported the church activities. Luz remembered her mother as being the center of her family and the one who provided the emotional strength in the time of family crisis. She noticed that her parents had continuous quarrels when she was about ten years old. Luz then discovered through the neighboring children that she had some half-brothers and sisters who lived on the other side of the town. At first it was devastating for her. Her admiration for her father cooled and her emotional ties to her mother increased.

As Luz went through her teenage years, she developed into a beautiful young woman and her suitors were many. One, Juan Jose, was particularly gallant. Her father virtually pushed her into the marriage—after all, Juan Jose was several rungs higher on the social ladder in their small town. In the first year or so, things went reasonably well between them. Within the first year of marriage a son was born to them, and they named him Juan Luiz.

Luz's inner delight was now unspeakable—she had proven to herself and the world that she was a real woman. She doted on her son, and he soon became the center of her life. Meanwhile, her husband began to be weary of the constraints of married life. Luz was shocked, deeply hurt, and angered when she found out through the grapevine that Juan Jose had a mistress. The husband and wife quarreled and argued frequently. At the end of two and a half years of marriage, Juan finally abandoned Luz and their son and left the area. Once again Luz was devastated. However, her mother comforted her with the words, "My dear, that is just the way men are. You must accept it. Let us go to the church and pray to the Virgin to comfort you in this time."

After some time, Luz decided to go to Quito, where she hoped to find a job that would enable her to raise her precious young son. She had a high-school education, so she was able to find a well-paying job. At first it was terribly lonely for her, but gradually she made friends. She also became more faithful in attending mass. When she felt lonely for her mother, she would pour out her heart to the Virgin and find great relief.

A year or so after Luz had moved to Quito, she met Pedro, a fellow employee. He was almost the exact opposite to Juan Jose—not particularly handsome or charming, but known among the employees as stable and responsible. He became almost obsessed with her feminine beauty, even though she appeared to be totally uninterested in him. Finally, however, Luz gave in to his persistent attentions. They decided to live together, but he was not interested in formalizing the relationship by marriage.

Pedro proved to be all the husband that her real husband was not. They got along reasonably well. He provided for Luz, her son, and the two other children that came along later. At times he would become irritable and angry with her, but she knew that he also adored her. He did spend time with his friends in the corner bar, but only on occasion did he come home drunk.

Luz had now lived with Pedro for almost ten years. Pedro, she knew, had occasionally indulged in some sexual escapades, but they were very short-lived. Luz had decided to ignore these in light of the material security that he offered to her and her children. She was bothered occasionally by the fact that she was not really married to him, but she reconciled the issue within herself by saying, "I'm happier now, not being officially married, than I was when I was officially married. Moreover, it is almost impossible to get the church to grant me a divorce from Juan, and until I do, I cannot marry Pedro." Luz became more and more devoted to the Virgin and set her personal goals to match the Virgin's purity. She had now become the emotional strength for her own family and was really the one who made the decisions.

Then Luz decided to attend an evangelistic campaign near her home. The first time she attended she became deeply aware of her spiritual need. The second time there was no hesitation on her part when the invitation was given. Her conversion experience was life changing. Pedro and the children saw a marked difference in her attitudes and behavior. After the campaign, Luz began to attend the Protestant church and continued to grow spiritually. Her mother, quite aged by now, was disturbed by the changes taking place in Luz's life. Upon occasion, however, Luz had gone to mass and prayed to the Virgin, especially when the burdens became too heavy.

Recently the pastor had announced the beginning of classes to prepare new Christians for baptism. Luz was delighted and enrolled immediately. She had done very well in the classes and was looking forward to being baptized in two weeks. However, the pastor had visited her yesterday and told her it would be impossible for her to be baptized until her relationship with Pedro was formalized by marriage. This had been a blow to her enthusiasm, but today she had ventured a conversation with Pedro about the possibility of getting married.

As Pedro's angry words flashed once again into her mind, Luz began to weep. "What should I do?" she asked Marilyn. "How can I get married when I am already married? How can I get a divorce when I have no idea where Juan Jose is? The Catholic church doesn't put any of these kinds of demands upon me, so why should the Protestant church do so? How could I ever leave Pedro? I've learned to love him now! Does God see me as a terrible sinner because of my relationship to him? Or would it be better to go back to the Virgin Mary and the comfort she can give? What is the real reason why Pedro does not want to get married, and what does it mean to be a 'real' man or woman anyway?" All these questions poured out as Marilyn sat listening silently, wondering what she should say to the distraught woman.

15

Onions and Wives
Roger David Heeren

Beth Jones down-shifted her Honda 125XL dirt bike into first gear as she wearily climbed the last hill into Kabala, a village in the northern mountains of Sierra Leone, West Africa. At three o'clock there would be a meeting of the Kabala Women's Agricultural Cooperative—KWAC—and Beth knew there would be trouble. The village chief (and husband of the president of KWAC) had used his wife's onion money to buy two more wives. Should she take the wife's side and save her friendship with the women, who were already angry at her? Or should she save her job as agriculture extension agent and side with the chief?

Beth thought back to the cross-cultural training she had received one year ago during her first month as a volunteer in a Christian development agency for work in Sierra Leone. They had never warned her about a situation like this. Before joining the agency, she had campaigned for the Equal Rights Amendment in her New England college. Now a man had actually used the money she had helped the women earn—to buy more wives to be used for work, almost as slaves!

Beth had arrived in Kabala one year earlier at the end of the dry season, determined to get her agricultural cooperative program off the ground within the first year. The relief agencies had declared this "the year of the woman," so she had no trouble in getting money, tools, seeds, and even surplus bulgur and oil from the United States. She organized the women of the village and helped them develop programs that would improve their conditions. These included maternity and child care, health, nutrition, basic education, and kitchen gardening. Beth had a particular interest in the last of these, for it enabled the

75

women to earn a little money on their own, money they could use to purchase clothing, toiletries, magazines, and other personal and family items. It also gave them a sense of dignity and independence.

Under Beth's guidance, many of the women that first year planted onion patches in unused land around the village. The project went along well through the rainy season. Meetings with chiefs and meetings with the women to distribute the food, money, tools, and seeds had about drained her of all her strength, but Beth saw the onions sprouting on time, at the end of the rains!

Beth slowly learned the Koronko language during those first months by staying in the village for two and three days at a time, living in the house of Abu, the village chief, and his wife, Isatu. Beth ran weekly meetings with the women of the village, discussing baby-formula problems and lack of medical facilities as well as local gossip. Isatu had spoken many times with the women about how they should use their cooperative earnings for a health center for a midwife. All the women agreed.

Beth learned to respect and love these people, especially the way that the women worked so hard without complaining. Isatu showed her many women's secrets, such as how to cook meals with oil, salt, leaves, and rice over a fire. Despite their cultural differences, the two became fast friends. Abu even joked that Beth was one of his wives.

Throughout the year, the chief was friendly and even contributed his own male laborers for the heaviest of the work, even if it was only for three days. Beth thought that it was a good token of his interest in the progress of women's rights in the village. Chief Abu Bakar was not one to be taken lightly. He was not pleased with a previous rice project sponsored by a development agency, and he had had enough political power to have the agency thrown out of the chiefdom.

Beth had been away from the village for only two weeks to attend a conference on "Women in Development" when she had received a barely legible letter from Isatu. In it Isatu stated that Abu had hired laborers to harvest the onion crop before it was even fully grown and had sold the crop. He had taken the money and arranged to buy two new wives. Isatu was furious, suspecting that Beth was tricking her and the other women by having planned the whole scheme for Abu's benefit. Beth had written that she would be back early to help work on the problem. Now she was returning to the village.

The meeting was scheduled for three o'clock. Beth pondered her circumstances. What should she do? With whom should she identify? If she refuted the charges of her consorting with the chief and sided with the women, she would not be able to continue the project, because the chief determined all work assignments in his chiefdom. If she chose to side with the chief, then the women would not cooperate with her anymore. Possibly she could be a diplomat and not take sides, trying to facilitate change, but then she might infuriate both sides. As Beth pulled into town, the sweat poured down her forehead, partly from the hundred-degree heat and partly because of the situation she was about to face.

16

Should Mrs. Leung Submit?
Ho, Kai-Ming

Pastor Wong said good-bye to his visitor, Mrs. Leung, and closed the door to his office. He would need to spend some time in reflection and prayer before he attempted to advise her. It was a complicated situation.

Mrs. Leung, a new Christian, had been wondering for some time about how she could continue to fit into the family business. She and her husband ran a small shop in a village not far from Hong Kong that sold incense sticks, containers, and candles for Chinese ancestor and temple worship. This small business had been passed on to them from Mr. Leung's parents. Now things were even more complex because her husband had suffered a stroke. He was paralyzed and could not work or even walk alone. This had seriously affected his temperament and his limited tolerance of Mrs. Leung's new religion.

Although their village was near Hong Kong and its modern commercial influence, the Leung family, until recently, had clung to the traditional Chinese religion. Any influence from the city had been mainly superficial.

The Leungs' home was quite near Pastor Wong's small church, and he had visited them faithfully, but it had taken a long time for them to show any interest. The first response was that the Leungs began to send their three children to Sunday school. This provided convenient baby-sitting for them while they were both busy in the shop. Also, as they were nonliterate, they began to depend on the pastor for his willingness to complete official documents for them occasionally.

The people in Pastor Wong's church prayed fervently that the Leung family would come to know the Lord.

One day Mrs. Leung became seriously ill and had to go to the hospital. Several young people from the church volunteered to care for the children so that Mr. Leung could attend to his business.

Pastor Wong visited Mrs. Leung in the hospital and used the opportunity to present the gospel to her again. She was impressed by the love and concern of the church people, and her heart was opened to their message. She received Jesus Christ as her Savior during her hospital stay and went home a new person—spiritually as well as physically whole.

Because he loved her, Mr. Leung tolerated his wife's change of faith and did not interfere seriously with her practice of it. But he would not allow her to be baptized.

Almost as soon as she came home from the hospital, disagreements developed between Mrs. Leung and her husband. She felt she could no longer take part in burning incense to the ancestors. Even the business in which the family was engaged was a contradiction to her newfound faith.

The couple was able to compromise on some things. She would no longer help in the shop but would concentrate on caring for the children, so as to leave her husband free for the business. Mr. Leung saw this as somewhat inconvenient, but he didn't want to quarrel with his wife, especially since she made an effort to be very submissive to him in other ways. Now Mrs. Leung joined the people of the church in praying fervently for her husband, but he continued to show no interest in the gospel.

Then Mr. Leung had the paralytic stroke, and the compromise fell apart. Some of the relatives and other villagers blamed Mrs. Leung's conversion for her husband's stroke. Mr. Leung became ill-tempered and critical of his wife's faith.

Mrs. Leung was perplexed about how to deal with the business. She could not consider taking it up again herself, because of her Christian commitment. She wanted either to hire someone else to work in the shop or to sell the business. But when she suggested this to Mr. Leung, he angrily refused.

Another conflict developed over the ancestor worship. Mr. Leung insisted that their five-year-old son burn incense and candlesticks to the ancestors now that he was unable to do it himself. Chinese culture demands that a son replace his father if he is no longer able to carry out such traditional duties.

Finding herself unable to reach a further compromise with her husband, Mrs. Leung had come this morning to seek her pastor's help. By this time she had decided that employing another person to work in the shop was not right for her either. Although only indirectly, she would still be involved in idol worship because she owned the shop.

On the other hand, if she sold the business, she faced two serious problems. The first was that her husband was fiercely opposed to it. She would be risking great conflict with him that could eventually break up the family. The second problem was financial. She was now the sole support of the family, and as a nonliterate her opportunities for work were very limited. The social welfare extended to residents of Hong Kong was not enough for them.

Mrs. Leung told Pastor Wong that her husband was adamant about their son's fulfilling his duties to the ancestors. "He only knows one verse from the Bible," she told him, "and that is the one about honoring your father and mother. He accuses me of disobeying my own Scripture if I refuse to let our son burn incense to the ancestors."

The pastor and the perplexed woman both realized that the Christian witness in their village could be harmed if the tranquility of the family could not be restored. And yet, how could Mrs. Leung continue in a business that was entirely devoted to idol worship, or let her small son become an idol worshiper?

After prayer with Mrs. Leung, the pastor promised that he would make it a matter of prayer for the whole congregation. Now that she had gone, Pastor Wong decided he must share this burden with someone. He picked up the telephone and dialed the number of the seminary in Hong Kong from which he had graduated three years ago. Perhaps his friend, Dr. Chan, the Professor of Pastoral Care, could help him with this problem.

PART 3

Traditional Customs

How should new Christians deal with the beliefs and customs of their cultural past? What should they do with the drums, dances, dramas, songs, initiation rites and funerals, carved images, art, and banana or palm beer that are a part of their non-Christian tradition? And who should make the decision regarding these practices—the missionary, the church leaders, or the people?

When the gospel comes to a new society, it comes to a people who already have all the essential cultural traits necessary for maintaining their lives. They have their own ideas about food and housing, disease and medicine, and spirits and gods. They know how to build canoes, fight battles, and cast spells on their rivals. They have their own leaders, doctors, and religious practitioners. In other words, the church never enters or exists in a cultural vacuum. How, then, should it relate to the culture around it?

In the past, decisions regarding existing customs were often made by the missionaries. Faced with practices they did not understand, they frequently branded them all "pagan," and forbade their practice in the church. Thus, drums were often prohibited in Africa, dramas in India, and dances in the South Sea Islands.

Several difficulties arose from this sweeping rejection of old ways. First, when the old ways were rejected, new ways were brought in to replace them. Most of the missionaries came from the West, and many assumed that Western customs were basically "Christian." Consequently they introduced their own cultural practices to replace the old. Because of this, the gospel became unnecessarily foreign, and Christianity was identified as a Western religion. This foreignness has been a major barrier in the spread of the gospel among people who love their own cultural ways. Although the gospel does call people and cultures to change, this change must not be equated with adopting Western ways.

Second, this approach turned the missionaries into policemen who had to enforce the rules they made. Because the new Christians were not directly involved in the decision making, they often did not understand or agree with the new rules. These rules, therefore, had to be enforced by those in authority. Because the people were not taught to make decisions, the churches were often full of merely nominal Christians.

Third, this approach did not eliminate the old customs. People simply practiced them in private, where the missionaries and church leaders could not see them. A Christian wedding was held in the church, and then the people went to the village or forest to dance and drink beer. Or mothers continued to tie magical charms to their children to protect them, but now hid them under the children's clothes. In time, customs continued in private infiltrated public Christian practices. The result was syncretism.

Reacting to the colonialism and ethnocentrism implicit in this uncritical rejection of traditional practices, some missionaries and church leaders advocated an almost uncritical acceptance of the old ways. All cultures were seen as basically good because they provided for the ongoing existence of their societies. To become Christians, therefore, little had to change in the lives of the people. The danger of this approach is that old customs are uncritically accepted into the church, and the result again is syncretism.

What other approach can we take? There is a growing awareness that what we need is a "critical contextualization," in which the old ways are studied and then judged in the light of biblical teaching. The missionary or church leaders must first lead their congregations in a study of the old ways and their meanings. Then the leaders provide biblical teaching on the subject at hand. Finally, they lead the people in testing the old ways in the light of Scripture. The people will usually decide that as Christians they can keep many of their old ways, that they do not necessarily have to discard all their old songs, stories, or eating practices. They may decide that some of their customs are evil and must be condemned and that other traditions must be changed to make them acceptable. New words can be given to old tunes, new meanings to old rites. The people may also choose to borrow some of the practices of the missionaries' church. Finally, they may create new practices to express their new faith. In the end they will create new, indigenous, Christian rituals, and they will have learned Christian discernment. Because the Christians as a community make the decisions, the missionaries and leaders will not need to police them.

The question of how the church should relate to its cultural surroundings is not confined to mission settings. It applies equally to old, established churches. Unfortunately, where the church has existed for a long time, it too often adapts to the culture around it and loses its prophetic critique of that society. Even where it has kept its critical voice, the question remains as to what in the surrounding culture it should adopt and what it should reject. Should the church in the West resist the spread of divorce? And if so, how? Should it accommodate to Western materialism, capitalism, nationalism, militarism, expensive funerals, or shrinking swimming suits? If the church ceases to critique the culture around it, it is in danger of becoming a "civil religion"—a religion that serves to justify the status quo. On the other hand, if it totally withdraws from the world around it, it ceases to be heard.

Bibliography

Hiebert, Paul G. 1985. *Anthropological insights for missionaries.* Grand Rapids: Baker Book House.

Loewen, Jacob A. 1975. *Culture and human values: Christian intervention in anthropological perspective.* Pasadena: William Carey Library.

Mayers, Marvin K. 1974. *Christianity confronts culture.* Grand Rapids: Zondervan.

Nida, Eugene A. 1975. *Customs and cultures: Anthropology for Christian missions.* Pasadena: William Carey Library.

Song, C. S. 1984. *Tell us our names: Story theology from an Asian perspective.* Maryknoll: Orbis Books.

Stott, John, and Coote, Robert, eds., 1980. *Down to earth: Studies in Christianity and culture.* Grand Rapids: Eerdmans.

Yamamori, Tetsunao, and Taber, Charles, eds. 1975. *Christopaganism or indigenous Christianity.* Pasadena: William Carey Library.

17

Can a Christian Celebrate Diwali?
Simon P. David

It was Diwali time in India. As dusk began to settle over the village of Dipri in Uttar Pradesh, Victor Pakraj, a Christian missionary from Madras, trudged along the street to his home. His troubled mood was not lightened by the lights twinkling merrily from the little clay-pot lamps that decorated most of the homes he passed. In fact, they were part of his problem! He was trying to find an answer for the question Dhuwarak Prasad had asked him the night before. Dhuwarak's voice had been respectful as always, but his eyes held almost a pleading look when he asked, "Why can't we light our house with beautiful little lamps and decorate our rooms at Diwali? Or, if we can't do it at our Hindu festival, could we do it at Christmas time?"

Two years had passed since Mr. and Mrs. Pakraj had come to Dipri from Tamilnadu. They had started their mission ministry by conducting Vacation Bible School. A handful of students participated, all of them from the Harijan community (untouchable caste that ranks at the bottom of the village society). During the summer, a number of them had accepted Christ as their Savior and Lord. Among these was twelve-year-old Dhuwarak Prasad. Dhuwarak's parents were happy for their son's conversion because they could see a real change in his life. In time, Mr. and Mrs. Prasad also wanted to become Christians, so they had come to the missionaries and were led to the Lord.

This had happened a few months before the annual Hindu festival of Diwali, which celebrates the victory of the god Siva over the powers of the evil god Narakhasura. The missionaries were encouraged by the

Prasads' conversion and did their best to strengthen them in the faith. They visited the Prasads often and invited them to their own home as well. The Prasads had been socially ostracized by the other Harijans when they became Christians, so they especially needed the fellowship of the missionaries and felt quite lonely when Victor Pakraj and his wife went to minister in other villages.

As Diwali approached, the villagers began to decorate their homes and prepare the many lamps they would place around them. They thatched their huts with new grass and bought new clothing to celebrate the festival, but this year, it was a depressing time for the Prasad family. Their own home was dark and undecorated. They were lonely and anxious for Mr. and Mrs. Pakraj to return from their ministry in a neighboring village. The missionaries finally returned on the evening of the day before the festival was to begin. The Prasad family had immediately gone to their house to welcome them home. It was while they were sitting together and Mrs. Pakraj was preparing the evening meal that Dhuwarak had asked the disturbing question. Mr. Pakraj had answered that he would think and pray about it. He invited the Prasad family to come again the following evening, and they would discuss it more.

As Mr. Pakraj neared his own home the next evening, he still was not sure exactly what he would say. He remembered that the first Christians in Europe had begun to celebrate the birth of Christ during the time of a pagan Festival of Winter because they were servants, and their masters gave them holidays at that time. After a while, the Christians had taken the pagan symbol of the evergreen tree decorated with lights and turned it into a symbol of their own evergreen hope for eternal life because of Jesus' coming into the world. Could the same kind of reinterpretation be applied to the Hindu festival of Diwali? Perhaps.

Victor Pakraj knew very well how important it was for new converts to make a clean break with Hinduism. If they did not really understand the difference, the Christian community might be absorbed back under the umbrella of Hinduism. Then its distinctiveness and its evangelical witness would be lost.

On the other hand, Mr. Pakraj also knew that he must help the Prasad family find a way to restore the joy of their salvation. He wondered just how he could do that.

18

Fit for the Kingdom?
Robert D. Newton

Missionary, what do you think? Should Sabado keep the vow he made before he became a Christian out of respect for his father? Or should he postpone his baptism?" The question had caught Eric by surprise. A special service had been planned for the following day, during which twenty-two of the thirty-five families of the village would be baptized. Eric had visited the village of Bicol (Papua New Guinea) many times in preparation for the event, but until today he was unaware that there was a problem.

Earlier, after arriving at Bicol, Eric and five others had seated themselves quietly around the fire while they sipped hot coffee from tin cups. It felt good to be out of the cold wind, relaxing with friends after a long day of hiking. Three of the men were elders of the village. The other three, two lay evangelists and Eric, had come from the Christian village of Tanu, a five-hour hike downriver. For the past six months they had faithfully come to meet with village leaders and their families, sharing with them about Jesus Christ. Particularly fascinating to these animistic people were the stories of Christ's power over spirits and the natural forces of wind, rain, thunder, and lightning. Though all of the people were pagans when the evangelistic team first came to Bicol, many now believed in the Lord Jesus and wanted to be baptized.

Finally, Dante, one of the village elders, had broken the silence. "Missionary, it is good that you brought us the gospel about Jesus. We are happy to know him and be a part of his clan. We also hope that soon all our village will follow with us so that we are like your families in Tanu. All of them are in God's clan. Isn't that so?"

"Yes, it is true. All of the families in Tanu are Christian. It brings strength and peace to the village when everyone walks together. At least that is what the people of Tanu tell me. But, Ama Dante, I am a little ashamed that you thank me for bringing God's love to you. I have done little to teach you. You know how hard it is for me to speak in your language. If my brothers here had not shared the message with you, I think you would still be in darkness."

"Missionary, what you say is true. So perhaps all of you will again help us with our problem. You have given sound advice before."

"Ama," Felipe, one of the evangelists, answered, using a term of high respect, "Our advice comes from the Book that God's servants wrote. We will look in the Book to help you with your problem if you want."

"Yes, that is what we want. The problem we have is hard. It concerns one of the elders in our village who wants to follow with us. The problem has to do with Sabado and his father, the *mabonong* [pagan priest]. What is your opinion of Sabado?"

"Wasn't he one of the first men in Bicol to believe the gospel?"

"Yes," Ama Dante answered. "He was the first to believe. He was also the one who told many of us about the gospel and explained some things that were too deep for us to understand the first time. It was his joy and faith that caused many of us to want to learn more about Christ. He has been looking forward to baptism for a long time. His wife and five children are also ready to be baptized. That is why this problem is so hard."

"Tell us the problem, Ama Dante," Eric answered. "We, too, have a burden in our hearts if Sabado is having a hard time. He was the first to open his house to us and encouraged us more than anyone else to continue to teach about Christ. We have met very few people who thirst to learn about God's Word the way Sabado does."

"Yes, he has been an example to all of us who want to be Christians," Ama Dante replied. "So I think you will understand that this is a problem we are all facing. I will tell you the story about this problem, and then you will give us good advice about what to do.

"The problem with Sabado started over one year ago, before you came and brought us the Good News. Sabado was sick with a high fever, and the hospital medicine could not help him. His father knew that it was a spirit that was causing the sickness, so he divined to find out the exact problem. It came out that Sabado's uncle, who had died during the war, was in need of a new blanket. His place in the other world was cold, and his blanket had become thin with age. Sabado's father called a feast, and they butchered fifteen pigs, two cows and a carabao. The day after the last pig was butchered, the fever left Sabado and did not come back. In thanksgiving, Sabado butchered a pig, and made a vow to his father that he would butcher another pig on the anniversary of his healing. The anniversary has come, and now Sabado's father is insisting that Sabado finish his vow. The father believes that if Sabado does not finish his vow, the uncle will bring sickness again, not only on Sabado, but also to him. He knows that he is accountable to the uncle to ensure that Sabado will butcher another pig.

"Sabado is stuck in the middle. He does not want to do this pagan thing. He does not believe that the uncle's spirit has power over him, because Jesus is stronger. But he is also afraid for his father. His father is afraid of the spirits and rightly so—he is not under the protection of Jesus. Sabado sometimes thinks he should postpone his baptism, finish the vow he made to his father, and then reapply for baptism. Other times he thinks that postponing his baptism will put a stumbling block in front of the young Christians.

"We have discussed this problem over and over, but we still do not have a satisfactory answer. We believe that if Sabado butchers the animal, he is going against Jesus. If he refuses to butcher the animal, he will go against his father. Both of those ways are not good to us. Does God want us to spit on our fathers in order to become his followers?"

"Sometimes we must go against our fathers in order to be Christians," Felipe answered quickly. "It says in the Book that we must be willing to forsake all, even our fathers, if we want to be fit for the kingdom."

Ama Geteb, the other evangelist, responded next: "Yes, you speak correctly, Felipe, when you say we must forsake all for Jesus. But the problem is not so easy. The Book also says that we must honor our fathers and fulfill our vows. That is what is troubling Sabado. Because he loves Jesus, he also wants to show love by honoring his father's request that he finish his vow. Anyway, Sabado does not have to be the one to butcher the pig. He only has to give the pig to his father to butcher. Maybe that is not wrong for a Christian to do."

"What do the other families in the village think about this problem?" Eric asked. "Maybe they can give us an idea."

"That is also a problem," Ama Dante answered. "The families who follow the ways of Jesus are divided. Some say that he should obey his father, and the others say he should push ahead and be baptized with them tomorrow. The pagan families are not divided. They all know that Sabado must follow the ways of our people and honor his father. The pagan families are mocking us because they are of one mind, but we are not. They say that Jesus has come to destroy our village, not to make it strong."

It was then that Ama Dante had asked Eric the troubling question: "Missionary, should Sabado keep the vow he made before he became a Christian out of respect for his father? Or should he postpone his baptism?"

"Let's spend tonight praying about this problem," suggested Eric. "God will show us a good way to follow."

"Yes, this is true," answered Ama Dante. "We have tonight. Sabado will not come for our decision until the morning. But we must be ready to give him an answer when he comes."

Now, as he lay quietly on his mat, Eric wondered what was God's guidance in this matter.

19

Banana Beer in Burundi
Nzohabonayo Ferdinand

The refreshing change caused by the beginning of the rainy season had given way to dreary days of endless drizzle. Muddy rivulets ran along the hillside paths, making them slippery and hazardous. The monotonous dripping from the banana leaves and grass roofs drummed into Missionary Coti's head and aggravated his anxious state of mind. What could he do to solve the banana-beer crisis that was brewing as the time for the Yearly Meeting in the month of June drew near? What would be the right verdict to pronounce? Should he give the green light to the use of the beer, or should he excommunicate two thousand church members? This decision was robbing him of his sleep and causing him to grow listless and thin.

"Ah, Bwana Cilisoni," he sighed, in his mind addressing the missionary who had preceded him with the title used by the *Barundi* (the people as a whole) that is equivalent to "Mister," with an added implication of "boss." "Why did you die in January instead of waiting until the Yearly Meeting was over?"

Cilisoni had been an easygoing man who had never gotten over his rather romantic view of Burundi and its people. The climate, with its average temperature of 70° F., suited him perfectly. The mountains are green all year because even in the dry season when the grass withers, the banana leaves remain green. The Cilisonis were delighted by the gifts of ripe bananas given to them as soon as they had learned to know some of the local people.

Coti smiled in spite of himself as he remembered Cilisoni's story about how he had discovered the banana-beer problem. One day Cilisoni had gone out to visit a *Murundi* (one Barundi person) by the name of Rugi. As he went along the hillside paths to his friend Rugi's house, Cilisoni had met many people who were obviously drunk. This puzzled and disturbed him, so he asked Rugi for an explanation. To Cilisoni's surprise, Rugi told him that the people were getting drunk on beer made from bananas. "Would you like to try some, Bwana Cilisoni?" he asked. Without waiting for an answer, Rugi asked his wife, Gati, to bring a calabash of banana beer for Bwana. Trying to hide his surprise, Cilisoni had politely refused to drink the beer.

Rugi had felt terribly hurt by the refusal, in spite of the missionary's effort to be tactful. By then, Rugi had considered the missionary to be his friend, and for a *Murundi* to refuse a drink offered by a friend is a great insult. *Barundi* babies are given beer during the first week of their life, and it is the center of all social activities among the people. Banana beer is used to entertain guests, to influence a superior, to pay a dowry, to stimulate discussions, and to give honor to those who have achieved status by doing good for the community. It can even be used to pay off debts incurred during initiation periods. And, if all that were not enough, it can be used to quench thirst. It is therefore almost impossible for a *Murundi* to understand a society where beer drinking is not the center of life and relationships.

Rugi got over the insult, however, when Bwana Cilisoni then invited him to be their houseboy. It was, after all, an opportunity for Rugi to become wealthy. Many other men living in the nearby hills had come looking for a job at the missionary's residence. They had also asked the Bwana to teach them to read and write. This pleased the missionary because he perceived their request as an opportunity to preach the gospel to them. Cilisoni agreed to teach them on three days of the week. During each lesson he told them more about Bwana Yesu who had died for their sins. For his part, Rugi spread the word that all who wanted to be Bwana Cilisoni's friend would have to deny that they drank banana beer.

Everyone wanted Bwana Cilisoni's friendship. Those who accepted Bwana Yesu as their Savior and denied drinking banana beer were treated well by the missionary. Soon hundreds were flocking to the mission house to hear the story of Bwana Yesu. Many of these were ready to lie to Cilisoni about their desire to become Christians, so that the *Muzungu* (white man) would help them to get rich and pay their colonial taxes. It was a mutually rewarding arrangement. While the people benefited materially—and it must be said that some of them grew spiritually as well—Cilisoni could naively write glowing letters home about how the Holy Spirit was convincing these uneducated heathen to become Christians.

By 1940, ten years after the first missionaries arrived in Burundi, four thousand people gathered to celebrate Christmas. After the service, secondhand Western clothing was distributed to those who had faithfully attended Cilisoni's classes. Not long after that, Missionary Coti and his wife came to help the Cilisonis start more classes and organize more churches for the *Barundi* who said "Yes" to Bwana Yesu.

Very soon, however, it became clear that the missionaries could not provide enough jobs and materials for the ever-increasing number of believers. It had become apparent that the true followers of Jesus were those who continued to attend classes and church, even if there were few material benefits. Also, because converts had to say that they had forsaken the drinking of banana beer, abstinence became one of the main requirements of church membership. Even the drinking of banana juice was prohibited.

Rugi had continued to be very interested in church activities and developed many skills. Bwana Cilisoni soon asked him to become the first native catechist. When he accepted, Rugi knew that he had to make a radical decision about banana beer. He would have to teach against it, but he knew that although beer was still the center of the culture of Burundi, there were many church people who were tired of the double standard on this issue. They might be ready to actually enforce the sanctions against beer drinking.

A real test for Rugi came two years after he had become the catechist. One day, Gaya, the father of Baga, brought a pot of banana beer to Rugi with the request that Rugi give his daughter, Yaje, to Baga in marriage. Rugi was greatly disturbed by the situation, but after talking to his wife, he went ahead and drank the beer with Gaya to seal the marriage contract.

Cilisoni died without knowing how hot the banana beer issue had become among the church people. Ironically, some people wanted to bring pots of banana beer to Cilisoni's home for mourning, and that is how Missionary Coti discovered it. They thought that perhaps Coti would be more lenient than Cilisoni and that the never-drink-banana-beer discipline might die with his predecessor. Pressured by members of the congregation, Rugi went to ask Bwana Coti to lift the sanction against beer drinking at the Yearly Meeting that would take place in June, the beginning of the dry season. Coti had not been able to conceal the shock he felt when Rugi came with the request. He had been totally unaware that the problem still existed and believed that all the banana trees that dotted the countryside were being used for nothing other than to provide income with which the population was paying its colonial taxes. After his initial shock, Coti was even more disconcerted to find that Rugi himself was not firmly against the beer drinking. In fact, Rugi informed him that more than half the members had sworn to leave Coti's church and join the Roman Catholics, or not attend church at all, rather than give up banana beer.

A noisy argument outside his window interrupted Coti's reverie. Two men whom he recognized as church members were in a fight with another, who was a stranger to him. The tone of their voices and their wild gesticulations told him more than he wanted to know. He would have to go and break up the fight so that these two would not be hauled into court. This was not the first time such disturbances had happened, as he had recently discovered. Coti started for the door with a mixture of righteous indignation and grim determination on his face. Perhaps he knew what he would say to the Yearly Meeting after all! However, as he negotiated the slippery path and got closer so that he could see the faces of the brawlers, he realized with a jolt that one of them was Rugi's son-in-law, Baga. "Oh God," he prayed, "how will this all end?"

20

The Communal Feast
Denis J. Green

J im was aroused from his preparation for teaching at the next day's Bible School by his wife, who reminded him that evening had almost come. With a start, he remembered the dilemma facing him, one that would require a decision within the hour. Would he accept his neighbor's invitation delivered earlier in the afternoon to attend the *slametan* feast just after dark?

Jim and Anne West had lived in a small rural Javanese town for over a year now. Before coming, they had learned to speak Indonesian with reasonable fluency and later had acquainted themselves with Javanese culture through observing and mixing with the people.

After moving to the town, Jim and his family did their best to integrate themselves into the local community. Jim established good relationships with the local officials—the civil administrator, the military commander, the police chief, and the locally elected town mayor. His ability to speak Javanese gained him immediate respect, and his position as chief pastor of several congregations also gave him status in the community.

Jim and Anne also found that having a family of three young children helped to establish relationships with their immediate neighbors. Soon after their arrival, they had followed the local custom of inviting all the neighbors to a housewarming so that they could formally introduce themselves. Thereafter they took every opportunity to chat over the fence and strengthen relationships in other ways. Living on church property, however, meant that non-Christians did not always feel free to visit them. Jim understood their hesitancy in what was a nominally Muslim society, but it made him feel as though there was still a lack of complete acceptance on their part. Perhaps that was a situation that could never be overcome completely.

Jim's thoughts turned again to the invitation that had suddenly faced him with a difficult choice. When his neighbor's teenage son delivered the verbal invitation earlier, Jim's first reaction was one of excitement and joy, because this was a sign that his neighbors had really accepted him and regarded him as a part of the immediate community. There was no need for an immediate reply, for guests are expected to accept automatically unless they are unavoidably prevented from attending. The euphoria quickly passed, however, replaced by more sober reflections on the implications of accepting or rejecting the invitation.

Jim had learned about the *slametan* during his language studies and by talking with other missionaries and members of the church. It was a simple meal arranged by a household at various times in connection with significant events in life, such as the birth of a child, circumcision of a male son, marriage, death, the building of a new house, the departure for a long journey, illness, or success in some important venture. In this case, their neighbor's wife had just given birth to a baby, and a son at that.

But Jim knew that the *slametan* held far deeper significance than just an expression of joy for another son in the family. Basic to the feast is the ritual designed to give protection from evil spirits. Even though the Javanese are nominally Muslim, their day-to-day lives are still very much influenced by fear of spirits and witchcraft. After the invited male neighbors gather (the *slametan* proper is an all-male affair, although women often gather in the kitchen or another room) and are seated cross-legged on woven-leaf mats spread around the perimeter of the room, the host begins with an introduction and an explanation of the reason for the gathering. Incense is burned and specially prepared food placed on mats in the center of the room. Normally the food consists of rice and two or three side dishes. In the center is placed a cone of rice representing a mountain, which in Javanese belief is regarded as the source of well-being.

The food is not primarily for the guests. It and the incense are offerings to the spirits. Sometimes, in his opening speech, the host mentions the various spirits, which are thought to be particularly concerned with this occasion and for which the food is intended.

After the speech is over, someone is called upon to offer a prayer, which is in the form of a Muslim chant in Arabic. Sometimes the local *modin*, or Muslim official, is specially invited for this purpose. At other times the prayer is offered by anyone persent who has learned the appropriate recitation. Its intent is protection against the harm that the spirits might bring (in this case, against the newborn baby). The guests indicate their participation in the prayer by holding their hands out with palms upraised and by saying "amen" at each pause in the chant.

After the prayer the host invites the guests to eat the food dedicated to the spirits, for the spirits have already been satisfied with the smell of the incense and the aroma of the food. Each guest takes some rice and a small amount of the side dishes, which he eats immediately. The rest is taken home to be eaten later. With that, the ritual is over.

The *slametan* serves two basic purposes. First, it reinforces the social solidarity of the community by drawing the neighborhood together on all important occasions. Second, it fills a felt need for protection from any misfortune that might be caused by the spirits. In a sense, the feast preserves a state of social and spiritual equilibrium.

As he reflected on all this, Jim could see the pros and cons of accepting or rejecting this invitation. On the one hand, to accept would do much to cement his relationship with his neighbors and show that he identified with them in what they regarded to be an important event in their lives. To reject the invitation would imply rejection of them and their cultural values. On the other hand, Jim knew that many missionaries, and some national Christians, had adopted a policy of not attending the *slametan*. They felt that their attendance would implicitly affirm their neighbors' belief in the efficacy of the ritual as a protection against the spirits. How could they participate in the prayer offered to a different god from the Christian God? How could they eat food offered to the spirits? These were the issues with which Jim struggled as the darkness closed in. The time for reaching a decision could no longer be delayed.

21

To Drink or Not to Drink?
Dennis Teague

It had been a long evening. What had started out as a real privilege had turned into a real disaster. John had already insulted and upset the Professor by refusing the aperitif, the wine, and the beer. Now, as they sat in the living room after the meal, Professor Piaget set a glass in front of John and began to pour the prized Brittany cider. Was it right for John to continue to anger, insult, and alienate his host—or would it be all right just this once to forget all that teaching in Bible College, forget his alcoholic father, forget what the Smiths would think and say, and drink a little cider, which did not contain much alcohol anyway?

John had spent the past two summers in France and now was enrolled at the University of Nantes. It was not an easy decision, but in obedience to what he felt to be the will of God, he returned in October and entered the beginning course in French. John had never studied French before. He found a room in the dormitory, hoping to make contacts with French students. He worked with the Smiths, who were starting a new church in Nantes. John had just graduated from a Bible College, a conservative school that took a strong stand against drinking alcoholic beverages. Besides, the Smiths had warned him about a few missionaries who had started drinking wine with the French and had later become alcoholics. John knew the suffering that alcoholism brought, because his father was an alcoholic.

One day John received an invitation to have dinner with his professor, along with three other foreign students. Professor Piaget had very graciously opened his home to them. John realized that it was a real privilege in France for French students to be invited to a professor's home, and an even greater honor for foreign students. When the night arrived for the dinner, the Smiths loaned John their car so that he could pick up his Japanese friend, Isao. The two students were excited as they arrived at the house. Little did John suspect that this would turn out to be such a problematic experience.

Dr. and Mrs. Piaget were very friendly and cordial. John spoke less French than any of the other students, but they had been very patient with him. After all the students arrived, Professor Piaget offered everyone an aperitif. Everyone accepted except John. He wanted to be a good witness for his Lord, so he refused. John thought the professor seemed ill at ease, because for a moment he appeared not to know what to do. After an uneasy silence he offered John some lemon drink and it was accepted. The awkwardness of the moment passed and John breathed a sigh of relief.

When dinner was served, John partook heartily of the beans and roast beef. But when Dr. Piaget began filling the guests' glasses with the customary wine, John politely refused his share. It was clear that this time the professor felt not only awkward but somewhat angry at this foreigner in his house who refused his hospitality. Though he offered John a Coke instead, the atmosphere had changed. Due to the length of French meals and the thirst of the people there, the host soon got more wine. Again it was only refused by John.

Dinner being finished, everyone sat around the table and discussed various subjects. Mrs. Piaget cleared the table of the last remains of dessert and coffee. It had been a great time for everyone except John and perhaps his host. John wondered, "Was it right to offend Professor Piaget the way I did? Was the Lord really pleased with what had taken place? Will I ever be able to share my faith in Christ with Dr. Piaget? Is it really so bad to drink just a little wine, and is it not worse to build a barrier between oneself and someone who does not know the Lord?" All these questions and more had run through John's mind throughout the meal and particularly now, when everyone was enjoying the conversation and relaxing.

It was then that Professor Piaget excused himself. He was gone for a few minutes but reappeared carrying a tray. On it was a large flask surrounded by neat-looking glasses. He began to tell his guests how good the Brittany cider was and, especially for John's benefit, that it contained only a little alcohol. The host set glasses in front of everyone and began to pour.

John became anxious as the professor moved closer. Should he refuse once again, even though the professor had pointed out for his sake that it contained little alcohol? Was he going to build an even-higher barrier between his teacher and himself? Or should he ignore the teachings of the Bible College and the warnings of the Smiths? When Professor Piaget paused before John and put a glass before him with a smile, John . . .

22

The Triumph of the Chiefmakers
Wilson Awasu

Dake had just returned to his home village in Africa. He had carefully avoided coming home for a number of years because of his Christian faith, but now he was sure there was nothing to worry about. It had not even occurred to him that this was Chiefmaking season.

After the usual exuberant reunion with uncles, aunts, nephews, nieces, and cousins, Dake decided to visit the old palace where he had grown up. His father had been the reigning chief of their royal line. Dake, however, was not allowed to daydream for long. He had barely seated himself in the palace when he heard the war cries at the gate. There was an onslaught of people surrounding the palace. Every outlet was blocked—there was no escape. The Chiefmakers were upon him!

Almost before he knew what hit him, Dake was smeared with white clay. A goat was slaughtered and the blood was sprinkled on him. The cries of triumph ascended and a stampede ensued.

The village had just installed him as its new chief. It was too late for Dake to regret coming home! It was all over. Dake was the new chief, and there was no way to undo what had been done.

The Council of Chiefmakers had not acted impetuously—they were carrying out a long-overdue assignment. As the youngest son of the reigning chief, Dake had been chosen for royal succession when he was only three years old. Until now, however, circumstances had prevented the council from carrying out their duties.

Dake's great-great-great-grandfather had won royal status for their lineage among these warlike people who lived in the mountains and had their own language. Dake's ancestor was made chief because of his bravery in battle against the dread Ashanti, whose forces were defeated and forced to retreat. He was made chief of a jurisdiction that included seventeen villages. Dake was the youngest son of the fourth chief of this royal line. He was carefully groomed in the intrigue and tradition necessary to carry out the duties of a chief.

Even when Dake was a boy, however, the royal succession was threatened. His mother was a Christian and had done everything she could to instill Christian principles in her son. Her great desire was that Dake would become a fine Christian man, educated and trained for Christian service. Her wishes began to be realized when Dake became a Christian during his high-school years.

Just a year after Dake's conversion, his father died. That was when the trouble started. Everyone expected that after the eight weeks of funeral ritual, Dake would be installed as the new chief. He would be expected to take part in all the rituals, beginning with the invocation of the ancestral spirits, through the veneration of his late father, the dances, the offerings, and the purifications. He would play his part by following, in shadow fashion, the movements of a senior elder, who traditionally replaces the old chief until a new one is installed.

Dake and his mother faced these proceedings with a great deal of consternation. How could he pour libations to the spirits and lead his people in the worship of ancestors now that he was a Christian?

A solution for them came with the help of Dake's mother's brother. This uncle was sympathetic and did not believe Dake should have to become chief against his will. At the dawn of the final day of the funeral, Dake's uncle whisked him away from the village.

Dake's absence became obvious immediately, and the funeral rites could not be completed satisfactorily. Dake's mother was blamed, and everyone expected that the ancestors would exact the normal penalty of death for the interruption of the traditional procedures. But that expectation decreased after two years passed without Dake or his mother being taken.

In the meantime, a regent occupied the throne. Dake, for his part, avoided the palace area during the special seasons when it is appropriate to enthrone a chief. He wondered if this would be the pattern for the rest of his life.

Dake went abroad for college and graduate school. He completed a Master of Divinity degree and then pressed on for a Ph.D. in theology. When he returned home from abroad, Dake married a woman from a tribe who were traditional enemies of his own. She was a medical doctor.

On the morning that Dake returned to his village, he felt quite safe from the Chiefmakers. It had been years since his father died. He was now a trained Christian theologian who had violated the "orders" and angered the ancestors. His wife was from an enemy tribe; she did not even come from a royal family. Surely his people would not want anyone like him for the throne! The ancestors would have to be pacified, and there was just too much against him in other ways as well.

Now, however, Dake's world had been completely shattered. He had been trapped and made chief. His people would expect him to pacify the ancestors as well as lead them in all aspects of the traditional religion. His marriage would be seriously threatened. What about his Christian faith and theological training? Could he force his people to accept Christianity? It seemed out of the question. What in God's name should he do?

23

The Threat of the Spirit Dancers
Georgia R. Grimes

Grace Mead had just come back to the village after three weeks at mission headquarters in Vancouver. The local people had been unhappy when Grace told them she had been ordered by her mission to leave, although the tribal elders agreed that it was dangerous for her to stay. Now she had returned, but the question—after what had happened before she left—was whether it ever would be safe for her to live in the village again.

Now Grace sat in the Big House, looking around at the people with whom she had lived for eleven years. Could she expect that they would ever give up the Spirit Dancing that was such a major aspect of their decimated native culture? After observing the dancing closely, she knew there was no other option if they were to become Christians. And what should be her own role in that process? Did God want her, a single woman, to stand here alone against this powerful force?

Grace had come to bring the gospel to a group of Coast Indians in western Canada in 1974. She had done her best with the help of two language informants to translate the Bible for them. The work had been hard, and for a long time Grace saw very few results. Finally, two years before, a breakthrough occurred when Joy, one of her language helpers, decided to follow Jesus. She was slowly growing in faith and in the understanding of the Christian Way. Joy's common-law husband, Daniel, who was the other language informant, had not yet become a Christian. He still had many questions and some old resentments, but he did allow Bible reading and prayer in their home.

Joy and Daniel came from very influential Indian families. Joy's father had been the last practitioner of native Indian medicine in the village. Before his death, he had passed on many of his skills and secrets to Joy. Daniel came from a large, prominent family and had ten children of his own. Seven of these already were Spirit Dancers.

It was the Spirit Dance Society that was a threat to Grace and her continued ministry in the village. This group enforces the norms of the culture by disciplining those who are not conforming to Indian ways. Initiates to the Society have no choice in the matter; usually they are chosen by close relatives who feel they are responsible to correct the erring ones. The initiation is so feared that even the threat of it is enough to bring some offenders back under the authority of the culture.

Grace knew quite a lot about the Spirit Dances. She had been allowed to attend many ceremonies during the dance season, which lasted from November to April. These took place in the Big Houses, the old-style dwellings that could accommodate up to a thousand people at a time. It was only the final part of the initiation process, where absolutely no outsiders are allowed, that Grace had not witnessed. She had heard enough about it, however, to know it was a terrible thing.

The group of men and women who initiate new dancers are called *germans*. In order to qualify, they must have been dancers themselves for at least four seasons. Just before "grabbing" the ones to be initiated, the *germans* meet, usually at night, and paint their faces with a mixture of burned bees' nests and petroleum jelly. All dancers wear facial paint, either the common black variety or a "more powerful" red color.

The leader of the *germans* carries a three-foot-long carved stick called the *klutsmeen*. As he faces the one to be initiated, he or she faints or is hit by the stick and knocked out. The initiate is then carried to the Big House to be ceremonially "worked on" for four days. This is the part no outsiders are allowed to witness, but most of the village gathers to watch.

An atmosphere of fear mixed with anticipation pervades the village during this time. The anticipation is for the dance and the powerful song *(siyawun)* that will be given to the initiate by the spirits. The fear is for the physical safety of the initiates. During the time Grace had been in the village, seven people from surrounding villages had died from the initiation rites.

The "work" goes on until the initiate *quns*—sings a song. It may take up to four days for this to happen. In the meantime, the initiate is kept on a strict diet of only lukewarm water or weak tea and no food. More severe treatment is administered to those who take more than four days to *qun*.

In 1977, a fifty-year-old man was "grabbed" by arrangement with his eighty-year-old mother. He endured four hours of torture before his son could get the government to send the Royal Canadian Mounted Police into the Big House to rescue him.

"My sides were like hamburger and my testicles were the size of lemons so that I could hardly walk," the man told Grace later. "My back was badly burned and the pain was terrible. My only relief came when I thought of Jesus with my mind. Then I would be aware of everything that was happening, but I was free from pain."

After an initiate *quns* and the *germans* learn his or her song, the new dancer is ceremonially "stood up." This is the critical time when a song and dance are put together for the first time. It ends with the initiate dancing around the fire alone. The family of the dancer watches anxiously to see if he or she has enough strength left to perform the dance. Everyone in the Big House sings the song of the initiate as he or she dances.

Grace had been present in a Big House several times when new initiates were stood up by the *germans* after they had *qunned*. She vividly remembered one occasion when a woman had been stood up. Her eyes had dilated, her face became contorted, and her mouth dropped open. The woman began to drool as she cried out her song. Her nose began to run and tears streamed down her face. The song, coming from deep within, became louder and stronger. Two other women had helped her up. Then she danced around the fire as if stalking someone, darting first one way and then rushing back the other, with arms outstretched and hands clenched like the feet of a bird on a thick limb.

Later that same night, a strong young man had clutched the edge of the bench with both hands and began to bounce up and down. Then he began to cry out in deep, strong yells with a pause between each. His head shook after each yell as the power within him grew stronger. Two men came and stood him up to dance.

The young man leapt around the fire as if someone held him by the shoulders and was bouncing him up and down. At times, he danced in a crouched position with one arm stretched out and downward, the other arm close to his face. As he pounced in one direction and then the other, his hands made motions like a striking eagle's talons. After dancing around the fire four times, he ran in a tight circle and then shot full speed ahead toward the men who had stood him up. They were waiting by his seat for him to "run home." They caught him in their arms and kept him from running headlong into the seats. It was nearly an hour before he became calm and stopped his deep, rhythmic yells.

The reason the mission had insisted that Grace leave the village for three weeks was that Grace herself was in danger of being grabbed for initiation. The risk remained if she decided to continue working here.

The trouble had started several months before, when there was an attempt to grab Joy, Grace's language informant. One cold Sunday afternoon in early January, Grace had been in Joy and Daniel's home reading the Bible with them. The phone rang, and someone on the line told them that the *germans* were coming to grab Joy.

The family went wild with fear. They took time for prayer and then Daniel told Grace to leave for her own safety. She ran next door to the house where she lived with Joy's seventy-two-year-old sister, Gwen. There Grace continued to pray with Gwen as the sounds of the dance grew louder and more frenzied.

Grace learned later that Daniel had tried to hide Joy in the attic above the ceiling, but she had fallen through and hurt her head. Then, in desperation, they had run out the back door, and he had driven Joy and their teenage daughter into a forested area some miles away. After leaving them there, Daniel had driven back to the house to face the *germans*.

It was just after midnight when eight Indian Spirit Dancers left the Big House and walked up the hill to Joy and Daniel's home. They found Daniel sitting in a chair facing the door with a loaded rifle on his lap. One of the dancers, who happened to be Joy's niece, asked where she was and then searched the house when Daniel refused to tell her. When they didn't find Joy, the *germans* went next door and threatened to grab Grace and Gwen if they refused to tell them where Joy was hiding.

Grace would always remember the calm that came over her and the way the words seemed to come to her without effort. She truly had experienced the grace that is promised to apostles in Matthew 10:19–20. It was not she who spoke, but the Spirit of her Father speaking through her.

As if one part of her was detached, she heard her own voice saying, "I will probably die if you grab me. The Holy Spirit of God lives within me. That Spirit will not allow any other power to control me. I don't want you to be responsible for my death. I want you to turn away from the evil spirits and worship the true God who can fill you with the Holy Spirit."

At these words, the *germans* melted away into the darkness. They satisfied themselves, however, by grabbing two of Joy's nieces, who then were duly initiated.

It turned out that Joy herself was never grabbed; she and Daniel therefore became the first members of the tribe to stand successfully against Spirit Dancing. Surprisingly enough, after a few weeks, Joy's sister-in-law, the old woman who had started the whole thing, came to apologize. She admitted that she was wrong for trying to grab Joy

without first consulting Daniel, and she even accepted the blame for
the injury to Joy when she had fallen through the ceiling.

It seemed as if Christianity had won a "power encounter" with the
traditional religion. The question was whether it would have a lasting
effect on the local people.

Just after this incident, the mission had insisted that Grace leave the
village. During her time away, she prayed fervently about her future.
She had dedicated herself to bringing the gospel to the Coast Indians
and translating the Scripture for them. Would it not be a defeat for the
cause of Christ if her personal safety kept her from going back? Or
would God provide for the work to be carried on some other way? After
all, she was a woman alone. Was it tempting God against good common sense for her to expect protection under the circumstances?

The mission executives in Vancouver told her that the final decision
would be up to her, although they were quite concerned that they
would not always be able to guarantee her safety, because of their
distant location from the village. They would stand behind her with
prayer, however, and use whatever avenues of influence that were open
to them on her behalf.

At the end of the three weeks, Grace still had not made a final
decision. She decided to go back to the village and put her case to the
Indian people themselves.

The day after she arrived, Grace approached the elders. "God has
put it in my heart to speak to the whole village to tell them why I want
to live here," she said. "Will you give me permission to do that?"

The elders advised her to put on a dinner for the whole village at the
Big House and, after everyone had eaten, she could talk to them. So
that is what she had done.

About 150 people came to the dinner. Even while they ate, there was
dancing going on in the other part of the Big House. After most people
had eaten, one of the elders got up and told the people that Grace had
serious words to say to them.

Grace stood and spoke to the people with an intensity that they
never before had heard in her voice. As simply and as comprehensively
as possible, she explained the gospel message to them. Then she told
them that she must decide whether God wanted her to stay with them
any longer. But now she was asking them how they felt about it. Their
answer would help her to understand God's will for her.

After Grace finished, another of the elders got up and translated
what she had said into the native Indian tongue. He concluded by
adding a few words of his own. If Grace did not stay with them, he said,
they would not only lose a friend, they would lose strong prayers, too.

Several other elders got up when he was finished and spoke, first in the native tongue and then in English. They all expressed the desire for Grace to stay and teach them. One woman even got up to apologize for the resentment she had felt against Grace during the last four years.

Another more-educated, middle-aged woman, however, got up to say that the Spirit Dancing was all they had left of their culture. The government and the church had taken everything else away from them. After she had spoken, there was a general murmur of agreement from the crowd.

Grace realized then that the answer for her question would have to come from a higher source. Should she stay? "Please show me, Lord," she prayed silently as, one by one, a number of her Indian friends slipped silently away to join the dancing at the other end of the Big House.

24

How Should Bashir Be Buried?
Syed Ratique Uddin

Tahir sat in a state of total shock. The wailing of his wife reached his ears, but he was helpless to respond to her or to even look on the too-tranquil face of his beloved only child, Bashir.

What a joy the eight-month-old baby had been to the whole family! Bashir was the first grandchild of Tahir's parents. How could any of them have guessed that their joy was going to be so short-lived? Just three days previously, the baby developed diarrhea. His bowel movements and vomiting had been uncontrollable. Bashir had died in the early hours of this morning. Tahir was finally roused from his stupor when his father spoke to him: "We must begin the preparations for burial. We must call the *Imam* [local Islamic priest] and send some people to dig a grave in the graveyard. Bashir should be laid to rest beside his other grandmother."

Tahir now faced a problem he had never anticipated. He and his wife had very recently become followers of *Hazrat Isa* (Jesus Christ). Would it be right for them to bury their son in the old Islamic way? Should they pray the *Namaz-e-Janaza* (Muslin burial prayer) over his body? If not, what should they do? How do the people following the path of *Hazrat Isa* bury their dead?

Tahir wished fervently that he could talk with Maulana Ahmed Ali. But today was Monday, and the Maulana (teacher) would not come until Friday. The burial must be done today, and his father was waiting for a response from him.

"Please be patient with me, father," Tahir said. "My grief has overcome me. Give me a few moments to control myself." His father nodded sympathetically and went into another part of the house.

As Tahir watched him go, the enormity of the situation almost overwhelmed him. His own parents were not even aware of his decision to follow the way of *Isa*. He had never told them about the fateful day four months before, when a teacher whose name was Ahmed Ali had come into his shop. The Maulana had been passing by and stopped to buy some puffed rice and sweets. He then sat down on the bench on the front veranda of the shop and began to eat. It was a hot day, so Tahir gave him a glass of water to drink.

Ahmed Ali lingered on the veranda to talk with Tahir. He asked Tahir if he prayed five times daily. Tahir mumbled that some days he did. Then the Maulana asked him if he was interested in learning how to pray so that he would get answers to the prayers. That interested Tahir, so Ahmed Ali invited him to come to Aminur Rehman's home on the next Friday, when he would be discussing the matter of the five-time prayer and how to receive answers.

Tahir was a shopowner and always interested in making more money in his business. However, since he always closed his shop on Friday like all the other merchants, he decided to go to Aminur Rehman's home to hear the talk about answers to prayer. Once there, Tahir found the Maulana had many new things to say—not only about prayer, but other things as well. He talked at length about Allah and his love for humankind. Then he introduced *Hazrat Isa*. This *Isa* (Jesus), said the teacher, was the Word of Allah. Tahir was quite surprised when the teacher was able to prove this from the *Quran* (Koran). He explained that *Isa* was the true revelation of Allah, and that no one could approach Allah except through *Hazrat Isa*.

The teacher also showed them the *Injil Sharif* (New Testament Bible). It was all quite astonishing to Tahir. Nevertheless, both he and Aminur Rehman agreed that after each *Namaz* (liturgical prayer) they would pray to Allah in the name of *Isa Masih* (Jesus Messiah) as the Maulana had taught them to do.

For a whole week, in fact, Tahir did exactly that. He prayed to Allah five times a day in the name of *Hazrat Isa*. Sure enough, his sales gradually increased as more and more people came to his shop. The jealousy of some of the other shopowners only served to sweeten the taste of his new success.

Gratefully, Tahir continued regularly to attend the Friday *Jama'at* (assembly) and prayers in the house of Aminur Rehman. Tahir was amazed at the Maulana's knowledge of various matters of religion. Each time, he learned more about *Hazrat Isa*. The teacher explained that *Hazrat Isa* had really died on the cross. That was very hard for Tahir to understand. He had always been told that Jesus was never crucified, that when he was being held by the Jews, Allah had miraculously delivered him. It was true that a crucifixion took place the following day, but the man who was crucified was not Jesus but another man who happened to look like him.

However, Maulana Ahmed Ali insisted that it was *Isa* who was crucified and that he had to die because of human sin. Tahir was deeply impressed when the teacher showed from the *Quran* that Jesus had actually predicted his own death. When the teacher asked him if he believed that *Isa* is the way, the truth, and the sacrifice for sin, Tahir asserted that he did believe it.

Tahir's wife, Amina, and Aminur Rehman's wife, Rukhsana, began listening to the teachings of the Maulana, too. They hid on the other side of a bamboo fence that divided the room where the men sat.

After about ten Fridays, the two men and their wives all decided to become followers of *Hazrat Isa*. They submitted to the ceremonial bath and washing. Maulana Ahmed Ali administered this to the two men, and they in turn did it for their respective wives.

And then, like a bolt of lightning from heaven, this catastrophe came upon Tahir and his wife: Allah took away their only son, Bashir. What about the prayers that had gone up to Allah in the name of *Hazrat Isa* for the well-being of their family? Their teacher, Ahmed Ali, had promised that they would be heard and answered.

As Tahir reflected on these things this morning, however, he remembered another teaching of the Maulana. It was the story of *Hazrat Ayub* (Job). The teacher had explained that in the time of terrible disaster, Allah remains present through his Spirit. How did these two teachings fit together? Tahir was not only in anguish, he was also very confused. If only the teacher were here to talk with him.

His father's voice in another part of the house brought Tahir back to the immediate problem he faced. How should Bashir be buried? To do it the Christian way, should not the Maulana be present? If the *Imam* did it in the Islamic way, of course, the prayers would be sent to Allah in the name of Mohammed. Had he not promised Maulana that his prayers would now always be in the name of *Hazrat Isa?*

Thinking of the local Islamic priest brought more anxiety to Tahir. What would he say to him? Any disclosure of his new faith at this time could only bring disastrous results. The *Imam* would refuse to bury his son. The entire village might decide to ostracize Tahir's whole family. His father, who was very old and weak, might actually die of shock if Tahir revealed that he had departed from Islam, the only true and straight path to Allah. Even the forthcoming marriages of his sisters would be put in jeopardy. If people came to know that their brother had changed his faith, the parents would not want such women to marry their sons.

Tahir sat with his head in his hands and heard with dread the approaching footsteps of his father. What would he say to him?

Postscript

The burial was done in the Islamic way. There was great controversy among the followers of the path of *Hazrat Isa* because of it. Some said it was wrong to bury the dead in the Muslim graveyard and in the Islamic manner. Others said it was all right to do so because the Bible does not give specific instructions about the burial of the body. In any case, each village has only one graveyard, so they really had no other choice.

PART **4**

Sickness and Death

The concept of missions is built, in part, on a love for people and a desire to minister to them in their needs. What these needs are, however, is often a point of discussion. The missionaries think of the need for salvation and eternal life, and for holiness and Christian community here on earth. The people to whom they minister think mainly about their need for food and shelter, for success in business or school, for good marriage partners, for protection from spirits, witchcraft and the evil eye, for healing from illnesses, and for comfort and meaning in death. These are the concerns that preoccupy much of their daily lives.

Certainly the primary message of the gospel has to do with eternal matters—with our relationship to God and the establishment of his kingdom in the heavens. But it also has to do with earthly matters— with our relationship to our fellow humans and the establishment of the kingdom of God on earth. Jesus became human not only to die for our sins, but also to minister to those around him. Similarly, in missions, we have a dual responsibility: to proclaim the Good News of salvation, and to minister to humans in their felt needs. Often, after we help people deal with the crises they face, they are ready to listen to what we have to say.

But what is the message we bring to people in their earthly needs? What do we say to people when they are gathered after the death of a

sick child, a young man killed in battle, or an aged mother loved by all?
What do we say when a young person is critically wounded in an
accident or a young mother is dying in childbirth? What do we say
when an earthquake strikes or a drought sets in and famine stalks the
land? What do we say when people are oppressed and poor, forced to
live in cardboard shanties and exploited by the powerful? These are
the daily questions that all missionaries face if they identify closely
with the people to whom they minister.

God does work in extraordinary ways, and we are called to pray for
people in their needs. But even here questions arise. Does God answer
the prayers of non-Christians for protection and healing? What do we
say when God does not heal the sick for whom we pray? Is it the will of
God that this young Christian die? Are we powerless? Or does this
young Christian lack faith? What is the place in missions for modern
medicine, agricultural technology, relief, development, and education? These questions and many more are the ones we face when we
seek answers for people in their needs.

Here Christ's incarnation must be our example. He was fully God
and brought us salvation. He became fully human and ministered to us
in our earthly needs. That tension between eternal and earthly needs
lies at the heart of our ministry in planting new churches.

Bibliography

Brand, Paul. 1983. A surgeon's view of divine healing. *Christianity Today*
27:14–21 (Nov. 25).

Burkle, Howard R. 1977. *God, suffering and belief.* Nashville: Abingdon.

Gerstenberger, Erhard, and Schrage, Wolfgang. 1980. *Suffering.* John E. Steely,
trans. Nashville: Abingdon.

Lindskoog, Kathryn. 1985. What do you say to Job? *Leadership* 6:90–97
(Spring).

Lawrence, Ray. 1980. *Christian healing rediscovered.* Downers Grove: Inter-
Varsity Press.

Packer, J. I. 1982. Poor health may be the best remedy. *Christianity Today*
26:14–16 (May 21).

Shorter, Aylward. 1985. *Jesus and the witchdoctor.* Maryknoll: Orbis Books.

Yancy, Phil. 1977. *Where is God when it hurts?* Grand Rapids: Zondervan.

25

Nemon's Death
Joanne A. Wagner

Peter stepped out of the hut of his friend Besi, his heart heavy and confused. Besi was ill and convinced he was dying. Peter felt a trip to the coastal hospital, a two-hour drive away, would restore his health. However, because of what had happened earlier, he did not know whether he dared suggest the trip and what the effect would be on his attempts to plant a church in the village if his advice failed again. As he stood looking out across the valley bathed in morning sun, Peter's thoughts went back several months to the time when he was leaving the hut of Nemon, his co-translator and dear friend, who had just died.

Peter and Lillian had come to Kwili village in Papua New Guinea to translate the Bible and plant a church. There they came to love Nemon, a national co-translator who helped them with their work. Then, on one occasion when they returned after an absence of a few weeks, Nemon was not at the door with his usual warm welcome. The villagers told the missionaries that Nemon was suffering from much pain and that he had been ill for two weeks. Lillian and Peter were shocked and saddened to see Nemon with a swollen jaw, a high fever, and in obvious pain. When they talked to his wife, Swenge, she told them that Nemon, a fine Christian leader in the village, was convinced that this sickness was going to kill him, and he had resigned himself to death.

Ruth, a nurse who had accompanied Lillian and Peter to the village, examined Nemon and diagnosed the case as an abscessed tooth. She recommended strongly that he be taken to the coastal hospital where he could see a dentist and receive medical care. When Peter relayed her recommendation to Nemon's family and reinforced it with his own, their reaction was negative. Nemon's kin felt that if he was taken to the *haus sik*, he would surely die. Moreover, he had already announced to them that he was going to die, and they did not want the death to take place away from the village, which would bring it a bad reputation. Among their people it was important for the mental well-being of the kinsmen and the person involved that he or she be at home when death came.

Nemon remained in his home, and his condition continued to deteriorate. Peter persevered in his attempt to convince the family that hospitalization was necessary for Nemon's survival. Finally they consented. Peter, Lillian, Swenge, and Nemon hastily departed on the two-hour drive to the coast.

It was Friday afternoon when they arrived, and Lillian felt a profound sense of relief when they admitted their friend to the hospital. Now, she felt, he was in good hands and would be cured. With confident hearts she and Peter drove back to the village, leaving Swenge to remain at the hospital with Nemon.

However, it was a weekend, and few of the medical staff were on duty at the hospital. Consequently the care Nemon received was minimal. He did not see a dentist, but an appointment was made for Tuesday morning. In the meantime the nurses tried to keep him comfortable. However, on Sunday evening, the abscess in Nemon's jaw burst, sending toxins to his brain, and he died.

When his body was brought back to the village, Lillian and Peter were shocked and grieved. Nemon's family was angry at them, claiming that Nemon died because they took him away to the hospital. Only when an influential relative of Swenge's rebuked the people for blaming the missionaries for the death did the accusations stop. Moreover, when the family observed the genuine grief experienced by the translators as they shared in the burial ceremonies in the village, they concluded that Peter and Lillian were not to blame for their relative's death. Later the family placed the blame on Jeremiah, a member of an enemy clan who had been a close friend of the deceased. Jeremiah, already stricken with grief at the death of his companion, was finally forced to leave the area and seek residence elsewhere because of the pressures placed on him by Nemon's embittered clan.

Peter's thoughts returned to the present as he heard Besi moan with pain. "No," he thought, "it is not a clear-cut matter. Should I try to influence Besi to go to the hospital—or should I step back and not interfere in this case?"

26

The Death of Manuel Vasquez
Larry W. Caldwell

Greg Baxter sat dejectedly in the driver's seat of the Land-Rover, parked in the shade of some coconut palm trees to avoid the intense heat of the Filipino sun. Even though it was only mid-morning, his *barong* was soaked. It was an inner debate that caused his perspiring, the same debate that had kept him awake most of the previous night. What was he going to say to Agnes Vasquez? Even now her family members were but a hundred feet away in her simple bamboo and thatch house, preparing her husband's body for the funeral. Greg, having the only vehicle in the area, had readily agreed to take Manuel's body to the cemetery. Manuel had died of tuberculosis despite Greg's prayer for healing. He had died a Christian, led to the Lord by Greg himself just a few days before his death. Agnes had refused to become a Christian at that time. She had instead made Manuel's healing the prerequisite for her own turning to Christ. Now Manuel was dead, and in a few minutes the family would place his body in the Land-Rover. What was Greg to say to Agnes and the rest of the family?

As he waited, Greg thought back over the past few months. Fresh out of seminary, he and his wife, Betty, and their year-old son had arrived in the Philippines, just eight months before. They had been assigned by their mission board to teach in Evangel Theological College, the mission's training school for national pastors and church workers. They had spent the first two months in Cebu City at their mission's headquarters. Here they adjusted to the climate and culture, underwent language study, and prepared for their move to E.T.C. The school, located in a rather remote area of the island and three hours' drive from Cebu City, was under total national administration. Greg and

Betty would be the only missionaries on campus. They arrived at
E.T.C. early in March, arranged their living quarters in faculty hous-
ing, and continued in intensive language study, aided by one of the
Filipino faculty members.

It was during this time that they met Agnes Vasquez. One morning
in late March, when Greg was at a meeting, Agnes knocked at the door
of their house, selling papaya. Betty used this opportunity to practice
her Cebuano, and quickly a friendship developed between them. During that first rather stilted conversation, the women discovered that
they were both the same age and had been married the same number
of years. Agnes, however, had two small children and was expecting
her third in September. From that morning on, Betty often invited
Agnes to the house for language practice during the mid-morning
break. Since the Vasquezes lived just outside the E.T.C. campus, on the
other side of a sugarcane field, it was convenient for Agnes to stop by
regularly.

Despite the women's friendship, neither Betty nor Greg was invited
to the Vasquezes' house. They discovered early on that this was because Agnes's husband, Manuel, was bedridden with an advanced case
of tuberculosis. Twice Greg drove Manuel in the Land-Rover to the
clinic ten miles away for X-rays and examinations. Each time, the
doctor's prognosis was discouraging: Manuel was dying. Greg used the
opportunities that these trips provided to explain the gospel to Manuel. Greg did give him a *Good News New Testament* in Cebuano, and
Manuel agreed to read it during his long hours in bed.

June came quickly, and Greg and Betty were thrown headlong into
the many activities of E.T.C. Greg had to teach four classes, and Betty
had two of her own. As a result, their time with the Vasquezes was
greatly reduced, though Betty tried to have Agnes over to the house at
least once a week.

One morning in late July, after Agnes had visited their house, Betty
found Greg and told him that Manuel was having violent coughing
spells. Agnes had asked if Greg would again take Manuel to the clinic
for more medicine. Greg immediately dropped what he was doing and
rushed Manuel to the clinic. There the doctor gave Manuel some medi-
cation for temporary relief but told him that death was close at hand.
At most he had but a few weeks to live, and there was nothing more the
clinic could do. It was best for him just to go home and try to remain as
comfortable as possible.

During the drive back to E.T.C., Manuel told Greg that he had been
reading the Bible Greg had given him. He also said that he wished to
become a follower of Christ before he died. Filled with joy, Greg pulled
the Land-Rover over to the side of the bumpy road. Then and there

Greg led Manuel in a prayer for salvation. Upon arriving back home, Manuel greeted Agnes with the words, "I will soon die, but then I will go to heaven. I have become a Christian." Agnes looked hard at Greg but did not speak. Once the two of them had gotten Manuel back into his bed, she brought Greg outside the house to talk.

"As you know," she began, "Manuel and I have two small children, and I am now big with a third child. Manuel will die soon, but he cannot! How will I and the children live on without him? I am desperate. So now I will make an agreement with God, with you as my witness. If God will heal Manuel and allow him to live, I, too, will become a Christian. But if he dies, I will turn my back on God forever."

Agnes's words, and the earnest look on her face convinced Greg of the sincerity of what she said. He tried, with his limited Cebuano, to explain to her that God could not be bargained with, that perhaps it was God's will for Manuel to die at such a time as this, and that, regardless, she herself needed to become a Christian. His words were in vain. Agnes refused. She ended the conversation with the words, "Will you not pray to God for my husband's healing?" Greg replied that he would seriously consider it and would pray about whether or not he should make that request of God.

Through discussions that day and the next with Betty and the other members of the E.T.C. faculty, and through his own prayer and Bible study, Greg became convinced that Manuel should be prayed for according to the model found in the Epistle of James. They all came to the consensus that Manuel's healing would be a form of "power encounter." It might convince both Agnes and others living in the area of the truth of Christianity. The following day, after fasting and prayer, Greg and two other faculty members went to the Vasquezes' house and explained to Manuel and Agnes what they were going to do. Manuel was greatly encouraged by their words. After the prayer he seemed better already. As they were leaving, Agnes reminded them of her "arrangement" with God. Again, they tried to explain to her the same things Greg had a few days before.

Three days later Manuel died. Greg and Betty heard Agnes's loud wail carry over the sugarcane field. They knew instinctively what had happened and they both began to cry. After composing themselves and saying a short prayer for Agnes and her children, they ran up the dirt road to the Vasquezes' house. By now, other neighbors had also arrived, and a crowd had gathered at the entrance. Inside, Agnes was being comforted by her older sister, Alice, who had arrived from the village the day after their prayer for Manuel's healing. When Greg and Betty came into the house, Alice motioned for Greg to leave. He left Betty there and went outside to wait for her. After a few minutes Betty came out and explained to Greg that Agnes could not bear to see him right now. Since the prayer for Manuel had failed, Agnes was blaming God and, indirectly, Greg. Not knowing how to respond, Greg returned home. Betty remained to help out as best she could.

The rest of that day was a terrible one for Greg. In between his classes, he spent the time in prayer and Bible reading. The same questions kept repeating themselves over and over in his mind: Should they have prayed for Manuel's healing? Why had God not answered the prayer? Why had Greg come to the mission field at all? What would he say to Agnes? Despite his fervent prayers, no easy answers came. Discussions with the other faculty members did not prove helpful either.

That evening, Betty tried to give Greg further information about Agnes's reluctance to see him. Betty related how she had unsuccessfully tried to explain things to Agnes, who still blamed God and Greg because the prayer for Manuel's healing had failed. Both Greg and Betty expressed their bewilderment at Agnes's reaction. When Greg shared with Betty his questions, together they sought the Lord in prayer. Still no answers came. They went to bed discouraged.

Now it was morning and Greg sat in the Land-Rover, waiting to take Manuel's body to the cemetery. Various responses to Agnes continued to fill his head. The funeral procession moved toward him from the house, carrying the wooden box that contained Manuel's body. Greg got out quickly and opened the tailgate. The box was placed on the floor of the vehicle. Agnes was helped into the passenger's side by Alice, who then sat beside her. Greg got in on the driver's side and closed the door. He turned to Agnes. The widow's eyes, red and swollen from crying and lack of sleep, looked up into his. Greg looked at her, and said . . . .

27

What Is Wrong with Auntie Mansah?
Daniel Tei-Kwabla

Kofi Ankomah was more than ready to leave the village and return to the city of Accra with his wife, Elizabeth, and their son, Andrew, when things suddenly fell apart. He had been looking in vain for his cousin, who had promised to give them a ride back, when they heard screams from the kitchen. Everyone came running. "It's Auntie Mansah!" someone shouted. "She has fainted!" By the time Kofi got there, the kitchen was full of people who were desperately trying to bring the old woman back to consciousness. They moved aside to make room for Kofi and he was suddenly aware that every eye in the room was fixed on him. In that instant it seemed that the two very different worlds he inhabited with varying degrees of discomfort came crashing together. Reading the looks on the faces around him was no problem. He knew they expected him to use the powers of his costly Western education to exorcise the evil spirit from Auntie Mansah.

The problem was that his education in Western theology had assumed a world in which there were no spirits. His Western self agreed with that; his African self wasn't so sure. But there was no doubt that he stood now in an African kitchen surrounded by people who lived in an African world. Perspiration beaded his forehead and he began to think he should never have come home.

It was 1969, and Kofi Ankomah had recently returned to Ghana after ten years of theological study abroad. His homecoming was the realization of the dreams and hard work of many people in his family.

Kofi was the second of four sons. His father, Opanian Buafo, had inherited a large cocoa farm. As head of the extended family, Opanian was responsible for his brothers and their families, for his divorced sister, Mansah, as well as for his own wife and children.

Auntie Mansah, as Kofi's father's sister was called by everyone in the extended family, had become a wealthy trader in cloth. In her travels, she had come to know about the Presbyterian mission in the market town some fifty miles away. After a while, she began taking classes in the mission school and was baptized as a Christian.

Auntie Mansah pleaded with Kofi's father to let him attend the mission school. At first her brother resisted, but when she brought back a new ready-made school uniform for Kofi as a Christmas gift, Opanian was quite impressed. "We must make Kofi a 'white man's child,'" Mansah said. "That is how he can become a wealthy and prestigious man in the tribe." Opanian did not argue; he agreed to let Kofi attend the mission school.

Kofi studied hard. He was in the top of his class and the headmaster took a special interest in him. Gradually, he also became interested in church activities, and a few years later he was baptized. Kofi's mother, brothers, and sisters were baptized at the same time. Opanian, his father, had refused baptism. He was sympathetic to Christianity, but he felt that as head of the extended family he must keep up his responsibilities as priest in the ancestor cult.

When Kofi began to attain physical maturity, his Auntie Mansah began to tease him about girls. She was quite serious, however, when she would urge him to be careful about "those Fanti girls." "Don't allow them to lead you astray," she said. "We will see to it that you get the most beautiful girl from our own Adukrom tribe." Kofi did not pay much attention at the time, for he was too preoccupied with his studies.

In the summer of 1953, a calamity struck the happy family. Opanian had worked all day in the cocoa field planting seedlings. It had begun to rain, but he continued his work because the planting had to be finished. That night he complained of having a cold, but no one took much notice of him. When the condition became worse, however, the family called the local pharmacist, who gave Opanian some medicines. These did not help, so Opanian insisted that they call the medicine man.

Auntie Mansah did not want to do this. Finally they asked a relative who was an elder in the church what they should do. He said that it would be all right to call the medicine man as long as they did not let the minister hear about it. Reluctantly, Auntie Mansah went with some non-Christian relatives to consult the diviner. He told them that Opanian had offended the spirits of the ancestors and that he must sacrifice a goat to pacify them. The diviner had agreed to come the next day to perform the sacrifice, but he was too late. Opanian had died during the night.

After Opanian's death, Kofi's mother wanted him to leave school and return to the farm, but Auntie Mansah held out against her. "What will the whole village say when your educated son returns to work in the fields? You will lose face, and our family will lose its hope of raising their prestige in the community," Mansah argued.

Kofi's mother gave in, but she told Kofi that he was lazy and useless and that it was time for him to raise his own family. His mother's attitude hurt him badly, and he decided that only Auntie Mansah understood him. Then he made up his mind to continue school, and he returned home only infrequently after that.

After Kofi's graduation, the mission made him a teacher in the market town. Soon after that, impressed by his performance, they granted him a scholarship to study in England. His departure caused a big stir in the village. The family called a prayer meeting in their home, and the pastor cited a prophecy: "The people that sat in darkness have seen a great light."

Turning to Kofi, the pastor said, "In the past, our tribe would have required you to fight in her wars and to bring home human heads as trophies. But we have been delivered by the blood of the Lamb. Today we send you to seek knowledge. Remember, the fear of the Lord is the beginning of wisdom. I have heard of young men from other towns," the pastor continued, "who went to the white man's country. But instead of bravely facing their studies, they went after the sweet things of the flesh. Some even married white women." The crowd gathered around him murmured its strong disapproval of such behavior. "A man who does that," concluded the pastor, "is lost to his people. He is like rain wasted on the forest. I would have suggested that you take a wife before you leave, but the time is too short."

Kofi remembered his pastor's words and studied hard in England. He acquired a Ph.D. in Theology at Oxford University. He was also a good student of the culture and soon was as adept socially as he was outstanding in his academic achievement. Apparently he forgot to heed his pastor's advice when it came to his social life. His British acculturation was crowned by marriage to a beautiful young woman from that country. In this matter, he quite forgot the pastor and his old-fashioned sermon.

After ten years, when it was time at last to go home, Kofi's excitement and anticipation of the homecoming knew no bounds. He sent a cablegram to inform his family of the time of his arrival.

Auntie Mansah headed the small delegation of relatives at the airport in Accra. Her first words to Kofi expressed her pride in welcoming him home as a "big man." If only Kofi's parents had survived to see this day!

The first sign of trouble came when Kofi's relatives realized that he had not come alone. His European wife, Elizabeth, and their son, Andrew, were with him. Then Kofi disappointed them even more. He said that they would not be coming directly to the village. Kofi had reserved a hotel room in the city; they would spend the night there and come to the village the next day. This was a bitter disappointment, particularly for Auntie Mansah, who had taken the responsibility for Kofi since the death of his mother.

Trying to make the best of it, Kofi's relatives returned to the village without him. Early the next morning, they began for a second time to make preparations for the welcoming feast. They had killed two fat sheep and a number of chickens for the feast, but because of the delay, much of the cooking would have to be done over again.

A big crowd gathered in spite of the fact that Kofi's kinsmen were complaining because they had not gone to their farms for two days. The Reverend Doctor Kofi Ankomah and his family did not appear until late afternoon. The Adukrom brass band was in attendance. It was nothing short of a festival. Old Pastor Mintah was there with all the rest and opened the service with prayer. Auntie Mansah's second son, who had finished high school, gave a brief welcoming address that praised his cousin for his brilliant academic achievements. Then the celebrations began in earnest with eating, dancing, and drinking.

The festivities showed no signs of coming to an end that evening when Kofi and his wife announced that it was time for them to return to Accra. It was while he was searching for the cousin who was going to take them back that Aunt Mansah collapsed in the kitchen.

Instinctively, Kofi sent one of his relatives to look for transportation to rush his aunt to the hospital. When the older folk heard what he was planning to do, they objected violently. "Auntie Mansah cannot be helped in a European hospital," one old man said contemptuously. "This is a case of spirit possession; someone must exorcise the spirit." As he spoke, all eyes turned to the Reverend Doctor Ankomah as if to say, "Well this is your opportunity; show us your newly acquired spiritual power."

Kofi was still determined that they would take Auntie Mansah to the hospital when his cousin returned with the news that there was no transportation available. He was trapped! There seemed to be nothing to cover a situation like this in the kind of Western theology that he had studied so hard. That theology demythologized all transcendent phenomena such as spirits and demons.

As these thoughts raced through his mind, and as if to add to his confusion, Kofi remembered the circumstances of his father's death. Were the African spirits only in the African's head? Or was Christianity powerless against the African spirits? Kofi wished at that moment that he had never come home. And yet, here he was, standing over his beloved Auntie, who was lying rigid on the floor while everyone in the village watched him carefully. What in heaven's name should he do?

28

A Sacrifice to the Goddess of Smallpox
Paul G. Hiebert

Venkayya felt the burning forehead of his young daughter. He had prayed fervently all afternoon, and still the fever mounted. The angry red spots on the child's face and body left no doubt that she had smallpox. Would she die like so many other children in the village? Did God really care? Or would giving one *paisa* to the goddess Misamma spare her life? Should he listen to his younger brothers and give in to the village pressure? What did the Bible mean when it said that a Christian should have no other gods but God?

Venkayya's problems began when a plague of smallpox came to Muchintala, a small village south of Hyderabad, in South India. The village elders called the government doctor; he distributed medicines and gave shots, but these had little effect on the disease. When a number of children died, the elders called the village diviner to determine the reason for the plague. He announced that Misamma, the goddess of smallpox who lived in a rock under a tree outside the village, was angry with the village. The villagers had offered her only two goats instead of the usual water buffalo at her festival five years before. Since then no feast had been held, and Misamma expected a sacrifice from the village every three or four years.

When the elders heard this, they hastily made arrangements for a water-buffalo sacrifice. Messengers were sent to every house in the village to gather donations to purchase the animal, since every household was expected to contribute something to satisfy the goddess.

When a messenger came to the house where Venkayya and his two younger brothers lived, Venkayya told the man that he and his brothers had become Christians three years earlier, so they could not make a contribution for the sacrifice. It was against their religious beliefs.

The messenger reported this to the high-caste elders, who became very angry. How could anyone in the village, especially an "untouchable" such as Venkayya, disobey their orders? They summoned Venkayya and demanded an explanation. He told them that he and his brothers had become Christians, and that Christians worshiped no gods but the God of the Bible. He would take care of them.

The elders said that they did not object if Venkayya and his family worshiped the Christian God. Everyone had a right to worship his or her own god *(ishta devata)*. But this was something different. Misamma was not a god like Rama, Allah, or the Christian God, who live in the heavens. She was only an earthly spirit who lived near their village. If the village did not keep her satisfied, she would continue to plague the children. Everyone in the village had to contribute something or she would be displeased. Besides, giving her something to eat was not worship. Even the Muslims, who worship only one god, gave money to buy the water buffalo so that their children would not die.

When Venkayya told the elders that a Christian could not offer a sacrifice, even to local spirits, they grew more angry. It was all right, they said, if he killed his own children by refusing to make the sacrifice, but he was to blame if other children in the village died. Moreover, he was disobeying the village elders, and that was an unforgivable offense. To show their authority and pressure him to change his mind, the elders placed Venkayya, his brothers, and their families under a village ban. No one in the village could talk to them, sell them goods, or marry their children—or he or she, too, would come under the ban.

The next week was difficult for the new Christians. They had to walk to the next village to buy food. Because they were forbidden to go to their caste well, the women had to fetch water from the stream a half-mile outside of town.

When more children died, the elders summoned Venkayya and told him that if he did not contribute a few *paisa* (cents) for the offering, they would bar him from working his fields. Again Venkayya held fast to his convictions.

The following week was unbearable. The young men of the village prevented Venkayya and his brothers from irrigating their pitifully small rice fields. Under the hot sun, the paddy began to wilt. If something was not done soon, there would be no harvest and nothing to live on next year.

Finally, Rangayya and Pullayya, Venkayya's younger brothers, came to him and said, "We must give in to the pressures of the elders or we will all die. God will understand if we give them a few *paisa*. We will tell him we did not give it as an offering to the spirit—but as a tax demanded by the village elders. Besides, Misamma is not a goddess living in the heavens. She is only a local godling living in a rock. Offering her a sacrifice is not worship. It is only food to placate her anger. It is like giving something to a belligerent official to keep the peace."

Four days later, his own little daughter came down with the dread disease that was taking so many in the village. Venkayya began to doubt his own judgment, so he went to see the missionary living forty miles away. The missionary prayed for the child and exhorted Venkayya to stand firm in his refusal to contribute to the sacrifice.

Today, he and the family had prayed all afternoon, but God seemed so far away. The medicine the doctor gave him made little difference to the girl's rising fever. Was he wrong in refusing to contribute even a few *paisa* to the elders? Clearly, local spirits like Misamma were not gods like Jehovah. Was it wrong, therefore, to feed them to keep them happy? They were little different from the officials who made life hard for everyone in the village and needed to be placated with gifts. Maybe the missionary was wrong. He really did not understand the village or the local spirits. Why couldn't he, as a father, pray for God's healing of his child, and give a *paisa* for the sacrifice at the same time?

As night came, Venkayya looked at his wife as she pleaded with God for the life of her child. Would God heal the little girl? And if God did not, what would he say when villagers scoffed at his God? Maybe his brothers were right. Maybe he should go to the village headman and give him one *paisa* to help buy a water buffalo for Misamma. Then his daughter might live. And even if she did not, he would not be blamed for the deaths of other children. Then he could work the fields and his family live in the village in peace.

29

Drought
R. T.

The fine dust was everywhere—on the floor, the pews, and the pulpit. Pastor Joseph knew that no matter how often he dusted it off, it would return. There had been no rain to speak of for three years, and the fields had turned into gray powder that penetrated everything when the wind blew. With the drought came dry wells and famine, and with the famine came death. Why had God not heard the prayers of his people? Was this his judgment? Or was he testing their faith and teaching them to depend on him? Did he not see their suffering and starvation? Did he not see the tensions this was causing in the church? And what should he as the pastor say about the village sacrifice scheduled for next week? As he prepared for the next day's sermon, Joseph cried to God for guidance.

The crisis began in 1976, when a drought hit parts of East Africa. When it continued a second year, the people used up the last of their reserves. When no rains fell the third year, the people had nowhere to turn. Their cattle died and their crops were blighted.

The elders of Kangoi village blamed it on the Christians. In old times, they said, they had never had a famine like this. Now that some of the people had forsaken their ancestors and tribal gods to worship a foreign god, the ancestors and spirits were showing their anger. To show them that they were not forgotten, the elders had arranged for a sacrifice on the high hill east of the village the following Wednesday. They sent word to all the houses that at dawn the able members of each family were to go to the hill. There the elders would slaughter a sheep. Its blood, mixed with the milk of a cow, would be sprinkled in the air with a cow's tail to show the ancestors and spirits that the village needed rain. Then the people would say together, "Let it be so," to show the spirits that they were all in one accord.

The decision brought divisions to homes with Christians. Kipkorir's younger wife, Jesang, and her children were faithful church members and close friends of the Christians. She said that she could not take part in the sacrifice. Jerubet, his older wife, was not a Christian and had no problem with the decision of the village elders. Kipkorir was torn. If he joined the village leaders, he would lose his Christian friends; if he sided with the church, he would be accused by the non-Christians of making matters worse. Either way, his family would be divided. Other families in similar situations faced rising tensions as the days passed. The issue was on the tongue of every villager.

The decision also caused division in the church. The new Christians questioned their new God. If he was powerful and loving, why did he not answer the many prayers of their church? Was he powerless in the face of their tribal gods? And could they not take part in the sacrifice to appease the ancestors and still continue to worship the Christian God? Was God against their ancestors?

Even the elders of the church were divided by their responses to the sacrifice. Some took a strong stand against participating in rituals they had forsaken when they became Christians. Peter, an old church elder who had participated in the tribal rituals before his conversion, explained the meaning of the sacrifice to the church members. He pointed out that the sacrifice was offered to the spirits and the dead, and that such practices would make God angry. He quoted 1 Corinthians 10:20–21 to show that Christians had to make a clear choice between God and the devils, and he urged them not to be lured into participating in such practices, which would lead them astray.

Other elders disagreed. Kiprop, formerly one of the leaders in the village, told people that there were various forms of worship and prayer and that the form itself did not matter. What was important was the spirit of the people when they prayed. He said that since God looks at the hearts and desires of the people, Christians could join the others on the hill but worship their own God while there. Moreover, both Christians and non-Christians needed rain, and God in the past had sent his rain on Christians and non-Christians without discriminating against the prayers of the non-Christians who prayed for rain. He said that it was God who gave the rain, and it was the ignorance of the non-Christians that needed their compassion, mercy, and forgiveness. Kiprop's allies quoted Romans 2:14–15 to show that even non-Christians can do what is right. They compared their tribal sacrifices to the Hebrew sacrifices in the Old Testament and concluded by saying that although Jesus Christ had become the end of all sacrifices, that does not mean that God refuses to hear the prayers of those who pray in Old Testament ways. Finally Kiprop pointed out that if Christians joined the village in the ceremony, the non-Christians would not be hardened against Christ.

Some of the younger men took a middle position. They argued that it was important for the Christians to identify with their fellow villagers in their common suffering, so all should go to the hill to pray for rain. But then the Christians could leave and the non-Christians could remain for the sacrifice. They wanted to preserve both Christianity and their tribal identity and heritage.

Two meetings of the church elders had produced no consensus. Each group became more entrenched in its own beliefs. Pastor Joseph heard that a few Christians had begun to question their faith in the Christian God. Maybe their non-Christian relatives were right. Maybe the ancestors were angry with them for having neglected them. Others were arguing that the Christians should do both: worship in church and sacrifice to their ancestors. One old Christian said that the drought was the judgment of God because the Christians had not broken totally from their old ways. Many of the children were confused by the accusations and uncertainty. No one could explain why the drought continued, and no one knew what to do about it. The people were becoming more and more confused by the continuing crisis.

All this went through Pastor Joseph's mind as he sought to prepare his message. Where was God and why had he forgotten them? What would God want him to say to his church on tomorrow's Lord's Day— especially to those who lived in homes divided by different faiths? And what should they say to their non-Christian relatives and friends who ridiculed their God?

PART **5**

Finances and Bribery

What is a bribe, what is a tip, and what is a gift? Mentally and theologically, we Western Christians draw a sharp line between them. Gifts have high value, higher than contractual exchanges or enforced payments. Their chief function is not economic gain but the building of social relationships, since the unsolicited exchange of economic goods is symbolic of affection and goodwill. Tips are a form of expected gift. Bribes, on the other hand, are evil. By giving such a private "gift," one person seeks to persuade another to give him or her special advantage in some economic or political decision. A man may try to bribe a judge. A woman may give the shopkeeper an added sum to hide some rice for her when it is in short supply. In a sense, a bribe is an attempt to circumvent the normal cultural rules for one's own benefit. It is to take unfair advantage of others.

So much for theory. What about real life? Here we face three problems. First, the distinction between gifts and bribes is often very fuzzy. Is it wrong for a landlord to rent an apartment to the person who gives him an extra sum in private? What if he adds this amount to the first month's rent as a renter's fee, much as a bank adds on "points" when granting a loan? What if he charges an outrageous rent simply because "the market will bear it." Or, to take another case, is it wrong for a shopkeeper to keep some scarce food or gasoline to sell to his relatives

133

and friends? This became a real issue during the gasoline shortage in the United States in the seventies. We must remember that such shortages are widespread and chronic in many parts of the world.

A second problem has to do with cultural differences. Western cultures emphasize what some have called "universal rules." We believe that the same rules should be applied equally and impartially to all people. A government official should be given a ticket if he is caught speeding. He should not be exempt just because he is an official. Many cultures, however, have "particularist rules." Such rules are applied selectively to different types of people. Ordinary people stand in line for their turn at the mission hospital. But when the mayor of the town comes for treatment, everyone (except possibly the missionary) expects him to go the head of the line. Similarly, during the colonial era, natives in India stood in line for railroad tickets, but a white man was invited in to visit with the stationmaster and given his tickets immediately. In these societies, what is seen as "fair play" is different from our Western concept. People are expected to give gifts to important people in certain situations, which to us might be seen as bribes. What is a biblical view of righteousness in such situations? Missionaries must maintain their integrity by being faithful to scriptural principles. On the other hand, must these always be interpreted in terms of universal rules and a Western sense of fair play?

A third problem in dealing with bribery is the fact that it has become a way of life in many parts of the world. The people in these cultures often agree on what is bribery and even admit that it is wrong. But what can a person do when everyone else is doing it? To get a driver's license, or permission to build a school building or import a car for mission work, the officials expect a personal payment. Then matters are expedited rapidly. Failure to give the amount, which is often small, leads to endless delays and wasted time. In such situations, how should a missionary act, particularly if she or he is in charge of a school or hospital and needs to construct a new building or get medical supplies? Is it wrong to give a little *dash* or *bhaksheesh* when everyone else is doing it? Here there is widespread disagreement, even among missionaries, on what to do.

A similar situation arises in countries that regulate their currencies. For example the official exchange rate inside a country may be five rupees to one American dollar. In the black market it may be ten to one. If you exchange money *outside* the country in the "gray" open market, it may be eight to one. But that nation may have a law making it illegal for you to bring rupees into the country. Can a mission agency with good moral conscience buy rupees in the black market or the open market and bring them in, on the moral rationalization that the local government is wrong in seeking to control its currency to its own advantage? After all, there will be twice as much money for the Lord's work! Or should the mission abide by the local laws, even when they seem unjust?

When it comes to money and economics, the question of what is moral and what is immoral, what is right and what is wrong, is not an easy one to solve, particularly when we go to other cultures that have different beliefs and practices from our own.

Bibliography

Beckmann, David M. 1981. The challenge of economics to the teaching of missiology. *Missiology* 9:99–112 (January).

Gould, David J. 1983. *The effect of corruption on administrative performance: Illustrations from the developing world.* Washington, D.C.: World Bank.

Holmes, Arthur F. 1984. *Ethics: Approaching moral decisions.* Downers Grove: Inter-Varsity Press.

Nooman, John T., Jr. 1984. *Bribes.* New York: Macmillan.

Nürnberger, Klaus. 1985. Ethical implications of religious and ideological pluralism: A missionary perspective. *Missionalia* 13:95–110 (Winter).

Smedes, Lewis B. 1986. *Choices: Making right decisions in a complex world.* San Francisco: Harper & Row.

Sproul, R. C. 1982. The relativity blitz and process theology: Understanding God or shaping God to accommodate our ethics. *Christianity Today* 26:50–51.

Yeow, Choo Lak. 1985. Theology's long march against corruption. *East Asian Journal of Theology* 3:199–201.

30

To Bribe or Not to Bribe?
Teg Chin Go

Pastor Luke looked with despair at the immigration official seated behind his large desk. He could offer the man a small sum of money and then receive the visa permitting Reverend John to enter the country, or he could refuse and no visa would be granted. The choice was his.

Pastor Luke was the elderly pastor of a large church with more than a thousand members among the Chinese in the Philippines. He had labored hard, but now he was in poor health and the load was too heavy. The people complained that they were being neglected, and he knew that the outreach of the church in the community had almost stopped. But where could he find help? He had searched widely throughout the Philippines for a younger assistant, but even in the Bible schools and seminaries there were almost no young Chinese training for the ministry. To find one in the country was almost out of the question.

In discussing the matter with other pastors, Pastor Luke found out that there were Taiwanese pastors willing to work in the Philippines. Their language abilities and cultural backgrounds were well suited to his Chinese-speaking congregation. So he and some church elders had traveled to Taiwan, where they found Reverend John, an able and willing worker.

However, when Pastor Luke applied for a work permit for the Taiwanese pastor, he ran into a serious problem. The officer in charge of immigration expected some money, and the pastor had heard that in some cases it had taken five to ten years for an application to be processed when no money was offered. With a suitable sum changing hands, the matter could be resolved in a matter of a few days.

When Pastor Luke brought the problem to the board of elders, most of them explained that the giving of money to an official should be thought of as a "gift" and not a "bribe." Many of them were involved in business, and they admitted that giving "gifts" to those in authority was a cultural practice in the country. They faced similar situations in business, and if they did not follow the accepted pattern they could not continue their work. Pastor Luke raised an objection. Were they not in danger of compromising with evil, of not speaking out against corruption, no matter the cost? Was the giving of money to officials so much a part of the culture that they should accept it as a church and comply in order to carry out the work of the church? Or were the elders right when they said that it was only a "gift" to the officials for their assistance? Throughout the years, he had been firm in his preaching that Christians should not be involved in bribery.

When Pastor Luke hesitated to go along with the elders who asked him to pay the money, they threatened to remove him from office and install the new pastor in his place. If, however, he agreed to give the money, would he not compromise his own convictions and lose the respect of those in the congregation who knew of his firm stand on the issue? Pastor Luke looked at the official seated before him and said . . . .

31

Elusive Justice
Keith Hinton

Bill looked at the police officer with uncertainty and frustration. The officer has asked him for 50,000 *rupiahs* for the return of his driver's license. It was Bill's twelfth weekly visit to the head-quarters since the license had been confiscated, and his resentment rose as he faced the possibility of yet another wasted week clouded with uncertainty and unpleasantness, unable to use his car. Must he sacrifice his principles in order to resolve the matter?

The problem began when Bill had returned from a missionary assignment out of town. He was coming into Bandung, West Java, along the main highway from Tjirebon, the same road on which he had left the city two days before. The chaotic congestion was about normal in this heavily populated part of town. Animals, trishaws, and people were weaving their way in and out among the motorized traffic that crawled along the road toward the urban open market. For some time Bill had been caught behind a slow-moving, overcrowded bus, and there was little chance of getting past it, even when it stopped to allow passengers to alight.

Suddenly Bill was jolted to attention when something hit the side of the car. Before he knew what had happened, he caught sight of a policeman approaching the car and shaking his fist. By the time the officer had picked up his baton from the street, Bill was out of the car and prepared for the worst. Fellow missionaries had warned him never to tangle with the police. In fact, it was missionary policy not to call the police, even in the case of a house burglary. Experience had shown that it was cheaper to sustain the losses of robbery than to bear the frustration of red tape and the loss of further property taken to headquarters to test for fingerprints.

Bill did not have to wait long to find out what he had done wrong. For several hundred yards approaching the market area, the highway became a one-way street. Buses and other public vehicles were permitted to use it in both directions, but private vehicles had to detour around back streets and rejoin the highway several blocks beyond the market. Bill pleaded that he had seen no sign and had simply followed the bus. The officer walked Bill back twenty yards and pointed out to him a small, mud-spattered sign obscured by a large parked truck. This did not seem to concern the officer at all. There was a law and a sign—and Bill was guilty.

Officer Somojo escorted Bill to the local police post in the market. Five other officers materialized from the stalls in the market, so Somojo began to explain how very embarrassing it was for him to have to prosecute a foreigner, and how he regretted that Bill had put him in this difficult position. After some time, Somojo suggested that the whole thing might be smoothed over quietly and without further awkwardness if Bill would pay a token fine of 500 *rupiah* (U.S. $1.20) on the spot. Bill had been expecting just such a request. Without even asking if it was a formal, legitimate fine for which a receipt would be given, Bill quickly protested that although he might be technically guilty, Indonesian law had a system of justice and courts where such matters were to be settled. He would go through proper channels and requested to be allowed to do so. The officer scowled and told Bill that he would have to hold his driver's license until the case was settled. Bill could come to the police headquarters the following week to get it back. Since no receipt was issued for the license, Bill secretly feared that he would never see it again.

The following week, Bill went to the appointed office, only to be informed that the license had been sent to another department on the other side of the city. After a slow trip by trishaw, Bill finally found his way to the other office. The policeman in charge had a record of Bill's offense and said Bill could talk to the captain who would probably be prepared to settle the issue for 1,000 *rupiah*. Bill suspected dishonesty and requested an official receipt for the money. The man just smiled. Bill told the policeman that he had come to Indonesia to build efficiency, justice, and a high standard of morality in the country. He would prefer to go through official channels. At that, he was told to return in a week's time. So week followed weary week, with hours wasted in travel and more hours spent waiting in offices. Each time the amount requested for settlement rose higher.

Bill worried about what he should do. He didn't want to be a troublemaker, but as a missionary he had to take a stand for honesty. His Christian witness depended on it. His whole upbringing as the son of an evangelical pastor had been one of strict integrity, and he had managed, so far, to maintain this standard in previous encounters with immigration officers and postal clerks. Yet, while he felt he had done the right thing, he still felt uneasy, for he knew full well that government officials were so poorly paid that they had to make at least double their official salaries on the side if they were to feed and clothe their families. The whole system was unjust, and he was caught in it. Bill talked to some other missionaries. They just laughed and said, "Let us know how you get on!"

Now it was the twelfth week, and he still did not have his license. Moreover, the amount being asked to settle the case had risen to 50,000 *rupiahs* (U.S. $120). Should he pay the official and end the case? Or should he appeal to a higher-level officer in hopes of a just settlement? Bill looked at the officer and said . . . .

32

Fuel for the Water Pump
Anonymous

Don answered the knock at the door. It was Ngoy, the man who ran the water pump for the mission station. "Bwana, we have only one day's supply of diesel fuel left for the pump. After tomorrow I will not be able to pump anymore." Don thanked Ngoy for keeping him informed. Before leaving, Ngoy told him that the young men in the next village had diesel fuel for sale. Don said that he wanted to think about the matter before giving him an answer. He knew that that fuel had been stolen, yet he needed fuel to keep the seminary and the high schools going.

After Ngoy had left, Don sat down to think things over. The mission station was the largest educational center for his denomination in Angola. In it were two high schools with boarding students, and a seminary. To have no fuel meant that a thousand people would be without water. If it were the rainy season, there would be no problem, because the people could catch the rainwater off the roofs. But it was June, and the rains would not come until October. Fifteen years earlier they could have used the river, but it was now polluted by the mines that had sprung up in the region, and besides there was now *bilharzia* (schistosomiasis) in the water. For this reason the mission had the mine owners drill a well to tap the underground water stream. A diesel motor was used to pump it into the reservoirs of the station.

When Don had come to Angola to teach in the seminary, he was also made responsible for the pump. At first there had been no problems, because the mission treasurer in the city a hundred miles away sent him the diesel fuel. The church had a quota with the oil company, for fuel had to be imported into the country. However, during the last few months, when the treasurer went to get the fuel, he found it had been diverted to someone else.

Don knew that without fuel there would be no water. Without water they would have to close the station. The last time they had been without water some of the students went to the river and became sick. He had then bought fuel from the young men in the village, and that had saved the situation. It was only later, through casual conversation with the African director of the seminary, that he learned the source of the fuel. The young men had an arrangement with the drivers of the mine trucks. The drivers would stop at the village to eat, and the young men would siphon off some fuel from their tanks to sell at a high profit. Don remembered how guilty he felt after he found out how the fuel was obtained. He remembered his pious upbringing. His grandfather was a great leader in the holiness movement, and Don himself had been raised in an atmosphere that emphasized holy living. Keeping one's witness and credibility as a messenger for the gospel was one of the cardinal values in his life. He forgave himself for having bought the fuel the first time, because he did not know that the merchandise was stolen. But now he knew.

"Don, it's time for the radio call," his wife, June, called out from the kitchen, and he went to the shortwave radio with which he kept in contact with the other mission stations. Perhaps another station would have spare fuel he could use. But all the other stations were facing the same problem, since they all depended on the quota in the city for fuel.

Don decided to see if he could find fuel in other places. He drove to mining headquarters twenty-five miles away. When Don explained the situation to the manager, he said, "I am sorry, but our mine quota for fuel is only enough for our operations. We can't help you." Don then tried the construction company that had built the buildings at the station, but to no avail. He went to the merchants, but found that they were operating on stolen fuel.

Don drove back to the station pondering the decision. He would either have to close the station down, keep it open and risk the health of the people as they went to the river for water, or buy diesel fuel he knew had been stolen. As he drove up to the house, Ngoy was waiting. "Bwana, did you find any diesel fuel?"

"No, Ngoy, I haven't," he answered.

"Bwana, do you want me to get some fuel from the young men in the village?" Ngoy asked.

Don thought a moment and said . . . .

33

Bonanza or Black Market?
Paul G. Hiebert

Sarah put down the letter and looked at her missionary colleagues on the finance committee. "It's up to us to decide," she said. "The home board says it doesn't know the situation well enough and wants us to make the decision."

"I think we should go ahead," said Philip. "It would be a real bonanza for our work, and we wouldn't have to cut back on evangelism or the schools."

Steve, the third member of the committee, was not so sure. "What if it's illegal or immoral? If it becomes known, this could bring shame on the gospel and possibly put an end to our work."

"What could be wrong with it?" Philip replied. "After all, we are only buying rupees on the open market, not the black market. Besides, there's little chance of getting caught. There is so much to be done, and we need the money to expand the work. It's the government that is robbing us by setting an unrealistic exchange rate for its currency. What do you think, Mary?"

Mary, the fourth member of the committee thought a long moment before she was ready to answer.

The Asian Evangelical Mission had begun work immediately after World War II and over a twenty-year period had managed to plant more than twenty small churches in the villages and towns. The mission had grown until it now had an annual budget of $135,000, raised in North America. This supported ten missionary couples, two single missionary women, and nine evangelists. It also covered the operating costs for two dispensaries and a dozen small village schools run by the churches to train their people how to read.

Over the years the mission had exchanged its dollars for rupees through the government bank at the official exchange rate. This had created no problem, for the official exchange rate was only slightly below the rate available on the black market. In the past two years, however, inflation had sharply reduced the value of the rupee. The government had increased the number of rupees it gave for a U.S. dollar, but this had not kept up with the declining value of the rupee. Now the official rate was four and a half rupees for one American dollar, compared to eight rupees for a dollar on the black market. The mission had had to cut back on some of its work because it was not getting full value for its dollars. Missionary salaries, paid in rupees, had had to be raised significantly to keep up with inflation, but this took more dollars and left less for the rest of the work.

The mission finance committee had been struggling with its shrinking budget when Philip met the treasurer of another mission. "What are you doing to deal with the problem of inflation and poor exchange rates?" he asked.

"We now exchange our money on the open market," the treasurer replied.

"Isn't that illegal?" Philip asked.

"It is if you use the black market in the country," the treasurer replied. "But we exchange our money in the States through an international exchange company."

"But it is also illegal to bring rupees into the country. You have to declare them in customs when you enter. If you were caught, you might be prosecuted or deported," said Philip. "Besides, if it were known, it would give Christianity a bad reputation."

"We don't bring them in," the treasurer said. "We give the international company dollars in the United States and they send us their agent in the country to give us the rupees. I don't know how they exchange the money, but I'm sure they know what they are doing. After all, the company advertises widely in American magazines and is well known on the international scene. Besides, *we* are not the ones bringing rupees into the country."

When Philip returned home, he called the finance committee together and explained to them the "new way" to exchange money. "Just think," he said, "if we use the free market, we would have plenty of money for our work. The government only gives us four and a half rupees for a dollar. The international agency gives us seven. That means we can get 945,000 rupees instead of 610,000. Each of our missionary couples gets $600 a month. If they used the new exchange rate, they would get 4,200 rupees rather than 2,700. That would make living a lot easier. And we would have 390,000 rupees for evangelism and church ministries instead of 250,000. We wouldn't have to cut back on the work. Or, if we as missionaries would be willing to live on 2,700 rupees a month, as we are now, we would have 590,000 rupees for evangelism and church planting—more than double what we now get. Think of all the things we could do with that money!"

Steve looked worried. "It sounds suspicious to me. The government is explicit. All money brought into the land must be exchanged through official government banks. It seems to me that somehow the international company is getting around the law. What if we are caught, and it is wrong? It would discredit Christianity in the whole country. You can imagine what the local religious fundamentalists would make out of that!"

"Other missions are doing it, and nothing has happened to them," Philip countered. "Besides, the government has no right to take our money and give us only half its value. And even if it is illegal, we aren't the ones bringing money into the country."

"But we don't want to give even the appearance of evil, for that would bring shame to Christ," Steve replied.

The finance committee had brought the matter to the full missionary fellowship, but there, too, there had been a division of opinion. In the end, the fellowship sent the matter back to the finance committee to decide.

The committee had written to the home board for guidance, and now they had received its reply. Mary knew that she had the deciding vote and that the missionary fellowship would go along with the committee's recommendation. It would be wonderful to have more money, but was it ethical? Finally she said . . . .

34

The Price of Ordination
Anonymous

Pastor Mulunda was confused and angry. The irony of the situation was incredible! The pastoral committee, representing the institution that stood most strongly against bribery in his culture, had just asked him for what amounted to a bribe. He had met with them for most of the morning. Now they had recessed for lunch, but later in the afternoon he would have to give them an answer. His ordination depended on his willingness to acquiesce to their request.

Three years before, Mulunda had heard a call from the Lord to minister in the poor, heavily populated capital city of his African country. He responded by beginning a three-year course of study at the national Protestant seminary. Mulunda's gifts were numerous, but academic achievement was not one of them. He persisted, however, with a dedication that he knew had been given him by the Lord. He often stayed up long into the night to complete his assignments while other students slept.

When he graduated, the pastoral committee assigned him to a large church in the capital city and also granted him a teaching position in one of the church's elementary schools. Since the congregation was poor and could provide Mulunda with only a fraction of even a modest income, a supplemental income was imperative. Most of his country's Protestant pastors were forced to do other things as well, because of the high incidence of poverty and unemployment in the country.

Mulunda knew, of course, that the choice placement and teaching position was no accident. The chairman of the pastoral committee, Elder Mukole, was also Mulunda's maternal uncle. As such, Mukole was simply fulfilling his obligation to his nephew by using whatever power or money was at his disposal to advance Mulunda's education and career possibilities. While Mulunda was at the seminary, Mukole supported him with tuition money and often with food. The latter became necessary when the seminary was unable to provide the students with their monthly ration of corn, manioc, sugar, and salt.

After his second year of studies, Mulunda married Mukaji. Again, it was his uncle who contributed heavily to the wedding dowry of goats, money, and bolts of cloth. He had done this in spite of the fact that many of the clan were upset because Mukaji was from a different tribe.

The first eight months of his pastorate were not easy, but Mulunda faithfully worked with all groups in the previously divided congregation. He saw the Lord add greatly to the church in numbers of members as well as in the depth of their spiritual lives.

In the eighth month, the pastoral committee notified him that they felt he was qualified to undergo the church's ordination examinations. He anticipated these exams with great apprehension, but it turned out that he passed all four of them and was recommended by the committee for ordination. All went well as he proceeded through the ordination process right up until the end of this morning's meeting. That was when he first learned of the committee's condition.

"Brother Mulunda," began one of the pastors on the committee, "many of the members have traveled long distances to attend the four meetings of your ordination exam. To be ordained, it is customary for the new pastor to pay the committee one goat for the trouble and expense we have incurred."

Feeling stunned and almost betrayed, Mulunda looked at his uncle for help, but Mukole's eyes had met him with an icy stare. Uncle was not on his side this time.

Now, as he reflected on what had occurred, Mulunda still could hardly believe it. His own Christian leaders were asking for a payment—a bribe! Their comments after the meeting made it quite clear that he would not be ordained until he gave them the goat.

Financially, the goat represented over two month's wages. But ethically it meant so much more! The problem of *matabishe* (bribery) was endemic in the national culture, but most pastors and lay evangelists preached strongly against it. Many of Mulunda's class discussions at seminary had been directed toward the questions of honesty, bribery, and the Christian witness.

The church would view such a forced payment as a bribe if they learned about it, and Mulunda would be seen by his own congregation as a "man of two words"—a hypocrite. How devastating that would be to the new converts!

The foreign missionaries who brought the gospel to Mulunda's country were the ones who first condemned the *matabishe*. Later it was also declared illegal by the national government. In the culture at large, however, people winked at the custom, and it was still widely practiced.

Mulunda had always been outspoken against the *matabishe* system. But suddenly, as his confused mind raced in circles over the dilemma he now faced, something else occurred to Mulunda. Was his attitude shaped more by the American missionaries' views than by the gospel message? He had often been hurt by their insensitivity to the customs of his culture. They often seemed to condemn things just because they didn't understand them—like the tribal respect for their ancestors, the temptations of a polygamous marriage, and the older people's fear of the spirits of sickness and lightning.

Matabishe was apparently not a part of American culture. Was it possible that the missionaries had condemned this part of Mulunda's culture without real Scriptural justification, and only because it was not a part of Western culture?

Mulunda realized he would have to pay the amount if he were to be ordained, and he had been quite sure of his call to the pastorate. And, of course, he owed his church placement and teaching position to the pastoral committee. More importantly, to refuse to honor the committee and its chairman—his own maternal uncle—was inexcusable. Why should a committee ordain a defiant candidate who would not submit to ecclesiastical authority? The non-Christians would soon hear about the disunity in the church, and that would seriously hinder their witness. No African wants to be associated with a fractured community.

Mulunda's mind raced over the teachings of Jesus; the Epistles; the Old Testament stories. Nothing seemed to speak to his situation.

But how could he pay what seemed to be a bribe to the committee and at the same time be exhorting his congregation to honesty? Was it bribery or was it gratuity?

Sweat rolled down Mulunda's forehead as the afternoon sun slipped downward through the hazy sky of the dry season. Outside he heard children racing noisily home from afternoon classes. Was there any way out of this dilemma that would satisfy both the committee and his own conscience?

PART **6**

Conversion
and Theology

Conversion and theology are central to the mission task. The gospel is the Good News of salvation for those who believe, and new believers must grow in faith and the knowledge of that gospel. But the mission task does not end with conversion. It must also be concerned with spiritual growth and maturity—with the long-range development of the convert and of the church as a corporate body.

In the case of the individual convert, we must begin where she or he is. To become a Christian is to turn around and move toward another center—to change allegiances. But converts come as they are, with their lives scarred by sins of the past. Their beliefs and world views do not change overnight. Consequently, the church must lead them into a growing understanding of the gospel and the transformation of their lives. It must minister to people from their births and their rebirths—until their deaths.

When considering the church as a body of believers that persists over time, the missionaries and leaders must plan for fifty and even a hundred years. They are responsible for keeping the church true to the gospel. Through constant renewal, it must maintain its missionary vision. And through prophetic voice, it must determine what it means to live as a Christian in a sinful world.

149

As missionaries we may spend a great deal of time studying the message of the gospel but relatively little time examining the means by which we communicate that message. We assume that when we speak, people will understand what we say, even though we come from another culture and speak their language poorly. We are often unaware that more than half of our communication in face-to-face situations is by gestures and body postures, tones of voice, facial expressions, the clothes we wear, the distance we stand from the people we address, and other paramessages. These signals tell people how we feel about them and the message we bring, and how we expect them to respond.

When we do study methods of communication, we focus on verbal media—preaching, teaching, printing, and radio and television broadcasting. Because of our Western orientation toward print as the chief means of storing information, we overlook the fact that people in nonliterate societies preserve their traditions and knowledge by means of songs, stories, bardic narratives, riddles, and proverbs. As Western Christians we underestimate the importance of such non-verbal methods of communication as rituals, symbols, dances, and music in many other societies. Consequently, we often do not understand the significance that rituals such as baptism and ordination, or birth rites, marriages, and funerals have in these cultures. We wonder why non-Christians may object to the baptism of their relatives but not to their conversion. We wonder why so much is made of bowing to parents at weddings, not realizing that most people use rituals to communicate their deepest allegiances and most fundamental identities to others in their societies.

The most basic problems we face in communication, conversion, and theology—and the ones we are usually least aware of—are at the "world view" level. Underlying each culture is a unique way of looking at the world. This can be seen in the assumptions a culture makes about the nature of reality and of what is "good." Since these assumptions are taken for granted, the people themselves are largely unaware of them. Yet these assumptions mold the way the people order their world. When missionaries from one culture go to another culture, they are rarely aware of their own hidden assumptions about the world around them, much less of the world view of the people whom they serve. Consequently, great misunderstandings arise, even when it seems on the surface as though the people understand the missionary's message.

Nowhere is this problem more evident than in Bible translation. The question arises as to what words in the local language should be used to translate the biblical words for God, incarnation, sin, salvation, and the like. The fact is, no language is theologically or philosophically neutral. All reflect the implicit assumptions of their cultures. It is impossible to make a translation that is one-hundred-percent accurate. Each translation loses some of the original meanings and adds some unintended ones, as can be seen in the case dealing with Bible translation in India (chapter 36).

Our hope is that communication will lead to conversion. But decisions are made in different ways in different societies. We in the West stress the importance of personal decisions because we live in a society that emphasizes individuality and self-realization. Other cultures see decisions as corporate matters to be made by a family or a tribe. What does conversion mean in such societies?

Finally, we need to deal with issues of theology. Mission activity is not complete until the church in a new setting reads and interprets the Bible in its own historical and cultural context. But this often leads to theological differences between new churches and their parent denomination. How should the missionary handle such differences? There is no easy answer, because theological commitments lie at the very heart of the missionary task. Yet to impose theological understandings on young churches is the deepest form of colonialism, which leads to a foreign Christianity in the country.

On one level, we need to teach people to turn to the Bible for their answers, trusting that the same Holy Spirit we know is at work in us is also in them, leading them in interpreting the Scriptures. On another level, we need to continue our dialogue with them, for the interpretation of the Bible is the task not of individuals but of the church as a hermeneutical community. And we and they are part of one church.

Bibliography

Costas, Orlando E., Jacobs, Donald B., et al. 1978. Conversion and culture. In *Gospel in context* 1:4–40.

Elwood, Douglas J., ed. 1980. *Asian Christian theology: Emerging themes*. Philadelphia: Westminster Press.

Hiebert, Paul G. 1985. *Anthropological insights for missionaries*. Grand Rapids: Baker.

Hiebert, Paul G. 1979. Sets and structures: A study of church patterns. In *New horizons in world mission* (pp. 217–242). D. J. Hesselgrave, ed. Grand Rapids: Baker Book House.

Kasdorf, Hans. 1980. *Christian conversion in context*. Scottdale: Herald Press.

Kraft, Charles. 1983. *Communication theory for Christian witness*. Nashville: Abingdon.

Nida, Eugene A. 1978. Linguistic models for religious behavior. In *Readings in missionary anthropology II*. William A. Smalley, ed. Pasadena: William Carey.

Nida, Eugene A. 1978. New religions for old: A study of culture change. In *Readings in missionary anthropology II*, William A. Smalley, ed. Pasadena: William Carey.

Ro, Bong Rin, and Eshenaur, Ruth. 1984. *The Bible and theology in Asian contexts*. Taichung, Taiwan: Asia Theological Association.

Schreiter, Robert J. 1984. Culture, society and contextual theologies. *Missiology* 12:261–274.

Stott, John R., and Coote, Robert, eds. 1980. *Down to earth: Studies in Christianity and culture*. Grand Rapids: Eerdmans.

Whiteman, Darrell L. 1984. Effective communication of the Gospel amid cultural diversity. *Missiology* 12:275–286.

35

Lily Liu's Baptism
James Chuang

What do they know about baptism? How can I bend God's command in order to please them?" Reverend Smith asked himself. As a young missionary to Taiwan, he had been looking forward to his first baptism in the small Baptist church outside Taipei when Lily's parents had come to his home, furious and demanding that he not baptize their daughter, Lily, the next day.

Reverend Smith thought back to what he knew of the bright young woman. Lily had grown up in a Buddhist home, seeing idols and smelling incense all her life. She first heard of Christianity from the Smiths when they moved in next door. They soon became friends. Not only Lily but also her entire family welcomed the new neighbors. After four years of fighting doubts and opposition, Lily made a solid decision for Christ. Her testimony was so dynamic that the youth group elected her to be their first woman president.

Mr. Liu was a faithful Buddhist who checked each evening upon his return from work to see whether the incense before the images was lit. As a bus driver, he did not want to offend his ancestors lest they cause him to have an accident. Like other bus drivers he also scattered paper money along the road when he drove over dangerous mountain roads in order to protect himself from the spirits of those who had died there in past accidents. Mrs. Liu, too, took her religion seriously. She was a loving mother who cooked, washed, cleaned, and said prayers for her children. Once she refused to allow a worker sent by the telephone company to put up a pole in front of her house because, she said, it might block the passage of her gods.

Although neither Mr. nor Mrs. Liu were Christians, they attended the church services on occasion. They also allowed Lily to participate freely in church activities. But they drew the line at baptism. Mr. Liu told Pastor Smith, "I like what you teach, but what do you think my ancestors will say if I accept your religion? They would be very upset, and how can I do anything to displease my ancestors?" He likewise refused to allow Lily to violate family tradition. Moreover, he needed her to worship his spirit after his death so that he would be cared for in his afterlife. Mrs. Liu's opposition to the baptism centered around Lily's marriage. Only two percent of Taiwan's population were Christians, and it would be much harder to find Lily a husband if she were a Christian.

Reverend Smith pondered the situation, for he knew that Lily would arrive shortly to seek his direction. Should he advise her to ignore her parents' orders? This would surely destroy the relationships he and his wife had so carefully cultivated with Mr. and Mrs. Liu and the other neighbors. Or should he suggest that she wait, thus denying her the opportunity to give a public testimony of her faith in Christ?

36

A Word for God
Paul G. Hiebert

Ivan threw up his hands. "What is more important—" he asked his colleague, "that people think of God as 'ultimate reality,' or that they think of him as a 'person' with whom they can communicate? Each of these, by itself, is a half-truth. Yet somehow it seems to me that we must choose between two words that carry these two meanings when we translate the word *God* into Telugu. What shall we do?"

After joining the Union Bible Society, Ivan had been asked to assist in a new translation of the Bible into Telugu. After settling down in the city of Hyderabad, he began to work with Yesudas, a high-caste convert who was also assigned to the project. Together the two had worked out many of the difficult problems they faced in translating the Bible into this South Indian language. But the most stubborn one remained unsolved. What word would they use for "God"? The choice they made was critical, for the nature of God lies at the very heart of the biblical message. To use the wrong term for "God" would seriously distort the Christian message. But although there are many Telugu terms for "god," none conveyed the biblical meaning.

At first Ivan suggested, "Let's use the term *deva*. That is the word the people use when they speak of 'god' in general terms."

But Yesudas pointed out, "The *devas* are the highest form of personal beings, but they are not the ultimate reality. Like all things in the universe, they are *maya*, or passing phenomena. In the end, they, too, will be absorbed into the ultimate reality or Brahman. Moreover, they do both good and evil. They fight wars with each other and with the demons, commit adultery, and tell lies. Finally, in Hinduism 'all life is one' [see figure 2]. In other words, gods, humans, animals, and plants

155

Figure 2   **A Comparison of World Views**

	Biblical World View	**Indian World View**
Ultimate reality:	God: being & creator	Brahman: force
Temporal reality:	spirit	gods
	humans	spirits
	animals	humans
	plants	animals
	matter	plants
		matter

all have the same kind of life. Consequently, *devas* are not fundamentally different from humans. They are more powerful and live in the heavens. But they sin, and when they do, they are reborn as humans, or animals, or even ants." Yesudas added, "Hindus claim that *devas* often come to earth as *avatars* to help humans in need, but because there is no difference between them it is like kings helping their commoners or saints helping their disciples. We, therefore, can use neither *deva* or *avatar*, for both destroy the biblical meaning of the 'incarnation.'"

"If that is the case, why not use the term *parameshwara*?" Ivan suggested. "That means 'highest of the deities.'"

Yesudas replied, "Yes, but this carries the same connotations as *deva*. In fact, all Telugu words for 'god' implicitly carry these Hindu beliefs! We have no word that means a supreme being who is the ultimate reality and the creator of the universe. Moreover, there is no concept of 'creation' as found in the Bible. The world itself is an illusion that does not really exist."

Ivan took another approach to the problem. "Why not use the concept of *brahman* itself? After all, *brahman* is ultimate reality—that which existed before all else and will exist when all else has ceased to be."

Yesudas objected. "*Brahman*," he said, "may be ultimate reality, but it is a force, not a person. True, some philosophers speak of *saguna brahman*, of *brahman* in a personal form. But even he is only a manifestation of *nirguna brahman*, which is an insular, impersonal force. It makes no sense to say that *nirguna brahman* reveals itself to gods and humans, just as it makes no sense to say that a dreamer speaks as a real person in his dream. Similarly, humans have no way of knowing about or communicating with *nirguna brahman*. Moreover, nothing really exists outside of *brahman*. The heavens and earth are not creations that exist apart from it. They are projections of *brahman* in much the same way that a dream is a projection of the dreamer. So, in fact, we are all simply manifestations of the same ultimate reality. This destroys the biblical idea of a creator and a real but contingent creation."

"What shall we do then?" asked Ivan. "Perhaps we could use the English word *God* or the Greek word *Theos* and introduce it into the translation. In time the word would become familiar, and it would not carry within it the implicit Hindu theology found in Telugu words."

"How can we do that?" asked Yesudas. "When we preach in the villages, no one will understand those foreign words. We must use words the people understand. Isn't that what the early church did when it took the Greek words for 'god' and gave them new Christian meanings?"

Ivan counterd, "Even if we do use *deva* or *brahman* and try to give them a Christian meaning, they will still be given Hindu meanings by the Hindus. And since the Hindus make up ninety percent of the population, how can a small Christian community maintain its own definitions of these words when the linguistic pressures for accepting the Hindu connotations are so great?"

"Well," said Yesudas, "we're back to square one. Should we use *deva*, or *brahman*, or 'God'? We have to use one of these."

The two discussed the matter for a long time, for they knew that their choice would influence both the evangelistic outreach of the church and also the extent to which the church would understand and be faithful to the biblical concept of God in the next fifty or hundred years. Finally they decided to . . . .

37

A Group Conversion
Paul G. Hiebert

Mark looked at the chief and elders before him and at the more than two hundred men, women, and children crowding behind them. "Have they all *really* become Christians? I can't baptize them if they don't each decide for themselves!" he said to Judy, his wife.

Mark and Judy Zabel had come to Borneo under the Malay Baptist Mission to start a new work in the highlands. They spent the first year building a thatched house, learning the language, and making friends with the people. The second year they began to make short treks into the interior to villages that had never heard the gospel. The people were respectful, but with a few exceptions none had shown any real interest in the gospel. Woofak was always around and had been from the beginning. In time he had become a believer, but few of the others took him seriously. He was something of a village maverick. And there had been Tarobo and his wife and four others. By the end of the third year, the worship services were made up of these seven baptized believers, Mark and Judy, a few passersby, and a dozen children.

That year an epidemic had spread through the highlands. For weeks Judy and Mark went through the villages, praying with the sick and dispensing medicines, until they thought they could go on no more. They wept with families faced with death and told them of the God who loved them and had conquered death itself. One village in particular had suffered greatly from the disease. Though the people seemed to appreciate the love shown by the two missionaries, they had shown no particular interest in the gospel.

Three months later, two elders from this village had come to the mission home, wanting to see the missionaries. "Can you come to our village and tell us more about your God?" they asked. "We want to know more about him."

Mark and Judy were excited. Their many hours on the trail in the rain and the weary days of ministering to the people were bearing fruit. Taking some food, water, changes of clothes, cots and nets, they set out for the distant village.

It was almost dark when they arrived. The village chief invited Mark into the men's long house where all the adult males of the village were gathered. Judy joined the women, who sat in front of their huts discussing the decision the village elders were about to make. She sensed that there had been much discussion in the village before she and Mark had been invited to come. Now there was a feeling of excitement and uncertainty in the air. Some of the women wanted to know more about this new God. Others said that it was best to stay with their ancestors who cared for them in the spirit world, and with the tribal gods who had helped them to be victorious over their enemies in the past.

In the long house the chief asked Mark to tell them more about his God. For three hours Mark told the men about the Jesus Way and answered their questions. Then the chief asked Mark to sit down on a log. Mark noticed that the men broke up into smaller groups, each made up of men from the same lineage. For half an hour there was a loud debate as men argued for and against following the new God. The arguments died down, and then the leaders from the various lineages gathered with the chief. Again there was a heated discussion. Finally the chief came to Mark and said, "We have all decided to follow the Jesus Way. We want to be baptized like Woofak and Tarobo."

Although it was late, neither Mark nor Judy could sleep after the meeting. The decision of the village, especially the way it was made, had caught them totally by surprise. They knew that tribal people often made important decisions, such as moving their villages or raiding neighboring tribes, by discussion and group consensus. But they never dreamed that people might use this method to choose a new god. All their theological training in their church and Bible College had taught the young missionaries that people had to make personal decisions to become followers of Christ. Here the group leaders had decided for all. What did that mean? Was it a valid decision, especially when it was clear from the debates that some had opposed the choice? How could they baptize the whole village when not all were agreed? Then again, what did it mean in Acts when the jailer believed and Paul immediately baptized him and his whole household? Moreover, if they did not accept the villagers as Christians, the villagers might return to their old gods. Judy and Mark knew that they had to do something before they left the next day.

As Mark and Judy searched for an answer, suddenly the great spirit gong in the men's long house rang out. Hurrying over to find out what was going on, Mark found the chief and asked him why they were summoning the tribal spirits, now that they had become Christians. "Don't worry," the chief said. "We are calling them to tell them to go away because now we have a new God."

Judy and Mark were still uncertain as they finally fell asleep, bone-tired and knowing that they would have to give the chief and the village an answer in the morning.

38

Conversion or Social Convention?
Paul G. Hiebert

Leela is already twenty-one, and by our customs she should have been married five or six years ago. It is not good for a woman to remain unmarried in the village. Already the people look down on Leela and suggest that she is cursed by the gods and brings bad luck. Soon the people will accuse her of prostitution. So it is urgent that we arrange a marriage for her right away. But we are now Christians, and there are no Christian young men of our caste for her to marry. We have searched widely. The only good prospect is Krishna, a young Hindu who is willing to become a Christian if we give Leela to him as his wife. Is it sin if we marry Leela to him? Is his conversion genuine if he becomes a Christian in order to marry Leela?"

Virginia Stevens looked at the anxious mother who was pouring out her heart to her. Then she looked at the young woman sitting expectantly on the mat before her. What should she say?

For years the Lutheran missionaries had worked in Andhra Pradesh on the east coast of South India. They had many converts, but most had come from the *harijan,* or untouchable castes. A few scattered individuals had become Christians from the lower clean castes, but none from the high castes.

Then a leading South Indian evangelist, a converted Brahmin from the highest caste, held meetings in the area, and five families of Reddys became Christians. The Reddys are farmers and rank high in the caste order. Because of their land holdings, they are wealthy and control much of the regional politics.

The new Christians met in a house church led by Venkat Reddy, one of the converts. He was well educated and could read the Scriptures, but he knew little about Christian doctrine and practice. So he contacted Sam and Virginia Stevens, Lutheran missionaries serving in Guntur, a hundred miles away. They visited the new church and encouraged it in its new faith. They also spent time with Venkat Reddy to help him grow in his understanding of Christianity. The church had grown spiritually and had won three other Reddy families to Christ, but one urgent problem persisted. How should the parents arrange marriages for their children?

Indian village culture requires that parents marry their children to members of their own caste. To marry outside of caste carries a great social stigma. Those involved and their families are put out of caste and shunned. Even the untouchables will have little to do with them. But there were few Reddy Christians, and many of the new converts could find no Christian Reddys to marry their children. There were many Christian young people in the old established churches, but they were all *harijans,* and it was unheard of for Reddys to marry untouchables. To do so would bring disgrace on the Christian Reddy families and cut them off totally from their non-Christian relatives. The door for further evangelism among the Reddys would then be largely closed.

Three years had passed since the Reddy congregation was formed, and the problem was becoming more acute as the young men and women grew older. One young man ran away from home and married a Christian woman he met in college. She was from an untouchable background, so they moved to the city of Madras where they could hide from the censure of their rural communities. But this had caused great pain to the young man's parents, who remained in the village.

Then a distant relative of Leela approached her parents about the possibility of Leela marrying their son. Ram and Shanta, Leela's parents, at first said no, that a Christian should not marry a non-Christian. But two months later, when the relative returned and said that Krishna, the young man in question, was willing to become a Christian and be baptized if the marriage took place, they began to reconsider.

Ram was not sure. "He will become a Christian in name only," he said.

"But he will listen to us and to Leela," said Shanta. "She is a strong Christian, and can help him grow in faith. Look at her! She's well past the age of marriage. If we pass up this opportunity, she may never get married. You don't want to condemn her to that, do you?"

Ram looked at Leela, his only daughter, and said, "I know. But we have always said that our Christian God would care for us in important matters such as this. Certainly he can provide us a Christian husband."

The next time the evangelist came to the village, Ram Reddy asked him if there were any Christian Reddy men in other parts of Andhra for his daughter. He also made several trips himself to distant towns in search of a husband. But none of his efforts turned up a suitable groom.

It was then that Krishna Reddy's father approached Ram and Shanta, urging them to arrange the marriage and reminding them that his son was willing to become a Christian and be baptized before the wedding. Ram and Shanta began to wonder whether this was God's way of opening the door for their daughter's marriage. Or was this a temptation they had to resist? Was such a conversion genuine? Did God want them to marry Leela to a Christian from an "untouchable" background instead? Could they bear the shame and ostracism that this would bring upon them in the village?

Now, as Virginia heard Shanta's story, she realized that the problem affected not only these parents, but also the future of the church among the Reddys. If Christians could not find spouses for their children, many Reddys would be afraid to convert. On the other hand, what did the Scriptures mean when it said that Christians should not be unequally yoked with unbelievers? Would Krishna's conversion be genuine if he took baptism so that he could marry Leela? What would happen if such marriages became an accepted practice in the Reddy church? And how would she feel if her own daughter were denied marriage because her mother herself had become a Christian? Virginia breathed a prayer before she responded . . . .

39

When Baptism Means Breaking the Law
S. J. Dhanabalan

Pastor Prabhudas was uncomfortably aware that Rukhmini's eyes often fastened on him as she sat quietly in the corner of the front pew, awaiting the outcome of the church-council meeting. Somehow he felt she would hold him most responsible for the decision. But he said very little, allowing the elders to carry on the discussion.

All she wanted was for the church to baptize her on the confession of her faith. How ironic it was, he thought to himself. The church prayed often and hard for Hindu converts, especially from among the castes that have been almost entirely resistant to Christianity. Now that they had an authentic convert from a high caste, the council was thoroughly perplexed about whether or not to baptize her. If, like the vast majority of Christians, she had come from the "untouchable" portion of society, now called "scheduled castes" in deference to the reforms of Gandhi, they probably would have baptized her immediately.

Pastor Prabhudas remembered his own joy when Rukhmini had come to his office to ask about baptism. He had heard something of her story from her college friends who were members of his church, but he listened gladly as she told him about her life and her conversion to Christ.

Rukhmini told the pastor that she was the eldest daughter of poor but high-caste parents who had sacrificed and struggled to send her to college so that her job and marriage prospects would be enhanced. They saw this, in the traditional cultural way, as a means to gain more income to support themselves and their younger children.

Once in college, Rukhmini became friends with some Christian students. They gladly drew her into their circle, although no one put any pressure on her to become a Christian. One reason for their "Christian presence" style of witness was that it is against the law in the state of Orissa to make converts from other religions. It is punishable by imprisonment.

Nevertheless, Rukhmini saw something in these Christians that was very attractive to her. She noted the joy and peace in their lives and wished it for herself. After a while, she asked to go to church with them. There she heard the story of Jesus and accepted him as her Savior. The experience transformed her life. She began to study the Bible with her college friends and grew in her faith.

For a while, Rukhmini remained a "secret believer," like other caste people, some of whom never take baptism because it would mean total ostracism from family and caste. In the case of a single woman like herself, it would mean that her parents could hardly find anyone to marry her, because there were so few Christian young men from the upper castes. No Hindu parents would give them a son, and for her parents to give her in marriage outside the caste would be unthinkable.

The time came, however, when Rukhmini decided that she could no longer hide her Christian faith. That was when she came to Pastor Prabhudas and asked for baptism. He had not tried to hide the consequences from her, and it became clear as they talked that she knew them only too well. Her parents would object strongly, and her disobedience to them would itself become a reason for criticism of Christianity. This would be seized upon by the local organization of the Hindu Samaj, who were fanatical in their opposition to Christians and used any breach of cultural norms to condemn them. And, of course, if it could be proven that the Christians had converted Rukhmini, the Samaj would bring a legal case against them. It was not unlikely that baptism of a high-caste woman would become an opportunity for persecution of the entire poor and largely powerless Christian community in that town.

Pastor Prabhudas had promised Rukhmini that she could put her request for baptism before the church's council of elders. Now they had spent almost two hours discussing the issues and seemed to be no closer to a decision. Some of them thought the whole church should be involved; others thought the decision should be made here and now by the council. The pastor finally let his eyes meet those of the young woman who sat patiently waiting for them to arrive at some conclusion. He knew it was time for him to enter the discussion. Choosing his words carefully, he began to speak . . . .

PART **7**

Walls That Divide People

Humans are social beings. We are members of families; neighborhoods; clubs; institutions such as churches, schools, and businesses; and nations. We belong to different races and are raised in different cultures.

Societies and social groups serve important functions. They enable us to work together with other humans to make life possible and meaningful. They provide us fellowship with other human beings. And they give us much of our sense of identity. We are fully persons only when we have significant roles and relationships with others in social settings.

But, because of sin, groups also divide humans into hostile camps. Tribes fight with other tribes on their borders or in the same town. High-class people disdain the poor. Ethnic groups and castes divide villages and cities into warring camps. And nationalism threatens to destroy the world through global wars.

The message of the gospel is one of reconciliation with God and with our fellow humans. As John makes clear (1 John 2:1–11), the two cannot be separated. The Great Commission finds its roots in the Great Commandment. The Old Testament prophets made it clear that the rich are responsible for the well-being of the poor, and God's people are to show hospitality to the stranger and foreigner at their door. In the

New Testament, Christ's last prayer is for the unity of his body (John 17:22–23), and Paul fought those who sought to divide the church (Gal. 2; Eph. 2:15).

How, then, does the gospel address the social walls that divide humans into hostile groups? What is the missionaries' responsibility when they see tribal tensions in Africa, caste divisions in India, class oppression in Latin America, and ethnic segregation in the West? Should we remain quiet about these divisions and merely proclaim the message of salvation, in hopes that when people are converted, they will be reconciled? But how long did it take for a degree of fellowship and unity to come between black and white Christians in the United States? How long will it take in South Africa, where white Christians use the Bible to justify their superiority? Should we rather speak out strongly and face possible expulsion from the country?

Equally difficult to handle are the social sins that enter our churches. All Christians should participate in local congregations to experience fellowship *(koinonia)* and to minister and be ministered to *(diakonia)*. It is good when they come as families and as communities, for then the church can strengthen and perfect family and community life. But what is our responsibility as missionaries when the local churches we plant exclude people from other families or communities? When a church made up largely of one tribe refuses to admit people from another tribe? When an Indian congregation made up of high-caste people does not allow "untouchables" to enter their church door? When a church of the rich makes the poor feel unwelcome? Or when a white church keeps out the blacks? What is our responsibility when ethnic, class, and cultural differences within a church threaten to divide it?

Today all human societies are becoming part of one world community. One result is an escalation of hostilities between human groups. More than ever, people need to hear a message of reconciliation with God and with each other.

Bibliography

Asian Theological Association, and Evangelical Fellowship of India, Theological Commission. 1985. Declaration on caste and the church. *Transformation* 2:1 (April/June).

Boesak, Allan. 1984. *Black and reformed: Apartheid, liberation and the Calvinist tradition*. Maryknoll: Orbis Books.

Cyster, Graham. 1985. Facing apartheid. *Transformation* 2:2–4.

Forrester, D. B. 1980. *Caste and Christianity*. London: Curzon Press.

Gnanakan, Ken R. 1985. Caste and the Indian church. *Transformation* 2:23–24.

Ramseyer, Robert L., ed. 1979. *Mission and the peace witness: The gospel and Christian discipleship.* Scottdale: Herald Press.

Smith, David. 1985. The church growth principles of Donald McGavran. *Transformation* 2:25–30.

Verkuyl, Johannes. 1973. *Break down the walls.* Grand Rapids: Eerdmans.

40

Peacemaker or Patsy?
Ron Priest

6:30 P.M. The calm of the evening in the southern highlands of Papua New Guinea is broken by loud, incessant yells. From one end of the village of Yan to the other, the air is tense as people wait to hear the reason for the commotion.

"Singing Out," as the yelling is called, is that culture's way of announcing emergencies, deaths, and other important messages from one village to other villages nearby. The persistent yelling always demands an inquiry. What has happened?

There has been a three-month lull in the tribal fighting between the Yan villagers on one end of the plateau and the Emsa people who live on the other end. The war has been going on for two years.

The Christian mission has planted churches in both places. Now, because of the war, congregations have been divided, buildings burned, and Christians are perplexed about their loyalties.

The Emsas now enjoy a 24-to-11 lead in the death toll, so the Yans are eager to settle the score. For most of these people, in spite of twenty years of Christian teaching, the war is not over until every death has been avenged. The mission has tried to remain neutral in the fighting. They have seen their role to be one of encouraging people to apply Christian principles so that peace will prevail.

7:00 P.M. The Singing Out becomes more intense, louder with increased participation. The road alongside the mission station is now bustling with Yan villagers hurrying to the local meeting ground.

Suddenly, mysteriously, the Singing Out stops. The only sounds are the pounding of feet on the road. Then it seems as if the gathering is complete. In the distance a muted muttering of many voices is heard.

The missionary has been a missionary for only nine months and is confused about what is happening. He stops a hurrying late-comer and is told that two Emsas have infiltrated a nearby village. Now they are hiding out just outside the mission property. Their presence spells trouble—death, rape, or burning. The villagers are assembling to devise a plan.

9:00 P.M. The missionary hears a nervous, demanding knock on his door. The local pastor is there to give him a report. One intruder is in hand; the other has escaped under the veil of night. The pastor is terribly agitated, because the captured man is his friend from younger days. He begs the missionary to go with him to the assembled villagers to plead with them to deal kindly with the captive. Perhaps they can even be persuaded to send him home unharmed. If they decide to do that, it could mean a pledge of peace. The war might come to an end.

9:45 P.M. After the pastor and missionary present their case to the villagers, the missionary goes home. He feels frustrated and extremely concerned for the welfare of the captured Emsa. Would the Yan villagers so quickly abandon their Christian teaching? Gathering his wife and three children, the missionary seeks the help of God through prayer.

10:30 P.M. The low mutterings from the assembly grounds have subsided. Has a decision been reached?

Suddenly, frighteningly, loud shrieks cut the darkness—shrieks of victory. The missionary peers out his bedroom window. Yan villagers are pouring into his front yard. Lighted torches illuminate two men carrying a lifeless form tied to a pole.

A spokesman for the jubilant Yans insists that the missionary himself return the intruder's lifeless body to his home village. The crowd insists that the axe-mangled Emsa deserved his end.

The missionary is stunned—horrified and grieved.

The spokesman again insists that the body must be returned to the enemy side. If not, the man's dead ancestral spirits could cause disease and death among the Yans. Also, the Emsas would be further outraged because a fallen warrior's body had not been returned.

The missionary asks and is told about the traditional way of returning a dead enemy. The victor locates a woman in the village who formerly belonged to the enemy's village but has married a Yan. The Yan warriors will take her and the body with them to face the enemy warriors at a previously arranged place. Because she is still free to mix with her own clan, she is left with the body while the others draw back. Her own clan then comes to retrieve the dead body.

Hearing this, the missionary is even more perplexed. If he does what they are asking, will it not be an approval of their hideous act? But not to do it may get him blamed for any future "curse" that comes upon the Yans. On the other hand, if he returns the body, will the Emsas feel some gratitude toward him? Or will they view him as an accomplice of the Yans? Or, even worse, as one who disturbs traditional customs and practices? Will he be seen as a peacemaker—or a patsy of the Yans?

Muttered threats against the missionary from some in the crowd pierce him like a cold wind rushing through a hole in the pit of his stomach.

11:00 P.M. Tired of waiting, the villagers dump the lifeless body on the ground and begin to leave. The few who linger mingle nervously, awaiting the missionary's answer. He has a question of his own. What is God's word to the Yans tonight? Whatever he does should point to that, but what should it be?

41

Unity and Diversity in the Church
Paul G. Hiebert

In the early summer of 1979, John Thompson argued wearily with himself as he looked out the tent at the hot road baked by the South India sun, and at the dust swirling around an oxcart passing under the shade of a large banyan tree. In a few minutes the delegation of elders from the Farmer caste led by Venkat Reddy would come to hear his decision. Would he force them to take defiled Untouchables into their new church? Or would he ask the Untouchables *(harijans)* to start their own church near their hamlet outside of town?

As he reflected, John thought back over the past few years. He and his wife, Shirley, had come to India six years earlier. Their mission board assigned them to pioneer work in the villages near Nellore. They managed to build a small bungalow and to hire three Indian evangelists to begin the work. For six to seven months each year—after the intense field work following the monsoon rains let up—they toured the villages with the evangelists, camping in tents and preaching in the village squares at night. In the mornings they visited homes, and Shirley was often invited into the inner rooms reserved for women. In the afternoons John held Bible studies with the evangelists and curious inquirers from the villages. After preaching one or two nights in a village, they moved on to the next, for John was responsible for evangelizing more than three hundred villages.

The pace was grueling, particularly in the hot summer months, but there were rewards. At first, few were interested in the gospel, but prayer and faithful witness bore fruit. A number of families from the

173

village of Konduru who belonged to the Farmer caste publicly became Christians. After their baptism, they wanted John to teach them more about their new religion. The Farmer caste was *suvarna* (clean) and ranked high in the village hierarchy of castes. John spent a week with them and taught them from the Bible, but he was concerned about their growth. Only two of them, an old man and a young boy who had been to the city, could read and write. However, there were other villages in which the people had never heard the gospel; there was no one else to go to them, so John moved on.

A year later, John returned to Konduru to hold meetings in the Untouchable hamlet a furlong outside the village. He had come to realize that if he preached in a main village, only people from the clean castes would attend. The Untouchables, who made up more than 20 percent of the population, rarely showed up in such places in the main villages because they were considered ritually defiling. A person belonging to a clean caste who touched one of them had to take a ceremonial bath before he or she could eat or enter the temple. If John wanted to evangelize the Untouchables, he would have to go to their hamlets which were located outside the main villages.

John's meeting in the hamlet near Konduru went well, even though the Farmer-caste Christians did not attend. They said they were too busy with field work at the time. Their church had grown to fifteen families, and they had built a small church building at the edge of the village near their homes. There they met fairly regularly for worship services.

The second night, after the meeting in the hamlet, several elders of the Leatherworker-caste led by Pappayya came to John and asked whether Untouchables, too, could become Christians. John joyfully told them that the Gospel was for everyone. He pointed out that in Christ all persons are equal, that there are no distinctions of caste, class, or race. Over the next few days, six families of Leatherworkers publicly converted to Christianity and were baptized. John was very happy.

However, when John told this to Venkat Reddy and the elders of the Christian Farmers and asked them to accept the new converts into their church, they were shocked. How could they as clean caste people permit Untouchables to enter into their church? They would be defiled and their fellow castemen would put them out of the caste. They would be shunned by their friends and relatives. They would not be able to visit or witness to them, to eat with them, or to exchange brides and grooms with them. They would have no place to marry their children.

John told them that the gospel made all people one, but they said that if he forced them to take the Untouchables into their church, they would return to Hinduism. They said he did not understand their place in the caste system in the village. They would return the next day to hear his answer on the matter.

John realized that all people live in social systems that regulate their relationships with one another. In India there was the caste system. John knew this system was rooted in Hinduism and that Hinduism would wither and die if it were abolished. At the top were the Brahmins, the Hindu priests who performed the rituals and sacrifices necessary for the salvation and well-being of the people. Below them were many castes of rulers, merchants, craftsmen and laborers. At the bottom were the Untouchables, those ritually so impure that they were forbidden to enter the temples or to live in the clean caste villages. It was their duty to handle dead animals, clean the latrines, and do other defiling tasks so that the upper castes, particularly the Brahmins, might remain pure. Without this purity, the Brahmins could not supplicate the gods, and destruction and disorder would follow. At its very core, Hinduism rejected the equality of all humans. Its scriptures declared that people were born unequal and that their station in life was determined by the good and evil they had done in their previous lives. Those who had lived good lives were born Brahmins and were closest to salvation. Those who had done evil were born Untouchables. Their only hope was to bear patiently their lot in life so that in their next lives they would be born clean.

John also knew that because of this caste system, millions of Untouchables lived in the most grinding poverty and oppression. They could not walk through the villages where the clean castes lived. They could not return goods they purchased or cook food for others, for they defiled everything they touched. Many were virtual slaves to their clean caste masters.

John wondered what the gospel had to say to all of this. If he tried to break down the caste system in the church by requiring clean caste and Untouchable converts to worship together, would he not drive the clean castes away, and leave a church that would itself be branded as Untouchable? Becoming a Christian would then be perceived by respectable caste Hindus as becoming a member of an exceedingly low segment of society. Would this not close the door to the evangelization of high-caste people?

On the other hand, if he organized separate churches for the two groups, would he not be allowing Hinduism and its caste distinctions into the church, and so undermine the gospel? Moreover, would the Untouchables be drawn to the gospel if the church offered them no deliverance from their bondage? Other churches in South India had found that where equality and a rejection of caste had been made a condition for entry into the church, many Untouchables entered. When the caste system was permitted inside the church, some high-caste people came, but the Untouchables stayed away.

John spent the afternoon and next morning in prayer and the study of the Bible. He reviewed Paul's teachings about the unity of the body of Christ in the face of animosity between Jews and Gentiles that threatened to split the early church. He recalled the divisions in the Western churches. And he thought about the realities of life in the Indian village and the ways in which its social organization affected the growth of the church.

Now the Farmer elders were coming for his answer. What should he say to them, and to the elders of the Leatherworker Christians? Should he force them to form a single church? If he did, the Farmers would probably return to Hinduism. Or should he encourage them to form separate churches and then seek to build fellowship between them over time? But what would this say about the unity of the body of Christ to both groups? These arguments were rushing through his head as he saw the Farmer elders come down the road.

42

Conflict During the Lord's Supper
Christopher John Singh

Pastor Prabhakar looked at the angry men shouting at each other and wondered whether he should proceed with the Lord's Supper. And how should he deal with the fundamental issue that had divided his congregation? The old men had demanded that he not offer the bread and the cup to Mr. and Mrs. Ramu Rajendra. But many of the younger men had threatened to leave the church if he refused to serve the young couple.

The problem was an old one. Pastor Prabhakar was in charge of a two-hundred-member, multi-ethnic church in South India. About half of them belong to the Nadars, a high-ranking caste. The rest belonged to the Parayas and Sambavars, who were considered "untouchables" and so ranked very low in the village. There were some caste feelings in the church, but the pastor visited the homes of all his members each month and was loved and respected by them all.

Among his members were Mr. and Mrs. Bhim Rajendra, wealthy Nadars who had three daughters and a son, Ramu, who had completed his Master's degree in English but could not find a job, even with the help of his influential father. The family had asked the church to pray about the matter. Ramu was a good musician and served as the choir director in church. It was at the rehearsals that he met and fell in love with Kamalamma, the beautiful daughter of Mr. and Mrs. Devadas, who were Sambavars. His parents noticed this and tried to break up the relationship, pointing out to their son that the woman came from a poor and "untouchable" family. But at the summer leadership camp that both attended, the young couple decided to be married.

When they returned from camp, Ramu and Kamalamma came to the pastor and asked him to marry them. He told them that he could not do so without the support of their parents. Kamalamma's parents agreed to the wedding, but Ramu's parents were adamantly opposed. When Ramu got a job in a nearby town, he rented a house. Then one day he and Kamalamma went to the court and registered their marriage. When his parents heard this, they would not allow the young couple into their home.

The church was divided on the matter. Many of the older people objected to the "love marriages" that were beginning to take place in the cities, and to the very idea of "register marriages." Many of the young people sided with the couple and noted that they were happy together.

Today, two months later, Ramu and Kamalamma were visiting their village on a Sunday and attending the morning church service. There was to be communion, and at the outset some of the leading members had asked the pastor not to let the young couple attend the service because they were sinners. He refused to send them away. After the sermon, when he asked that only believers who were in right relationship to God and ready to take communion remain in the sanctuary, Ramu and Kamalamma stayed. At this, the older men rebelled and asked the pastor not to give them communion, and the younger men began to argue loudly that the church had no right to condemn them. Pastor Prabhakar had to shout to get the attention of his angry congregation. When they were finally quiet, this is what he said . . . .

43

Caste Violence Among Christians
A. Raveentharan

Pastor Victor slapped the newspaper down on the table and rose with an angry scowl on his face. Premila, his wife, and Sunder, his pastoral assistant, looked up with surprise that turned to shock when he began to speak. "What's the use?" Victor exclaimed. "Now the whole town can read in the newspaper about how the Christians fight with each other. Yes, they call themselves 'Christians'—sometimes I wonder if they know the meaning of the word. Anyway, that does it for me! I'm going to resign and leave this town—I don't want to show my face here after Christians make headlines like this."

The offensive headline in the paper of the municipal town of Angol proclaimed, "After Short Growth Spurt, Local Church Splits Along Caste Lines." The article went into detail about how families of the Reddy caste had been attacked with knives, staves, and crowbars by young men of the Mala caste who were their fellow church members.

Premila watched Victor anxiously as he strode from the room. The last few months had not been easy for her husband. She avoided Sunder's eyes as she said with a note of despair in her voice, "How can I help him? I am partly the cause of his trouble." Sunder hardly knew what to say, so he allowed himself only a deep sigh as he reflected on how things had changed in the short time since he had become one of Victor's converts to Christianity from Hinduism. It was only a little more than a year ago that Victor had started the fellowship group in his home that had now expanded into an established and growing church.

Victor's family was Christian and belonged to the Reddy community in the town of Ramaputnam. When he began his evangelistic ministry in Angol, Victor went to the Untouchable Malas, rather than to the clean middle-caste Reddys who were his social equals. He had a strong conviction that the church should transcend caste lines and was determined not to limit his counseling, ministry, or fellowship to any particular group. Within a few weeks, four Mala youths were baptized and forty others were preparing for baptism.

The town of Angol was 80-percent Christian. Of these, 25 percent were Catholic, and the rest belonged to the Church of South India. The CSI members were divided between the Malas and Reddys, with the latter group being slightly smaller. Caste distinctions were strictly observed by both groups, and there was often tension between them. Victor soon realized that there were many who were only nominal Christians.

After being in Angol for two months, Victor began Sunday services in his home. His earliest opposition came from other Christians. On the first Sunday morning he held a service in his home, the bell was also rung in the CSI church for the first time in many months. The people were confused as to which church they should attend. The pastor and elders from the CSI came to his home and angrily asked him to leave town. However, their threats to have him evicted were futile, because Victor's landlord was someone he had led to Christ a few weeks earlier.

Soon many people came to Victor's services. They also came to him individually for counseling, prayer, and fellowship. Many found new life in the fellowship and began to help Victor with evangelism. It was during this period that Sunder was converted and began to serve the church as Victor's assistant. While Victor's own caste background was initially unknown to the local people, Sunder was known to be a Reddy. He was, of course, theologically naive, but he was eager to learn and earnestly committed to the work of spreading the gospel.

Sunder had a great burden for his own relatives and caste people who lived in the street that was next to the one where the church was located. In fact, it was really because of Sunder's work that many Reddy Christians began to attend the prayer fellowship and, later, the Sunday worship.

After a while, Victor left the work in the hands of his able assistant and went home to Ramaputnam to spend some time with his parents, who were becoming quite concerned about arranging his marriage. Although Victor had now told the people in Angol that he was a Reddy and promised them that he would marry a low-caste girl, he was not prepared to disobey his parents. While he was with them, they arranged for him to marry Premila, a Christian from their own Reddy caste.

Newly married, Victor returned to his church in Angol and arranged a reception party. For convenience sake, the couple invited the Malas to their home in the morning and the Reddys in the evening. This was felt very keenly by the Malas, and the pastor was thought to have discriminated against them because of their caste. From that time on, it seemed that they were against everything he did.

Victor obtained the money to build a church building with the help of a missionary friend by the name of Bill Steward. He hoped that by building it in the street of the Malas he could overcome their grudge against him. Even that did not seem to make much difference to the Malas, however, and they continued to criticize their pastor for favoritism.

The Reddys came to the new church building for worship, even though it meant that they had to come to the street of the Malas. They did not come, however, on the third Sunday of the month, which was regularly scheduled for the observance of the Lord's Supper.

Finally Victor tried to placate the Malas by appointing a young Mala whose name was Kumar to be in charge of the youth ministry. Kumar had just graduated with a B.D. degree from the seminary in Ramaputnam and was a relative of Victor's landlord. The Malas were happy to have a respected member of their own caste put in that position, but the Reddys were not at all pleased and asked Victor to send Kumar to another church.

This request was what made the Malas so angry that they attacked the Reddy families with weapons and made headlines in the local paper. The town buzzed with expanded versions of the story. Not only Hindus, but some other Christian groups, enjoyed hearing about the humiliation of Victor's church.

Now Premila and Sunder looked up anxiously as Victor came back into the room. What had he decided? Would he actually carry out his impulsive threat to resign? Even if he stayed, with so many problems to solve, what could the three of them do to make Victor's dream of a living, united church in Angol come true?

There was a new look of determination on Victor's face as he turned to the other two and said, "I've decided that running away is not the answer. I'm going to stay, and here is what I'm going to do . . . ."

PART 8

Church-Mission Relationships

The ultimate purpose of missions is to plant churches. So long as the missionaries are unsuccessful in doing that, they can continue their ministries and give little thought to administrative and organizational concerns. But once they are successful, many questions arise regarding their relationships to their converts and to the local church. For example, how should one disciple new converts? Must they learn to read and write? What must change in their lives? How should their churches be organized? How long should the missionaries remain in charge of churches, schools, and hospitals? When should the local church take responsibility for itself and for evangelizing the people in its territories? And how should the transition of responsibility from mission to church be made?

The answers we give to these questions must take into account the history of modern missions and the beliefs and feelings of both missionaries and national leaders that this history has generated. Until World War II, the mission movement was closely identified with colonial expansion by the West. Many missionaries believed their task was to "Christianize," "civilize," and, in some cases, "commercialize" the "natives."

With colonialism came a sense of cultural (and often racial) superiority. Missionaries often treated local converts as children, even after they grew to be mature Christians. In situations where missionaries and local Christians worked together, the former were usually in charge. To say this is not to deny the love many missionaries had for the people among whom they served, the great sacrifices they often made, or the fact that God used them to plant churches around the world. They were people of their times, just as we are people of *our* times.

In the last century, two missionary statesmen, Rufus Anderson and Henry Venn, had called for an end of colonial attitudes in missions and advocated the planting of autonomous churches. They emphasized the need for three "selfs." The first of these was *self-governance*. Missionaries began to see their task as planting churches, training leaders, and turning over responsibility for the work to these leaders as soon as possible. Despite this emphasis, the transfer of power to young churches has often been slow. Some missions still find it hard to give up control of the churches they plant. Consequently there are often deep feelings of resentment and hostility between the leaders of young churches and the missionaries.

Along with self-governance came an emphasis on *self-support*. "If the churches are going to govern themselves, they should support the work," many missionaries argued. But many of the institutions that the missions built were too costly for the new, small, and often poor churches to maintain. The churches' response was, "We did not build these institutions, and if you want them to continue, you must fund them."

The question of financial relationships between churches in the West and those in the other two-thirds of the world requires careful consideration in our day. On the one hand, it is important for all churches to be "self-supporting," in the sense that they are not dependent on others for maintaining their own spiritual life and ministry. On the other hand, if we push self-support too far, it leads to a separatism that can seriously hinder the expansion of the universal church. The churches around the world belong to one body and should not be divided by nationalism into new tribes. The task they face is so great that they must work together, and this often calls for financial assistance.

The third "self" advocated by Venn and Anderson was *self-propagation*. The young churches, too, should have a missionary spirit. From the outset, they should help evangelize their own areas and, as soon as they are able, should be involved in missions to other regions and peoples. A missionary spirit, however, must be taught. Church history shows us that a zeal for missions does not automatically emerge when people become Christians. Missionaries must not only lead people to

Christ and plant churches. They must instill in these new churches a missionary vision.

The emphasis on self-propagation raises a number of important questions. After a church has been planted, should the mission move out into some new area? How strong should the young church be before it is left to do the work on its own? And if the young church does not evangelize those around it, does not the mission have a responsibility to continue evangelizing in the region? Or, if the church continues to evangelize its own people but neglects other kinds of people living in the same area, should the mission work among the latter, even if the local church objects? These are current questions that have generated strong debate.

Past discussions about the relationship between mission and church have centered around self-governance, self-support, and self-propagation. Today the question of a fourth "self" has been raised, namely *self-theologizing*. Do young churches have a right to interpret the Bible in their own cultural context? Does the Holy Spirit lead them just as he leads the sending church and its missionaries in their understanding of Scripture?

Self-theologizing raises profound questions regarding the nature of theology and truth. What should missions do if the churches they plant disagree with them theologically? If they force their own theological positions on the local church, are they not theologically colonial, and do they not hamper the maturation of the young church? On the other hand, if they keep silent, are they not partly responsible when an immature church slides into syncretism? These are the questions increasingly being raised with regard to mission-church relationships.

Bibliography

Anderson, Gerald. 1974. A moratorium of missionaries? In G. H. Anderson and T. F. Stransky, *Crucial issues in missions today* (pp. 133–142). Mission Trends no. 1. Grand Rapids: Eerdmans.

Bergquist, James A., and Manickam, P. Kambar. 1974. *The crisis of dependency in third world ministries.* Madras: Christian Literature Society.

Coggins, Wade T., and Frizen, E. L., eds. 1977. *Evangelical missions tomorrow.* Pasadena: William Carey Library.

Neill, Stephen. 1959. *Creative tension.* New York: Friendship Press.

Scherer, James A. 1964. *Missionary go home!* Englewood Cliffs: Prentice-Hall. (Reprinted in *Crossroads in Missions.* Pasadena: William Carey Library, 1979.)

Samuel, Vinay, and Sugden, Chris. 1982. The two-thirds world church and the multinational mission agencies. *Missiology* 10:449–454.

Tucker, Ruth A. 1983. *From Jerusalem to Irian Jaya: A biographical history of Christian missions.* Grand Rapids: Zondervan.

Wagner, C. Peter, ed. 1972. *Church/mission tensions today.* Chicago: Moody Press.

44

What Price the Gospel?
Carl K. Kinoshita

At exactly the appointed hour, Second Lieutenant Seichi Miyazaki knocked on the office door of Carter Jackson, pastor of the Kalakaua Baptist Church. With military discharge only eight months away, Seichi needed the pastor's advice on a decision crucial to his future.

In the over thirty years he had been a pastor and missionary in China and Hawaii, Jackson had counseled many men about entering the Christian ministry. From what he had learned about Seichi since they first met three years ago, Jackson did not think the decision would be difficult to make. After all, the twenty-two-year-old air-force officer had made good grades in college, was popular as a Sunday-school teacher and counselor of junior-age boys, and was an active leader in the young people's department of the church. And although Seichi had been a Christian and church member for just two and a half years, more than a few members had expressed their feeling that he should consider the ministry as a vocation.

Seichi and Jackson had talked about all of these things two months earlier. But today the more information Seichi shared about his family, the more Jackson understood the reason for the worried look on the young man's face. These were some of the data Seichi gave his pastor. . . . He was the first of seven children born to Kazuo and Matsue Miyazaki and was raised on Molaka, a small island of predominantly Japanese and Filipino people who worked for the most part as laborers for the Del Monte Pineapple Company on the island of Oahu. He was taken to the Buddhist temple most Sundays until his years at the high school he attended in Honolulu on the island of Oahu. At this point in his story, Seichi stressed the fact that his mother started working in the pineapple fields to help pay for his education at Lolani School, a private, college-prep, boarding institution. Upon finishing there, Seichi had enrolled at the University of Hawaii and lived with an aunt in Honolulu. In the meantime, his family moved to Kahjaluu, a rural community on Oahu, and leased five acres of land for truck farming. But when heavy rains ruined the crops on two consecutive years and put Mr. Miyazaki near bankruptcy, Seichi decided to drop out of college, find a full-time job, and help his family financially. But Mr. Miyazaki insisted that Seichi remain in school in pursuit of a business-administration degree, an order impossible to disobey after being reminded of three facts: (1) for a quarter of a century Seichi's father (whose own parents had died while he was still in his teens) had dreamed of running a family-owned store; (2) the second son, Fumio, who was a year younger than Seichi, was born mentally retarded; and (3) the last son and youngest child, Hitoshi, was also showing signs of mental retardation.

Relating the incident of two weeks ago was most painful for Seichi. His mother's father had died, and a Buddhist funeral service was held at the Kukui Mortuary. At the part of the service when family members and, later, everyone else in attendance were asked to light the incense sticks, Seichi had refused to participate. What he did out of a strongly felt loyalty to Christ resulted in severe criticism of his parents by relatives. And that, Seichi said, had hurt him deeply.

Until today, Pastor Jackson had known very few of these details. Now he realized that no longer was Seichi's dilemma just a matter of discovering God's call to a Christian vocation. How could he help the young man sort out the conflicting demands on his loyalty in a way that would be true to his Christian commitment?

45

The Reverend Chu's Decision
James Chuang

What am I going to do? No matter what I do, one of them is going to be hurt very seriously." Reverend Chu, capable chairman of the Taiwanese National Church Union, was at a loss for words for the first time. The air was unusually tense. On the faces of the weary committee were signs of frustration and despair. It was already the fourth meeting, yet they were exactly where they started four meetings ago.

The Gospel Church, one of their local congregations, was desperately in need of a pastor. The former pastor had left some time ago, and the church was experiencing a serious decline in attendance. It brought a great hope and excitement when one of the missionaries, Reverend Johnson, located Mr. Wang, a willing and able worker. The case was quickly presented to the executive committee and it voted eight-to-one to approve the proposal. The missionary had exclaimed, "Great, let us install the man as pastor immediately." But Chairman Chu said, "No, we cannot." The only negative vote came from Reverend Mah, the former chairman. What would he do if they installed Mr. Wang as pastor?

By far the greatest difficulty for the growth of the church in this particular field was the serious lack of qualified workers. Out of 2,300 Protestant churches in the country, there were more than 300 without full-time pastors. It took at least four years to train a new worker. Therefore it was a special discovery when the missionary located Mr. Wang, who at the time was working in an orphanage as a chaplain. He was a very sensitive, friendly, and experienced Christian worker. He felt the call of God to be a pastor of a local church and was looking for an opening. Reverend Johnson felt that it was God's guidance for him to become acquainted with Mr. Wang just at the time when he was open to a new appointment and when the Gospel Church was in need of a pastor.

Chairman Chu was a highly respected leader who always took into consideration every aspect of the matter in question. He was particularly sensitive to this case, because a few months before he had been elected chairman of the National Church Union over Reverend Mah, who had served as chairman for more than two decades. The latter had ended up being the vice-chairman, and this made things more complicated.

Mah was also a very respected leader. He had been with the denomination from its beginnings. Although he sometimes tended to be more subjective than objective, he had proved himself a faithful servant of the church. He had led the churches in their early years, and brought them to their present state as a body of autonomous, self-supporting congregations.

The committee took Mah's opposition to the selection of Mr. Wang as pastor very seriously. It chose two representatives to conduct further investigations into Wang's background. They returned with positive reports, finding nothing that would disqualify him for joining the National Church Union. However, they heard from another source that Wang's wife once worked for Reverend Mah and, on an important occasion, had failed to fulfill her responsibilities, causing a serious problem for him. Ever since that incident, her former employer had labeled her as "unfit" for God's service. Although many years had passed, Mah had not forgotten the experience.

The missionaries, who had had no part in the decision-making processes, were impatient with the delay. They remarked at times that they had turned the responsibilities over to the national leaders prematurely. Privately they told Chu to ignore Mah and to install Wang on the basis of a majority vote. But the chairman knew that this would not work. In the Chinese culture, interpersonal relationships were very sensitive and most important. Although each member of a committee was given one vote, not every vote carried an equal weight. In this case Reverend Mah's vote was of great significance.

Chairman Chu knew that he could say to the committee, "Dear committee members, Reverend Mah has been chairman of this committee for the past twenty years. He knows what is best for our entire church organization. Let us support his decision and make our vote unanimous." Most of the members would go along with such a recommendation. After all, maintaining unity was one of the highest values in Chinese culture. Moreover, if the committee members were forced to choose between Reverend Mah and Mr. Wang, they would be obliged to side with Mah who was an older insider. But if Chairman Chu allowed such a showdown to occur in the committee, and the committee supported Mah out of respect, it would become Mah's committee! Moreover, such a decision would be fair to neither Mr. Wang nor the Gospel Church.

On the other hand, if Chu ignored Mah's opposition, he knew that there would no longer be unity and harmony within the executive committee. Moreover, since the church organization was small, Mr. Wang would soon feel the tension, and would not be able to work at peace within the church.

Looking around the table at the weary committee members, Chairman Chu said . . . .

46

Partnership or Separation?
Richard C. Pease

Are you really saying that if the mission sends the Parks to Japan, there may be no more official cooperation from the church?" the Reverend Robert Adams asked.

"Yes, we are sorry, but that is what we mean." replied Reverend Tanaka.

"Then we as missionaries must make a decision, and I must call the mission headquarters in California immediately and notify them." said Adams.

The four missionaries drove down the winding road to the village, past rice paddies where farmers were finishing the laborious task of planting rice seedlings by hand. In the town at the foot of the mountain, they stopped at a Japanese restaurant. The heat and humidity seemed even worse in the valley. As they ordered lunch, each was deeply disturbed by this turn of events. The Parks were due to arrive in Japan in six weeks. Should the missionaries order the home office to delay their coming?

Adams's mind raced over the events of the past six months since the Parks were officially appointed. He remembered the long hours of private conversation he had had with the church leaders and the two joint meetings of the church and mission. How could something that seemed to be the leading of the Lord bring the church and mission to this crisis? He thought back over the key factors in the case.

The Faith Union Mission had worked in Japan since the turn of the century. The thirty-five churches and thirteen preaching points that made up the Faith Union Church were the fruit of the missionaries' work. The mission had helped build a Bible College and a Christian camp, but the church was now autonomous and self-supporting.

In the early 1970s, the mission developed a policy for working in partnership with its overseas churches. In order to respect the equality and autonomous nature of the national church organizations, plans for cooperative evangelism were drawn up. These were called Joint Working Agreements. The committees that drew up these agreements were composed of the governing committee of the national church, the field governing committee of the missionaries, and representatives from the mission headquarters in America.

In 1979, the Second Five Year Working Agreement was signed between the Faith Union Churches of Japan and the Faith Union Mission. The church and mission agreed to cooperate in areas such as church planting, the Bible College, literature work, and the camp program. There would be two joint-committee meetings scheduled each year to discuss these areas of cooperation, as well as any other areas of mutual concern. All missionary assignments were discussed at the joint meetings. So far, these arrangements had worked out well.

The problem arose with the appointment of Reverend and Mrs. Park. Both were American citizens of Korean ancestry. Both had lived in Japan. In fact, Mrs. Park was born there. Both were fluent in Japanese as well as Korean. During his theological studies in America, God gave Reverend Park a deep burden for reaching Korean people living in Japan. The local Korean church affiliated with the Faith Union Mission was also concerned about the Koreans in Japan and pledged itself to support the Parks' ministry there. When the Parks applied to the Faith Union Mission, the board was impressed with their qualifications and high recommendations.

Shortly before receiving the Parks' application, the Faith Union Mission had made a major shift in its policy. It decided to begin evangelistic work among ethnic and social groups in which there was no significant Christian witness. The six hundred thousand Koreans living in Japan were just such a group, and the Parks seemed the ideal couple to head up this new venture of faith.

When the possibility of the mission's launching of a new ministry to reach Koreans in Japan was first presented to the Faith Union Church, Reverend Kashiwagi, its chairman, was not enthusiastic about the idea. Nevertheless, he promised missionary Adams that the church would discuss it. A month later, in a private conversation, Kashiwagi said that he thought the appointment of the Parks to Japan would cause problems within the church and consequently between the church and mission. Some of the church's main objections were that historically there were problems between Japan and Korea, and that the Koreans in Japan felt that the Japanese discriminated against them. The church felt it would be like mixing oil and water to have Koreans and Japanese in the same national church organization.

After hearing the church's objections, the mission came up with what it felt was a compromise solution. The Parks would work in Japan among Koreans, but their work would have no organizational link with the Japanese Faith Union Churches. When, however, Reverend Tanaka became chairman of the Faith Union Church of Japan, he opposed the new work more strongly.

Hearing of this opposition, the missionaries and home office reconsidered their plans. They were concerned about working harmoniously with the Japanese church, which was the philosophy behind the Joint Working Agreements. At the same time, the mission was deeply burdened about the Koreans in the country who had little Christian witness among them. While the mission had the right under the terms of the agreement to launch a new ministry, they hesitated to do so over the objections of the national church. The Japanese leaders said that they had no plans for a work among the Koreans in Japan, but that when such a work was begun, they wanted to initiate it and be involved in selecting the personnel. After all, they were Japanese, and this *was* Japan! Moreover, although they had given a special status to American missionaries—for it was through the missionaries that they had come to know the Lord—they could not give the same special status to someone of Korean ancestry.

The home office felt deeply that the mission should begin a new work among the Koreans and that God had called to Parks for that ministry. The Parks, too, believed that God was leading them to Japan. They had sold their home and furniture and were preparing to leave for Japan.

The missionaries were strongly supportive of the idea of launching a new ministry, but they were saddened to see a breach developing in their own working relationships with these Japanese brothers and sisters. What would it do their own ministries?

When the home office and missionary council agreed to launch the new ministry despite the objections of the church, the Japanese felt the mission was not treating them as equals. At the next joint committee, Robert Adams explained the decision of the mission. He pointed out that the mission felt a responsibility for the Koreans in Japan, but that it did not want to offend the Japanese church. Consequently, the Parks would be assigned to another area of Japan and would be completely separate from the Japanese church. Reverend Tanaka said that having the Parks work separately was "an American way of thinking." He added, "If the mission sends Reverend and Mrs. Park as new missionaries to Japan, it will be difficult for the church to continue working cooperatively with the mission." It was then that Adams had asked, "Are you really saying that if the mission sends the Parks to Japan, there may be no more official cooperation between us?"

"What shall we do?" Reverend Adams asked the other three missionaries seated around the restaurant table. "The Parks are due to arrive in Japan in six weeks. In this matter the home office will go along with our decision because we know the situation best. So what shall I say when I call headquarters tonight?"

47

Between a Rock
and a Hard Place
Jerry C. Wilson

The motor was silenced as the boat slid onto the bank of
the river. During the three-day return trip, Arnold Green had dreaded
this moment. Just as he feared, Esteban was standing on the shore,
waiting for the news. "How was it resolved?" Esteban asked as the
missionary disembarked. But all Arnold could hear was the report
being read by the council secretary: "Esteban cannot be a member of
the church. He cannot continue teaching the adult Sunday-school
class. Nor can he serve on the local church board, or hold any other
office in the church."

That had been the final decision, by vote, of the mission council.
What was he to do? How could he tell the tribe, and especially Esteban,
what the mission council had done, when he did not agree with the
decision? And what would all this do to the Aguaruna church?

Missionaries had worked among the Aguaruna Indians in South
America for over forty years but with very little success. There seemed
to be neither a sincere commitment to Christ nor a real change in the
lives of the people. Some would join the church for a short time and
then leave. There was no Indian pastor and only one small congregation pastored by the resident missionary. When the missionary
went to the coast for supplies and rest, the church would disappear or
fall into open sin. Some missionaries thought these Indians were inca-
pable of making lasting commitments of any kind.

As a last attempt to establish a church, the mission decided to start a
Bible Training Center in the jungle for the Indians. If only a few young

men could be trained as preachers, maybe a church could be planted. Arnold Green and his wife, Sarah, had volunteered to start the center. They decided that the school had to be as self-supporting and as adapted to the Indian culture as possible. They built a simple house and school, cleared land for raising crops, and began classes.

The missionaries felt they had to learn more about the beliefs of the tribe—about the spirit world, about good and evil, about God or gods—in order to better minister to the people. Their curiosity brought them in contact with Esteban, a bilingual Indian who had worked for a time with some Bible translators in a neighboring region. Because of this training, he was made director and teacher in the government school in Chippe, a few miles down the road.

Esteban had a deep interest in his people. He sat around the fire in the early mornings and listened to his grandfather and father tell the stories of their tribe and its history. Esteban knew more about the Aguaruna and their history and culture than any other young man in the area. His interest in the tribe and his friendliness had earned him the respect of the village elders. His introduction of several government projects for the betterment of the village won him the admiration of the young people.

Because of Esteban's knowledge, and the Greens' interest in knowing more about the culture of the Indians, they became good friends. As they shared together, Esteban began to show a marked interest in the things of God. They often spent long hours talking about God and comparing biblical truths to the beliefs and ways of the tribe. Esteban began to attend church services. When he came, so did nearly all the village. The Greens began to pray that Esteban would be truly converted. They felt that he could be the key to the conversion of the village, and the church could get a foothold in the tribe.

God answered their prayers. Esteban came forward and gave his heart to God. His life was so transformed that all, even his superiors, noticed the marked change in his life. He began to teach Bible classes in the high school and to help in the church services. Because of his growing Bible knowledge, the Greens offered him the adult Sunday-school class, which he took on with fervor. It seemed that God had finally made himself known to these people. At the annual church meeting, Esteban was elected chairman of the board, Sunday-school superintendent, and treasurer. He never showed any signs of wavering from his newfound faith in God.

The missionaries on the coast were elated with the news. It seemed to them that the Bible Training Center was bearing fruit. All went well until the mission director visited the Greens. He wanted to meet Esteban and his family. When the director arrived at Esteban's house, he was shocked. Esteban had two wives! How, he asked, could Esteban be living in sin and serving God at the same time? Arnold explained that Esteban had both wives before God saved him, and he would have to stay that way until one of them died.

A few weeks later, Arnold and Sarah were called to the coast before the mission council to answer for this breach of Christian morality. Arnold explained to them the beliefs of the Indians on marriage. Esteban could not get rid of one of his wives. He had paid a good sum for them, and the father-in-law would not return the bride price. More important, if he were to put away one of the wives, she would have to commit suicide, for she would be considered a failure and a disgrace to her family, especially her father. Because her husband did not want her, it would be interpreted that she was not a good wife. Why else would her husband put her out? If she did not commit suicide, her father would most likely kill her, or she would be left to starve to death.

Arnold argued that in time God would reveal to these Indians the need for monogamy, but, for now, this was not a problem for them. They did not yet have guidance from the Holy Spirit on the matter of polygamy. He explained that the Indians were very responsive to the leading of God, who was revealing himself in many ways to them. They were growing spiritually. Could not the renunciation of polygamy be considered a part of spiritual growth rather than of conversion?

Arnold's pleading fell on seemingly deaf ears. One member said, "If the Indians are attuned to the Word of God, show them how wrong polygamy is."

"But how, then, shall I explain to them the admonitions against divorce?" the young missionary asked.

"Divorce has nothing to do with this case," said another council member. "Esteban is only straightening up his life—a kind of restitution."

"What if one of the wives commits suicide? Are we not guilty of murder?" Green asked.

"You are overreacting. Esteban told you this to get what he wants. He's just playing on your sympathy," another commented.

Arnold's final plea was, "After all, has not God saved Esteban with two wives, and could not God sustain him with two wives? Moreover, what will happen to our new church, which is just beginning to take root among the Aguaruna?" But when the vote was in, Arnold was ordered to put Esteban out of the church until he had gotten rid of one wife.

On the long journey back upriver by canoe, Arnold and Sarah had struggled with the question of loyalties. What were their responsibilities to the mission agency that sent and supported them in their work? If they broke with the mission, how could they continue the work? And what were their responsibilities to the new Christians among the Aguaruna? They knew that the answer they gave Esteban would depend on how they resolved this dilemma. Now the boat had come ashore, and Esteban and the elders of the church wanted to know the answer they had brought.

48

The Authority Dilemma
Mark Danielson

Eileen Thompson, a North American missionary in the San Isabel Valley of Mexico, was committed to working within the structures of local church authority. It was important to her that the church be an indigenous expression of God's kingdom, so she was glad to submit to national leadership. The problem was that there were competing indigenous authorities who laid claim to her ministry. Eileen had just completed her furlough and was getting ready to return to Mexico. First, however, she and her mission board would have to decide where she would next be assigned to work.

Several different local groups had great plans for Eileen's life. She could not choose any of the options without offending people who wanted her to serve elsewhere, and her decision carried the potential for long-term consequences. Eileen had been put in the position of either defying the authority of the local Mexican church, to the possible detriment of its future growth, or dropping a fruitful ministry among some 15,000 migrant farm workers. To complicate things further, the hospital where she had worked during her first term as nurse-anesthetist and evangelist also had designs on Eileen. According to the doctor in charge, the zeal for evangelistic outreach at the hospital had diminished considerably while she was away on furlough.

During her first years of ministry, Eileen had been assigned to the hospital, but she also began to evangelize the valley's migrant farm workers, whose ethnic identity was Indian rather than Mexican. Just before her furlough, after ten years of work among the Indians, she had begun to reap the fruit of her ministry. Several small congregations sprang up in a number of the Indian villages.

Eileen had carried out this ministry to the farm workers under the authority of the local national Baptist church. At the time she left, the infant Indian congregations still depended entirely on the Mexican church for leadership, support and nurture. Eileen trusted that the relationship would continue in the same way without her.

Soon after Eileen went on furlough, something else happened that seriously affected the Indian work. The pastor of the Baptist church left, and his successor gave very low priority to the Indian work. Pastor Gonzalez believed that attention should be focused instead on the Mexicans.

A group of national nurses from the mission hospital had tried to preserve the ministry to the Indians by teaching classes at the various camps throughout the week and arranging transportation to the Mexican church on Sundays. Because of the hospital's isolated location, however, it was difficult to keep their staff. So, within four months of Eileen's departure, two of the three nurses working with the Indians left the valley. The third nurse complained that her zeal for the Indian ministry had waned considerably for lack of support. She had tried to get incoming hospital staff interested in helping her, but it became harder and harder. The ministry to the Indians gradually slipped downhill.

When the Indian ministry went into decline, the leaders of the Indian villages took unprecedented action. They met together and drafted a letter to the mission board that sponsored Eileen, asking them to send her back to the valley to renew the ministry she had begun among them. Eileen was certainly willing to do that, because she had come to love the migrant Indian workers. Her mission board was also sympathetic to their appeal.

The problem was with the pastor of the local Baptist church. Pastor Gonzalez insisted that if a woman missionary were to be in the area, she would have to be under his authority. He would assign Eileen to playing the piano for church services and teaching a women's Sunday-school class in the Mexican church. He gave two reasons for not allowing her to work with the migrant Indians. First, he believed it was wrong for a woman to teach men; and second, he emphasized the fact that his own ministry was to the Mexicans and not to the Indians of the valley.

Members of the Mexican church expressed a desire for a missionary to come and work with them because they felt the church was dying and in need of rejuvenation. The pastor, on the other hand, was cold to the idea of *any* missionary coming to work with the church, citing some bad experiences with North American missionaries in the border town from where he had come. He complained that the missionaries "always came in and did things their way" without heeding his authority.

Some church members who were close to the pastor expressed the fear that if Eileen came to the valley and carried on her own ministry outside the authority of the pastor, it would reinforce his negative feelings about missionaries in general. This would further diminish their chances of ever getting a missionary to work with their church again.

Eileen now faced one final meeting with her mission board, during which they would have to make a decision regarding her assignment. She still could not see a way to resolve the conflict of other people's agendas for her ministry. It was still her deep desire to work within the national church structure. But now the Indian work also represented the "national church." Which national church had priority—Mexican or Indian? She hoped and prayed that her mission board would be able to help her make the right decision.

49

West African Church
Dean S. Gilliland

The general council of the Benue Valley Church of Northern Nigeria was in a special session. It was a meeting called by the field secretary of the mission, John Greenwood. The African chairman of the church, Pastor Yusufu Bawo, said before the meeting began, "If the white people call a meeting, it will be *their* meeting, not ours."

For weeks the missionaries had been saying that if relations between the mission and the church did not improve, they would seriously consider returning to their homes in South Africa. Finally, Yusufu Bawo looked directly at the five missionaries present, shrugged his shoulders, and said, "We believe Peter Ewing was right. He said we have been controlled and impoverished by the mission. And we believe, further, that you, Reverend Greenwood, were influenced by your mission board in South Africa to terminate him because he spoke the truth. Now whether you go or whether you stay makes no difference to us. Do as you please."

The Benue Valley Church. The Benue Valley Church was known as the South African Mission until the missionaries renamed it in 1962. The first missionaries came in 1926 from several denominations, including Baptist, Methodist, and Anglican. Little had been done in medical and educational work due to the high cost factor. As the spirit of nationalism grew in the 1950s and political independence came in the early 1960s, such missions generally began to transfer administration of the churches to African leaders.

The Benue Valley Church felt it lagged behind other denominations in being granted positions of leadership in their church. After forty years of missionary control, in 1966 Pastor Yusufu became the first

African to hold the office of chairman. His two years, thus far, had been turbulent ones for mission-church relationships. At every meeting where missionaries were present, the same questions were being asked:

"Why are there no funds, even for church buildings?"

"Have you purposely not built us a high school in order to control us?"

"Do you want us to feel shame when we compare ourselves to the other churches around us?"

"Is it not true that even in South Africa, the black man is a mission field for the whites?"

Attitudes toward South African influence. Benue Valley Church was a poor church, even by Nigerian standards. Unlike neighboring churches, Benue Valley had received no subsidies or grants from its home mission board located in South Africa. The missionaries of Benue Valley had taught a strict rule of self-financing for the church from the beginning of its existence. However, while the Methodist and Lutheran missionaries had a comfortable life financially, the white staff at Benue Valley lived almost at poverty level. They and their sponsoring board had nothing to give, except what John Greenwood called "gifts of love and service."

Pastor Yusufu had been calling for a change in mission policies both in administration and finance. He also demanded African autonomy at every level and pressed the missionaries to build a high school and enlarge the medical work. In this he reflected the changing attitude of the Nigerian government, which had recently taken a hard line against all white South Africans. One example was that the prestigious Dutch Reformed Church Mission of South Africa had been evicted from the country six years before because their mission was regarded as an extension of the apartheid state church. Further, a nationwide daily paper described the D.R.C.M. in headlines as "the mission we do not want."

The arrival of Peter Ewing. The long-standing problems of slow growth in membership, poverty, and mission domination sparked a new crisis when Peter Ewing arrived from Johannesburg. He had been assigned to train the laity for evangelism and to do continuing education for pastors. Though he used as his base the leadership-training school in which he taught during the rainy season, Ewing moved about frequently. He was an impressive person, tall, with a strong physical build. His commanding presence was further strengthened by a gift for the Nigerian language.

Within a month after his arrival, he warned John Greenwood while visiting him in his home that unless a change of attitude and corresponding new programs came from the mission, there was little hope the mission would survive.

John admonished Peter that "to raise false hopes is immoral. We have a long history, which has been built on trust and service. Our board has no funds and we have no funds, and to act as though we do is courting disaster. Moreover, we have always encouraged self-support."

To this Peter replied, "How can you say this to any African, when he has been told over and over again by his own government that white South Africa is the richest nation in the world?"

John answered with obvious impatience. "Be reasonable, Peter. Look who we are. You are a part of us and belong to our history. The leaders of the church, especially Pastor Yusufu, must not be misled by promises that we know we cannot keep."

The termination of Ewing. After two years of service, Peter Ewing returned to Johannesburg for furlough. Almost immediately, the Benue Valley Church was informed by the South African headquarters of the mission that his services had been terminated. Embittered and angry, Peter Ewing's African following believed and circulated the word that John Greenwood and the other missionaries had requested the board to terminate Peter's service in Nigeria. Greenwood denied the charge.

In desperation the missionaries felt their presence may have now become a hindrance to the church. They decided to call together the general council of the church to seek a solution.

"Greenwood's meeting." As the special council opened, Pastor Yusufu stepped out from behind the chairman's table and stated that this was "Greenwood's meeting." Following several hours of charges and sharp exchanges, John Greenwood stood to ask his final question: "In the light of all you believe we have said and done, and because our only reason for being here is for the good of the Benue Valley Church, shall we missionaries remain with you or should we leave the country?"

Pastor Yusufu replied that whether the missionaries chose to stay or to return to South Africa was of little interest to him or the church members.

John Greenwood was still standing when Yusufu, motioning with both hands in the direction of his African colleagues, said flatly, "We are waiting now for your decision. Do you go or stay?"

50

When a Woman Should Be a Man
Frances F. Hiebert

Karen White stared out the window of the bedroom-cum-office in her home. Snow had fallen softly during the night and settled on the pine branches that framed the window. Now the sun was shining brightly, and the day glistened with all the promise of a winter reprieve. But Karen was only half aware of the winter wonderland outside. She was, in fact, quite deeply troubled about the future of her mission organization.

It was *her* organization. She had begun it and for several years had been its director. The purpose of the organization was to provide interim medical personnel for mission hospitals and clinics. Doctors and nurses from the United States took their vacation time, sometimes extended, to serve in place of missionaries who had gone on furlough. Karen's organization recruited the temporary workers and put them in touch with missions that needed them.

Karen worked with a volunteer committee of Christian doctors in the Boston area. At their last meeting, one of them, Dr. Brown, threw a bombshell into the discussion—at least from Karen's perspective. He raised the issue of having men under the authority of women, citing a radio preacher he had heard that day. He asked whether, now that the mission was well established, they should not consider recruiting a man to be in charge. Karen, he said, could certainly remain as assistant director and would be invaluable in training the new male director. But, with a man in charge, the mission would be in line with their evangelical constituency and with Scripture.

The rationale given for this proposed change of administration had caused turmoil in Karen's mind all week. Her background, training, and present commitment were to the full authority of the Bible. It had never occurred to her that she was doing anything "wrong" when she answered God's call to missions and administered the agency that she was sure God had called into being. The discussion in the meeting had left her thoroughly confused. She was a single woman. Did the instructions to wives in the New Testament mean that all women were subject to all men? Were they universal, for all time and every place? Or were the injunctions about women addressed to a particular situation for a particular reason?

Dr. Fleming, another member of the committee, at the same meeting had voiced concern about changing to a male administrator. With things going so well, he asked, why should they risk the slippage that is an inevitable part of change? He admitted that he didn't know quite what to think about the biblical issues and the church intepretations, but he did know about a real situation that was very much like this one.

A number of years ago, Dr. Fleming told the committee, a young woman named Julie Smith, who had been his wife's close friend while he was in medical school in Canada, had worked on various university campuses for a well-known campus-ministry organization. She was also very interested in foreign missions and did her best to interest the students with whom she worked. She participated with great enthusiasm in the Urbana Missions Conferences.

During the time she worked for the campus ministry, the Lord gave Julie a vision for a need that she felt was not being met. Many young people committed themselves to missions but had little guidance as to how they should go about getting involved. Julie felt called to set up an organization that would help match the gifts and abilities of young people with mission organizations and agencies overseas that could use them.

Then one of the board members whose opinions she respected told Julie that it was time to turn leadership of the organization over to a man. He recommended a certain man for the job. Julie was reluctant about choosing that particular man only because he had no overseas experience. She was no "feminist." If a man would be more acceptable to the evangelical public, she was ready to go along with the change. Besides, it would free her to concentrate on improving the service.

It was not long after this man took charge, however, before the organization was in deep trouble. Julie had built up a large file of well-prepared applicants, and many others had already been placed in ministry positions overseas. But, soon after she turned over the leadership, the placement counseling was eliminated and the service dwindled to almost nothing. Financially, the organization was now always broke, although Julie was still out doing the fund raising.

Friction arose because Julie was still the *de facto* head as far as the evangelical community that supported them was concerned. Because of her long overseas experience, invitations to speak in churches about their mission came to her rather than to the man in charge. He had no missions expertise.

The small board was too far away and too busy to know what was really going on. Tired of the financial problems, the board finally decided to dissolve the organization.

Julie—on the recommendation of local mission leaders and her pastor and feeling a strong sense of call from the Lord—in the same week that the old organization was dissolved, incorporated a new one with the same goals. This time the board was composed of local people with whom she could stay in close contact. They rejoiced with her over how promptly God provided all their needs and how quickly the new organization became even more fruitful than the earlier one.

"This difficult experience has made Julie more sympathetic to women in leadership," said Dr. Fleming to Karen and the other commitee members. "And I think there are some valuable lessons for us in her story. We should be careful not to repeat past mistakes."

The mention of women in leadership had made Dr. Brown bristle, and Karen herself flinched, because she always tried to avoid that discussion. She wanted to get on with the work of evangelism and avoid being embroiled in hassles over who should be in charge.

"And yet," Karen thought, as she reached for her coat and scarf, "I *am* in the middle of it just because I am a woman—whether I like it or not." When she opened the door, a fluff of snow landed on her head. She thought of 1 Corinthians 11:10 and smiled in spite of herself. Was the snow a sign that her authority was on her own head? No, she would need more concrete guidance than that.

Her heart lifted as she took in the grandeur of the day. But the weight of the decision she must make was still on her. Should she resign and be submissive in the way that she, like many other evangelical women, had been conditioned? Or should she follow the new urging that she had been convinced was a call from God, and continue the work that God had begun in her?

As she walked away from the house, leaving a trail of footsteps in the soft snow, Karen realized that her decision, like Julie's in the story told by Dr. Fleming, would be a precedent for many other women who were struggling to live out their calls to mission and ministry, in spite of misunderstandings and traditions in some sectors of the contemporary evangelical church. As she looked at the brilliant sky and the snow-crowned earth around her, Karen suddenly remembered the words of the psalmist: "I will trust and not be afraid."

PART 9

Loyalty to Church and State

Christians belong to the kingdom of God. They also live in human kingdoms, whether these be tribes, feudal states, or nations. The result is a conflict of loyalties. Earthly kingdoms demand our unswerving allegiances. They demand that we be proud of our country or clan and hostile to those who oppose it. They expect us to kill and die for their defense, even when we disagree with their policies. They denounce us if we have higher loyalties, although these be to God.

What loyalties should missionaries have to their home countries when they are abroad? Should they publicly defend their nation when others condemn it for doing wrong? Should they leave the mission field when internal fighting occurs? Should they look to their own country to rescue them in times of war?

Missions have been badly hurt by the strong nationalism shown by many missionaries. This is particularly true of those who come from the United States and share the widespread belief that their homeland has a "manifest destiny" and is uniquely led and blessed by God. At its best, such nationalism erects a high wall between the missionaries and the local people who love their own country. At its worst, as we saw in Vietnam, it equates Christianity with foreign policy of the United States.

Christians, missionaries in particular, are called to be international people—citizens of the world. Their highest loyalties are not to their nations, however good they may think these are, but to God and to the people of the world for whom Christ died. Only then can they overcome the curse of nationalism that now divides the world into warring camps.

A second set of problems related to nationalism has to do with the relationship of missionaries to their host countries. Missionaries today are guests in the countries in which they serve. Is it right, then, for them to speak out against the human injustices that they see? On the other hand, as Christians, how can they keep quiet? Should missionaries in South Africa speak out against apartheid, knowing that they will probably be expelled if they do? In other countries should they speak out against the blatant corruption in government, the misappropriation of relief supplies and development aid, the male and female prostitution that attracts the tourists and their dollars, the oppression of minorities, and/or the slaughter of tribals to clear the forests? All of these violations are now found in various countries around the world.

Nationalism raises still another set of problems for missionaries who live in occupied countries. Should they side with the ruling nation or with the people who are seeking their independence? For example, prior to 1947, missionaries in India had to side with either Britain or the nationalist movement that represented the people. Unfortunately, most chose the former and justified it by saying that British rule maintained order, thus keeping the doors open for missionary service. In fact, their actions only confirmed in the minds of most Indians that Christianity is part of Western colonialism and missions are a means to keep native peoples submissive.

Similar questions face missionaries from the United States now serving in Central America, South Africa, and Korea. Among certain groups in those countries there is strong resentment against the United States. How should these missionaries respond to the desires of a people for freedom and justice?

In all of these cases, we must consider what we are saying to the people about the nature of the gospel if we keep quiet, if we speak out, if we take strong actions, or if we join revolutions. In a world of growing nationalism and its wars, how does the missionary proclaim the good news of the gospel of salvation, justice, and peace for all people?

Bibliography

Adney, Miriam. 1984. *God's foreign policy: Practical ways to help the world's poor.* Grand Rapids: Eerdmans.

Anderson, G. H., and Stransky, T. F., eds. 1979. *Liberation theologies in North America and Europe.* Mission Trends No. 4. Grand Rapids: Eerdmans.

Bosch, David. 1980. Witness to the World. Atlanta: John Knox Press.

Corson-Finnerty, Adam D. 1982. *World citizen: Acting for global justice.* Maryknoll: Orbis Books.

Costas, Orlando. 1982. *Christ outside the gate.* Maryknoll: Orbis Books.

Escobar, Samuel, and Driver, John, eds. 1978. *Christian mission and social justice.* Scottdale: Herald Press.

Habegger, Howard. 1980. Toward doing justice in Christian missions. *Mission Focus* 8:1–9 (March).

Ramseyer, Robert L., ed. 1979. *Mission and the peace witness.* Scottdale: Herald Press.

Sider, Ronald J. 1977. *Evangelism, salvation and social justice.* Bramcote, England: Grove Books.

West, Charles C. 1981. Christian witness to political power and authority. *Missiology* 9:423–448.

51

Christian Witness in Vietnam*
Paul G. Hiebert

Harry Miller looked beyond the rice paddies bordered*by the tropical jungle to the distant columns of smoke rising from the villages controlled by the Viet Cong as he listened to the deep rumble of the bombs dropped by giant B-52s invisible in the cloudy sky. The destruction only heightened the unease that had come over him as he prepared his message for tomorrow's meeting of the Joint Council of the South Vietnam Mission and the South Vietnam Evangelical Church. His earlier confidence that the mission had chosen the best of strategies had been shaken. Had they indeed presented the whole of the gospel and presented it in the right ways? What would he recommend to the missionaries and national leaders now, when it seemed likely that the North Vietnamese might win the war? And how would he have done it differently if he could do his missionary service over again?

Harry had come to Vietnam twenty years earlier, confident that God was using America to establish the Pax Americana and had set before her an open door to evangelize the world. Even after the war arrived, he had seen the church grow and was certain that American armed forces were necessary to keep the doors open for evangelism and protect the young Vietnamese church from prosecution.

However, as hostilities continued, he became increasingly troubled. Harry's relationships and those of his fellow missionaries with other expatriates in Vietnam, including the U.S. military officers who occa-

*Based on materials found in Wilbert R. Shenk, ed., *Mission Focus: Current Issues* (Scottdale, Pennsylvania: Herald, 1980).

212

sionally helped in the mission's programs, helped determine their identity within the country. The common people in Vietnam identified Catholic Christianity with France and evangelical Protestant Christianity with the United States. As the war progressed, evangelicals became increasingly identified with violence and militarism.

Moreover, the close alliance between the United States and the Thieu regime identified evangelical missions with the Saigon government. Although Harry knew that preaching the gospel sometimes meant potential conflict with the political ideology of a country, he decided to boldly declare his Christian convictions despite opposition. In the early years the missionaries took strong stands in challenging their converts to obey their Christian convictions. But, as Vietnam became more politicized and the government's propaganda barrage increased along with the war, the missionaries became less aggressive. They justified their "neutral" stance by pointing out that they would be expelled from the country if they took too bold a position and that it was more important for the church that they stay.

When American policies concentrated on the pacification of the people through the WHAM program ("Win the Hearts and Minds"), the missionaries did not want the gospel to be confused with American propaganda. Their policy was to help all Vietnamese alike on the basis of need. But, because security and logistics made it impossible to help both sides equally, the benefits were reaped largely by the Saigon government. Some critics even charged them with prolonging the war and increasing the pain. By supplying the people's necessities, the missionaries freed the government to use more of its funds for destruction. The tension in Harry became particularly sharp when he realized that while the missionaries saw themselves as giving bread in the name of Christ, the Vietnamese saw them as Americans with Saigon government permits, handing out U.S. surplus goods for the interests of both those governments. All of their work as missionaries had political import. Even evangelism was seen by many as supporting the cause of South Vietnam.

For a moment Harry's thoughts turned to the young South Vietnam Evangelical Church. What would happen to the Christians if the war was lost and the American presence removed? Had the missionaries done all they could to help prepare the Vietnamese church to live under a radically different political system? The Catholic Church had experienced alternating periods of persecution and toleration from the state. The Protestant churches had generally seen themselves existing alongside the state, showing little interest in the government and giving it no official support. Individual Christians could involve themselves in the affairs of state, and members were encouraged to fulfill the "duties of a citizen," but these were usually defined by the state. Nevertheless, there was an implicit assumption, brought largely by the missionaries, that the church could thrive only in the context of political freedom and governmental goodwill.

But now the Thieu government had cancelled military deferments for religious studies. The Catholics and Buddhists protested in public, but the president of a leading Protestant denomination urged the students at the Bible institutes to follow government orders and join the army.

Harry wondered what he should say to the Joint Council. What was the most effective missionary witness in such a context? Was it to adjust to political realities or was it to take a bold stance in opposition to the governments and their questionable practices? How could missionaries avoid being identified with the war, and what would be best for the Vietnamese church? He thought long and hard, and then he began to write his message for the council . . . .

52

Protest or Inaction?*
Stuart Willcuts and
Helena Eversole

Ian Cox and David Sellers looked at each other in silence as their hotel room door closed and all became still. Finally Ian spoke, "How can I make such a decision by tomorrow noon?"

As they sat in silence, Ian reviewed in his mind the past four days that they had spent in Honduras, which now seemed like a lifetime. They had both come from the Latin American headquarters of Development Aid to assist the local staff in assessing the needs of Salvadoran refugees who were crossing into Honduras, and to decide whether or not a relief project should be initiated. Ian headed the survey team and David provided the logistical support.

They were joined in Honduras by Mario Perez, Development Aid's staff person responsible for the local office and the projects in that province. It was the province receiving most of the refugees. Mario reported that several hundred refugees had been discovered along the 125-mile section of the Salvador-Honduras border. Due to the unusual and emergency nature of this situation, the director of Development Aid in Honduras asked Ian to design the response strategy. Mario was assigned to work for Ian on this survey.

When Ian and David first flew into La Esperanza (the capital of the isolated province and the only town there with a landing strip) they made contact with local military officials who were governing the province, to obtain information about the refugees' situation and to

---

*From *Together: A Journal of World Vision International* 2 (1984):13–15 and used by permission.

secure permission to survey the area. From the information provided, they learned that the refugees' condition was fair: they received basic foods and shelter from Honduran families living near the border; their clothing was adequate; and their health was "normal"—i.e., fair to poor.

"There is no official position from my government regarding these refugees," the local military representative warned Ian. "However, we consider them to be illegal aliens. Any aid given them will only encourage their continued immigration to Honduras. You realize, don't you, that they are the major cause of the problems in El Salvador, and we do not want them here?"

Most of the border between Honduras and El Salvador is made up of rivers. They range from 50 yards wide in the dry season to 150 yards during the winter rains. This was winter, and still the refugees—mainly old men, women, and children—were trying to enter Honduras to escape the bloody war and the political intolerance in their homeland.

Ian, who was born and raised in Bolivia and had worked in Central America for four years, was well aware of the historical sensitivity of the border. A war had been fought between El Salvador and Honduras twelve years ago and no official peace had been signed. After exhausting their resources, the two countries agreed on a cease-fire, but without resolving the conflict over territory. They simply accepted the good services of the Organization of American States. This international body established and monitored a "free zone" which was a strip of land between Honduras and El Salvador that could not be controlled or entered by the military of either country.

Mario reminded Ian and David that "Since the monitoring has been more symbolic than enforced, the free zone has been an ideal place for Salvadoran freedom fighters to train their fighters and to harbor their families. The near proximity of the freedom fighters and the constant threats of Salvadoran military retaliation in the free zone has kept the Honduran government in a state of nervous tension."

Development Aid began community development projects in El Salvador and Honduras five years prior to Ian's visit. The development work was not conducted through or directly with these governments, but relationships with both of them were cordial. The governments' recognition of Development Aid was mandatory for their work with the poor to continue.

Shortly after their arrival, Fr. Waters came to visit Ian, David, and Mario. He had lived and worked in La Esperanza for many years. After hearing who they were and what their interest in La Esperanza was, he said, "Would it be possible for us to cooperate in this work, as we share the same concerns for these needy people?"

Father Waters took them to his church compound and showed them some empty classrooms and a warehouse. He offered Ian the use of these rooms for storing relief supplies, food, or anything else he might have for these poor refugee people. He then added, "If you need to live in these rooms, you are welcome to them. And if transit refugees need a home, we can take them too, temporarily."

Four days later—the day before Ian and David were to return to headquarters—Father Waters visited them in their hotel room. He held a letter in his hand. After Ian, David, and Mario shared the information from their survey of the refugees, Father Waters asked,

> Are you aware that a massacre occurred ten days ago when 614 Salvadoran refugees trying to cross in Honduras were shot to death in the river? We have proof that the governments of Honduras, El Salvador, and Guatemala conspired to stop these people. This massacre occurred shortly after a conference between the presidents of all three countries. Initially 800–1000 old men, women, and children set out to cross the river, but the armies of the three countries stood on the banks and shot them until the survivors turned back to El Salvador.
>
> The first evidence of this atrocity was discovery, by a fisherman, of the body of a five-year-old child in his net. The child had been shot to death. Other bodies began to wash up on the river banks and were found by members of our diocese. Then we began interviewing local residents, survivors and refugees who had returned to El Salvador but crossed the border a few days later. Their stories all concurred. We documented the measure by photographing the bodies.

Father Waters produced a small group of papers from the envelope he carried.

> A group of us Christians," he said, "clergy and lay people, who cannot let this incident go unnoticed, have written this document. It describes the massacre, documents its occurrence, gives the number of people that have died, and gives eyewitness verifications that all three armies were involved.
>
> In this document," he went on, "we are exposing this massacre to the world and condemning it. Christians throughout the world should join us in making these governments accountable for this atrocity. We are asking church leaders, business people, and other governments to support us in this denunciation that will be published worldwide.

The priest stopped. He put his head in his hands and sat silently for a few minutes. Then, raising his head he said, "Do you realize that many

of the dead were the brothers, sisters, cousins, or parents of the people
with whom I have lived for fifteen years?"

He then turned to Mario. "As a Honduran friend, a brother in Christ,
and a representative of Development Aid in this area, would you please
add your signature to ours?"

Then to Ian and David he said, "As Christians and as representatives
of a powerful international Christian humanitarian agency, would you
also give your support by signing this document?"

For two hours the four men talked and prayed together about their
many fears and concerns. Finally Father Waters rose, saying, "Good-
night, my brothers. I will return tomorrow before you leave to receive
your answer."

After he left, Mario was the first to speak. "Ian, should I sign? How
can we do anything else but show the world that we know what has
happened and, as Christians, speak out against it? In Jeremiah 9:3,
God condemns the Israelites for not speaking the truth: 'They bent
their tongue like a bow; falsehood and not truth has grown strong in
the land; for they proceed from evil to evil, and they do not know me,
says the Lord' (Jeremiah 9:3).

"But we *do* know the Lord, so we must speak out in his name."
David quickly responded,

There is no way we can sign that. As representatives of Development
Aid in Latin America, we do not have the authority to speak for Development Aid internationally. Our African and Asian colleagues could interpret our signing such a document as radical, pro-leftist behavior which
would not be a true reflection of Development Aid's stand. Besides, in my
five years with Development Aid, much of our success in working under
all different types of governments has been due to the fact that we have
not become involved in local politics.

Furthermore, signing it would threaten the very existence of our
work, and possibly the lives of our national staff in Honduras and perhaps in the other two countries. We believe we have been called by God to
a ministry with the poor here. If we sign this, knowing the high risk of our
being expelled from these three countries, would that be following our
call to ministry?"

Mario shook his head,

Jesus took risks for the poor, those Catholic priests are taking risks,
how can we do any less? We Hondurans are well aware that people have
"disappeared" for speaking out against the government, but I live here,
my brothers, and I am willing to take that risk. Jesus commands us not to
be concerned with saving our lives but to seek first the kingdom of God.

He then departed, saying, "I will follow your lead tomorrow, Ian."

"How can I lead?" thought Ian as he sat in the utter stillness. He broke the quiet by saying, "David, I believe this massacre occurred. Father Waters' evidence confirms the statements we received from the refugees we interviewed and agrees with the facts we have gathered in our survey. Personally, I want to sign the document because I believe Jesus would. As a Quaker and as a U.S. citizen I want to uphold Mario, these poor Salvadorans and Father Waters by speaking out against this violence. But what would the results be to our ministry around the world?"

Once again the room fell into silence.

53

The Buddha Pedestals
Lee-Lim Guek Eng

I don't know what to make of them," Stephen said to himself as he thought about the statues of Buddha he had seen in the homes of the church elders. "Are they idols, or are they symbols of national loyalty? In either case, do they not undermine the local Christians' allegiance to Christ? And what should I do? Should I raise the issue in the annual meeting of the churches next week, or should I leave it up to the elders to decide on the matter? But do they as new believers really understand what is at stake here?"

Stephen Ling, an American-born Chinese, had come as a missionary to Nong Pai in northeastern Thailand to minister to the new Thai Christian community there. With a theological degree and training in evangelism and discipleship by a Christian organization in his background, he was excited about his new assignment. He had worked hard on learning the local language and culture and now felt at home in the administrative center where he lived.

The work had been started five years earlier by Jerry and Sue Lannin, American missionaries. It had grown to 550 believers in 49 congregations that met in local homes. Each church was composed of from two to twelve families and led by an "elder." Staff at the administrative center, located in Udon Thani, the capital city, coordinated the work of the existing churches and planned new evangelistic outreach. When the Lannins retired, they invited Stephen to take charge of their work. One of his chief tasks was to train the elders. Each week he visited a number of them in their village homes and helped them prepare for the services they would conduct in their homes the following Sunday.

Stephen's first visit was to the home of Seum, the young elder of Nong Pai, to help him study the apostle Paul's doctrine of grace. Seum ran a general store and lived in the quarters attached to the rear of the store. Worship services were held in his large living room. In the entry Seum had hung two rows of pictures. In the top row were photographs of the military graduation class of one of his family members; the queen of Thailand, the king, and the crown prince; a collective picture of the head monks of the Thai monastic order and Thai military officers; and a military recruiting poster. Under them hung magazine and calendar pinups of pretty Thai girls in bathing suits. On the far right of these was a statue of the Buddha. In later visits Stephen found that this was typical of most village homes, including those of Christians, for in the minds of the people in that part of Thailand there was a close tie between Thai nationalism, the royal family, the military, and Buddhism.

At first Stephen had hoped that the weekly Bible teaching would persuade the Christians to get rid of their Buddha pedestals. But most of them, including the elders, kept the pedestals as an act of patriotism and an expression of political loyalty to the king. Stephen realized that local history played an important part in their decisions. The northeastern part of Thailand had a long record of invasions and political and military instability, and the people wanted to affirm their allegiance to the government that had brought them peace and stability.

Now, four months later, Stephen was making his regular visit to Nong Pai to meet with Seum and several other elders. When Stephen asked them why they kept their Buddha pedestals, Seum pointed out that neither he nor his family performed rituals at the Buddha shrine in order to gain merit. Though he affirmed the biblical teaching that Jesus Christ eliminated the need for merit—making, he said, "I am a Thai and a loyal subject of our king. So I keep the Buddha pedestal to show my solidarity with my neighbors, my town, and my country." Wassana, a senior elder, defended Seum's position by appealing to Paul's doctrine of Christian liberty found in Galatians and his discussion of eating meat offered to idols in his letter to the Corinthians.

Back at the center, Stephen questioned the decision of the elders, and wondered whether such a decision should be left in their hands. They looked to him for biblical instruction, yet in this matter they seemed sure of themselves. The annual meeting of the churches would be held in a week. Could he as the missionary let the matter lie? If not, what should he do? He did not want the Christians to be accused of disloyalty to their country, but he knew that non-Christians would

222 Loyalty to Church and State

consider them Buddhists if they kept their Buddha pedestals. Moreover, in the long run it would open the door to syncretism. Finally, after considerable prayer and study of the Scripture, Stephen decided to . . . .

54

Summons by the Police
A. A. S.

Malika walked alone down the narrow, crowded streets of Cairo. The chatter of women and arguments of men, the shouts of little children, and the sounds of cars and radios filled the air, but she heard nothing except the voices arguing within her. Though the morning was unbearably hot, she was trembling in cold fear, trying to convince herself that what had happened the night before was but a dream. The feel of the summons from the Minister of Interior in her hand assured her that it was not. It stated that she would have to appear at the chief investigator's office before Lieutenant Mohammed Hassan at ten o'clock. Her Christian faith would be tested by fire, and in the process she could easily jeopardize the safety of other believers.

Malika, a baptized Christian, converted from Islam, was often invited to give her testimony in churches and home meetings. The night before, she was speaking to a large crowd gathered in a house when someone whispered in her ear, "There are three secret policemen waiting for you in the front room. I begged them not to interrupt the meeting." Malika continued her testimony of how she had been converted from Islam to Christianity, but word of the presence of the policemen spread among the people, creating confusion and anxiety. Some people wanted to form a barrier to keep the policemen away from her. After Malika calmed the people down, she found her way through the crowd and greeted the policemen warmly. They were surprised by her friendly behavior and, fearing a riot among the angry audience, merely handed her the summons and left.

The meeting continued for another hour in turmoil, as the people argued about what to do. When they had gone, Malika was left to make her decision alone. Lieutenant Hassan was known to be a zealous Muslim who cruelly persecuted Muslim converts and those who ministered to Muslims. Malika knew that as a Christian follower of the Way of Truth, she would have to answer his interrogation honestly regarding her Christian associates. But what would this do to those who had been involved in her conversion? There was the Anglican hospital, where the English missionaries had ministered to her during her illness, and where she had come to experience the love and healing power of Jesus in her life. It already had a reputation for converting Muslims and had come under severe attack from orthodox Muslim leaders and government officials alike. And there was Nadia, the Christian teacher who had befriended her and later taken her to an evangelistic meeting, where Malika opened her heart to Christ as her personal Redeemer and had become his disciple. It was Nadia who had given Malika her first Bible and taught her how to read it. And there was the evangelical church and the elderly Pastor Morkous, who risked his life and that of the church when he baptized Malika and several other converts. He had been questioned and his church closed down before. What would happen to all of them if she were forced by the officials to tell about her conversion?

For a moment Malika's thoughts turned to herself. Could her faith stand the fire of interrogation and persecution? She would be asked about her beliefs about Muhammed and the Koran. What would happen if she were to deny these and confess her faith in the Bible and the deity of Christ and his death and resurrection? Would she be imprisoned?

Malika knew that her father and older brothers, too, would be summoned. Had she not brought enough shame on them because of her conversion? They had tolerated her new faith so long as she kept it secret outside the family. But now she would have to face their anger, grief, and shame, because her faith would be announced officially and publicly. So far she had managed to keep her relationships with other Christians hidden from her family but now they would know who her friends were. What would her relatives do to them?

Malika thought also of those whom she had won for Christ in her meetings. Would they be offended at her cowardice if she went into hiding? And would not her testimony be ruined if she did not live up to her own preaching? The police would be looking for her, and word of their search would reach every church and every meeting. She would have to live a life of fear as the police pursued her. No church and no house meeting could ever invite her to speak again. Even her Christian sisters would be influenced by their parents and church leaders and told that it would be wise to avoid persecution by not seeing her again.

Much of the night she had struggled with these questions in prayer and in the study of her Bible, but no clear answer seemed to emerge. Now the hot sun and the noise of street life brought her mind back to the present. The hour had come for her to make her decision. She could not put it off any longer.

55

Goodwill Guerrillas?
C. A. Guang

It was Sunday morning at about 11:15 A.M. on the island of Ferrengi. The leader of the church worship service had just said, "Now it is time for our sermon. May God bless us and our missionary pastor, Reverend Smith."

At that moment, six young men dressed as government soldiers entered the church. They came quickly, almost running down the main aisle, showing holstered machine guns, and sweeping their eyes from one side to the other. While the congregation sat immobilized by shock, the "soldiers" sat down in the front pew.

Then a member of the congregation shouted imprudently, "They are not soldiers; they are guerrillas—from the Blue Blazers."

The pastor cut him off sternly. "Be quiet," he said. "And nobody leave the chapel." Even as he spoke those words with full authority, an unnerving incident popped into his mind.

Only a few weeks earlier, a different pastor had had to face a similar situation. A few members of a guerrilla band had entered his church during the worship service, looking for protection. One of the church members immediately ran out of the church to look for help. After making several phone calls, the man was advised to call the national police and ask them for protection.

The police had come and surrounded the church. The guerrillas and the police began to fight. Before the day was over, more than thirty persons had been killed, including the pastor and all the guerrillas.

Pastor Smith pushed that picture from his mind and forced himself to begin the sermon. He could see that most of his congregation was praying as he preached, and a few women were sobbing quietly.

The sermon was a basic presentation of the gospel message. As he concluded, the pastor invited those to come forward who wanted to be reconciled with God by receiving Jesus Christ as Savior and Lord. There was an extra measure of earnestness evident in his voice.

At first, no one responded. Suddenly two of the six guerrillas came forward, and knelt to pray. The pastor then led the congregation in audible prayer. But as he raised his eyes and prepared to dismiss the congregation, one of the guerrillas stood up and began to speak.

Standing between the pastor and the congregation, he said, "I would like to say a few words before leaving the church. I am a Christian, too. Someday I would like to be a member of your church."

Pastor Smith watched the shock wave electrify the church. What? A Christian guerrilla? Impossible!

The guerrilla continued: "As you all know, the common people on our island identify Catholic Christianity with Spain and remember how that country oppressed us during the colonial times. Now our people identify evengelical Protestants with the international politics of the United States. Some of you may know that the United States is using religion as well as sports, money, and material goods to keep control of our country. Do you know why? It's because for every dollar they give to us, they are collecting two or three more from our poor island."

The congregation was mesmerized by the man and his speech. And he was not finished. "As a Christian, I know that it is not God's will that the children of God be oppressed—to live in poverty, ignorance, and all kinds of afflictions. At the same time, our governors, who are backed by United States interests, are living in luxury and opulence. That is the real reason revolutionary movements are growing in this country and many others. We revolutionaries are using the Bible, too. We have our religious ceremonies. But we will never use the American theology that teaches submission and obedience to our corrupt governments."

The guerrilla had finished, so he sat down in the pew again. In the deep silence that followed, his words echoed loudly in the minds of all who heard. No one moved.

The missionary pastor stood looking out the window, and a rapid-fire succession of thoughts shot through his mind. He had come to this country only to preach the gospel, not to be involved in politics. But here he was, very seriously involved. He knew the government was corrupt and certainly had never wanted to be identified with it. The guerrilla's words revealed to him how much, in fact, he *was* identified with it. He had been brought up short to face what he had been trying to ignore. The close alliance between the United States, the national government, and the evangelical church was perceived as cooperation in the political affairs and practices of the country.

People on the island knew that American financial aid to the local government was used largely by the army for repression, political persecution, and—in the end—for the destruction of the country. Why should they not believe that the aid from the mission related to those purposes as well? After all, it came from the same source.

Pastor Smith realized in that moment that one of his own long-standing assumptions might be flawed. He had always believed that the church could thrive only in the "freedom" guaranteed by a government that was backed by a strong army.

What brought his mind back to the present situation was the swift realization that the police of the present government had the right to kill guerrillas any time and any place. What if a shoot-out occurred at any moment here in his church? How could he cope with the presence of the guerrillas and also ensure the safety of his congregation?

Postscript

The pastor conferred briefly with several of his mature church members. They decided to ask the guerrillas to change into clothes they would provide for them. Each guerrilla was assigned to a different family from among the members and left the church with them, to be dropped off in different parts of the city.

In this case, no one informed the police, and no one was hurt. If they had been discovered, the church members would have been guilty of subversion, because of the law against helping guerrillas.

After a few weeks, Pastor Smith left the country.

Editor's Note

The issues raised by this case are still very much alive in many countries where the United States has influence.

In some of these countries, guerrilla warfare has become a way of life. No matter where their political sympathies lie, people cannot escape the effects of the political system on their day-to-day existence. Missionaries and national Christians are involved whether they like it or not, for to be "neutral" is itself a strong political statement.

Many American missionaries are not preparing the national church to live and witness under different political systems. Many also continue to defend American enterprise and politics as the will of God and the manifest destiny of the United States. Even if they tried, however, it is unlikely that these missionaries would be able to avoid being identified with American policy in those countries.

At least two vital issues must be dealt with. What stance should a missionary take *vis-à-vis* his or her own government? And how can the national church be prepared to witness to the kingdom of God, regardless of the kind of political system under which the people live?

56

Kidnapped!
Paul G. Hiebert

We have to decide now," said Gerald, chairman of the mission's executive committee. "It is Wednesday, and it takes two days to get the money to the kidnappers. The deadline they gave us was Sunday."

"I vote against paying the ransom," said James. "If we give in now, it will encourage terrorists everywhere to kidnap missionaries for ransom. Besides, we can't agree to their condition that we take our missionaries out of Mindanao and abandon our new converts. That would sentence them to persecution, possibly even death."

"I know," said Sarah, "but what about Mark? I believe they will kill him, just as they did Pastor Manuel last week. They mean business! And what about Rachel and the children. What about all the relatives and the members of the Hansons' church? They will never forgive us if Mark is killed. I can't blame them. I know how I would feel if someone let a person I loved die. I am convinced we must negotiate with the kidnappers on the ransom. If necessary, we can move the missionaries to Devao. They would be safe in the city, and the young Christians in the villages could still meet with them when necessary."

Gerald realized he held the deciding vote. The committee had discussed the various possibilities many times over the past three weeks since the kidnapping took place. Now they had to make a decision.

The crisis began when the executive committee of the Mindanao Muslim Mission received word that the Reverend Mark Hanson, one of their missionaries, and Pastor Manuel had been kidnapped by the Islamic Jihad, a radical Muslim movement in the Philippines. Mrs. Hanson was in Manila with her two young children when the kidnapping occurred. The kidnappers demanded $50,000 and a promise that the missionaries would leave the area. They gave the mission two weeks to respond. The year before, the general board of the mission had adopted a policy not to negotiate with terrorists, so the executive committee rejected the ultimatum. At the end of the two weeks, it received word that the kidnappers had killed Pastor Manuel and had set a new deadline for Mark Hanson's death two weeks hence.

Immediately after the kidnapping, the mission had informed the relatives and Hanson's church of the mission policy regarding kidnapping. Although they agreed that paying the ransom would only encourage terrorism in the future, they encouraged the mission to continue negotiating with the kidnappers for Mark's release. Special prayer sessions were organized in the churches for both Mark and Pastor Manuel.

After Pastor Manuel was executed, however, the family members urged the mission to pay the ransom secretly. When the executive committee reaffirmed the board policy, the family members, with the help of the pastor of Mark's home church, began to raise the money and contact the terrorists on their own. They also called upon the United States government to urge the Philippine government to seek Mark's release. Some of the church members, unhappy with the committee's action, said they would withdraw their support if the mission did not negotiate to save Mark's life. They also contacted members in other churches, who then phoned the mission office to express their concern for Mark Hanson's life.

The U.S. State Department contacted the mission and urged it not to pay the ransom. It offered to assist the mission board by putting pressure on the Philippine government, but the mission, wishing to avoid a close identification with the United States government, asked it to wait.

When the press heard of the kidnapping, newspaper reports began to appear—branding all Muslims as fanatics and terrorists, and calling on the government of the United States to offer commandos to the Philippine regime to recapture Reverend Hanson. Despite the mission's pleas that the press keep silent on the matter, so as not to antagonize the kidnappers and other Muslims, inflammatory articles continued to appear in the local papers.

The executive committee kept in contact with the kidnappers through its field director in the Philippines and tried to negotiate a peaceful settlement. But the kidnappers remained adamant—the mission would have to pay the money and leave the area. If they refused, there would be other reprisals. None of the missionaries would be safe.

Gerald contacted the chairman of the mission board, who pointed out that there was no time to call a board meeting. Besides, the board members knew little about the situation. He said that the executive committee was authorized to act in times of emergency.

Now, as Gerald looked at James and Sarah, he thought of Mrs. Hanson and her children, and of the mission and its commitment to evangelize the Muslims in Mindanao. If a nation expected its people to die for the nation, should the church not expect Christians to give their lives for the cause of Christ? But did this situation call for such a sacrifice? Gerald breathed a prayer before he spoke . . . .

PART 10

Everyday Problems of Missionary Life

In our preoccupation with the great issues of missionary services—evangelism, church planting, Bible translation, contextualization, confrontation with non-Christian religions, and so on—we often forget that many problems in missionary service have to do with everyday living. Finding and cooking food may be a time-consuming process because it must be done over a wood fire that must be lit and stoked, because everything must be boiled or soaked in permanganate in order to kill endemic amoeba and bacilli, and because the chickens are still running around when we buy them in the market. One study showed that it takes five and a half hours in many countries to cook a day's meals, which in others would take an hour and a half. Laundry is a full day's job. Cleaning the house and yard, marketing, making long trips to distant cities for medicines and other supplies, and going to the bank soon fill up a missionary's days. There seems so little time left to do the things for which we have come.

One solution is to hire servants, particularly in countries where this is a normal and expected custom. They can relieve the missionary of many of the day-to-day tasks that take up so much time and generate so much frustration. But having servants is often a mixed blessing. We must ask ourselves, "What message does hiring servants give to the people among whom we minister?" Does it distort the gospel message we seek to bring? Does it open or close doors to personal relationship?

We ourselves must also learn how to work with servants. Many Christians place a strong emphasis on egalitarian relationships. It is hard for us to assume the role of masters, particularly as that role is defined by some other cultures. We want to be casual and friendly and avoid the strong disciplinary measures exercised by masters in the local community. But those working for us often misunderstand this as an invitation to become friends. Consequently, they may stop doing their work and expect us to continue supporting them.

Equally frustrating is the loss of privacy. Some cultures place a high value on privacy at home. We are not used to having people come unannounced into our bedroom or living room. We want to be alone as a family or as a person. Even if we do not have servants who come and go in the house, we find in most cultures that it is hard to maintain this type of privacy. In many remote tribal and peasant societies, the people are curious about us and our ways. They look in the windows, handle our belongings, pinch the cheeks of our children, and ask an endless stream of questions. At first we are pleased, for this opens doors for building relationships and communicating the gospel, but in the long run there come times when we cry out for solitude.

Another solution is to live as much as possible as the local people do. To some extent we need to do so in order to identify with the people for the sake of the gospel, but "going native" has its limitations. People in many societies spend much of their time on the daily routines of survival, and adopting their ways leaves little time for ministry. Moreover, there are limits to our abilities to adapt to other cultures. The psychological energy spent in adopting totally new ways of living may be so great that we have little left for the work we are assigned to do.

Another set of problems has to do with our children. Where should they go to school? Do we expect them to identify with our home culture, or to become a part of the culture where we serve? What about their sex education? And what about their dating and marriage?

Furlough and retirement pose still other questions. Where shall we live? How do we maintain family life when we move so often or go on deputation? What is our responsibility to our children if they remain in our homeland to go to college? And how will we support ourselves when we grow old? The fear of retiring and having no place to go, nothing to do, and nothing to live on is very real among many missionaries, and not without reason.

Some of the most difficult problems of everyday life have to do with crises such as illnesses, accidents, terrorism, and war. How do the local people act when we kill a person in an automobile accident? What obligations do we have to the relatives of the deceased? Finally, what does one do when terrorism, military coups, or wars come close?

We may be very successful in solving the great questions of ministry in another culture, but if we do not solve the problems of everyday living, we may not be around to put those solutions into practice.

Bibliography

Missionary Children

Boyce, Everett R. 1981. Schools for missionary children: How good are they? *Evangelical Missions Quarterly*. July.

Danielson, Edward E. 1984. *Missionary Kid—MK*. Pasadena: William Carey Library.

Hill, Brian V. 1986. The educational needs of the children of expatriates. *Missiology* 14:325–346.

Lockerbie, D. Bruce. 1975. *Education of missionaries' children*. Pasadena: William Carey Library.

Moore, Raymond and Dorothy. 1981. *Home grown kids: A practical handbook for teaching your children at home*. Waco: Word Books.

Preheim, Marion K. 1969. *Overseas service manual*. Scottdale: Herald Press.

Stevenson-Moessner, Jeanne. 1986. Cultural dissolution: "I lost Africa." *Missiology* 14:313–324.

Useem, Ruth, and Downie, Richard. 1976. Third culture kids. *Today's Education*. September/October.

Wagner, Richard E. 1980. Advantages of home instruction. *Evangelical Missions Quarterly*. January.

Werkman, Sidney. 1977. *Bringing up children overseas*. New York: Basic Books.

Missionary Adjustment

Dye, Sally F. 1974. Decreasing fatigue and illness in field work. *Missiology* 3:79–109 (January).

Kane, J. H. 1980. *Life and work on the mission field*. Grand Rapids: Baker Book House.

Smalley, William, ed. 1978. *Readings in missionary anthropology: II*. South Pasadena: William Carey Library. (Particularly see Parts VIII & IX, pp. 693–912).

Williams, Kenneth L. 1973. *Characteristics of the more successful and less successful missionaries*. Doctoral dissertation, U.S. International University.

57

Cross-Cultural Marriage
Wen-An Andrew Su

I don't want to leave the Gospel Mission Society," Greg said again and again, "but I must marry her in three weeks or my witness will be ruined."

"I understand, I understand, my dear brother," Reverend Anderson said gently, as they drove to Elder Tsai's house from the train station where Greg had picked him up. "Now, tell me, how does Miss Tsai feel about the whole thing?"

"We were only allowed to talk on the phone. I explained our mission rules to her many times," Greg said sadly. "She insisted that she already considered herself a staff member of the G.M.S., and the ministry she is doing proved that. She also assured me that after we were married she would be able to help the ministry of the G.M.S. even more. These were her words: 'Greg, just like the others, I cannot understand the difficulties of your position. However, I do love you and trust the Lord will open the door for us. Don't worry. Let me talk to Reverend Anderson and everything will be okay!'"

"How can I hurt these enthusiastic young Christian workers?" Reverend Anderson asked himself. "On the other hand, she is not yet a staff member. How can I go against mission policy?"

Three months earlier, Greg Watson had called Reverend Anderson from Yu-Li, the remote town at the foot of the mountains where he served, to announce that he had fallen in love with a Taiwanese woman. As district director of the mission, Anderson's immediate question was, "Can she be considered as one of our staff members?" The rules of the G.M.S. required both partners of a married couple to be full-time staff workers. If a single person on staff wanted to get married, he or she should either marry someone already in the mission or delay marriage until the future spouse be accepted as a full-time staff member. Although outsiders often could not understand the need for this rule, the mission leaders were convinced, on the basis of the ninety-year history of the mission, that it was necessary and reasonable. "After all, the family is the basic unit for missionary service," they said. "This is the principle behind the rule."

"Can she be considered as one of our staff members?" Reverend Anderson asked again.

"Sure!" Greg replied on the phone. "I've known her for two years, and we've always worked closely with each other. Undoubtedly, she will be a brilliant Christian worker."

"Be careful and patient! And keep it an absolute secret!" Reverend Anderson warned. "Why don't you set up a time for me to meet her when I visit your field two months from now? Just hold on a couple more months, okay? You understand the seriousness of this, don't you?"

Two months later, Reverend Anderson came to Yu-Li. As in previous field visits, he recognized that Greg was an outstanding and fruitful young missionary. His ministry was so successful that at the end of the next year the church of Yu-Li would be ready to be independent from the mission and taken over by local Christians. But he was disappointed at the widespread rumors of Greg's romance. Almost every Christian he met reported to him the "good news" about Greg and Miss Ling Tsai.

"I was very, very careful," Greg explained. "Actually, besides serving together, we've never gone out on a date. Except one incident—one night we were planning an evangelistic meeting, and it was too late for her to go home alone, so I had to give her a ride with my motorcycle. Unfortunately, we ran into some teenagers from the church. This is a small town, you know, so word got around."

The expatriate agricultural experts, Dr. and Mrs. Meyer, who were counselors to the local government and helpers in the G.M.S. church, told Reverend Anderson that Ling Tsai was an excellent schoolteacher and a great leader in the church. "In fact," they pointed out, "she contributes a great deal to the success of Greg's ministry. Everyone in Yu-Li, even the non-Christians, believe that the two make a perfect couple."

After meeting Miss Tsai, Anderson agreed with her positive evaluations by others. He sent her an application form and wrote that as soon as he received it, he would present it to the administrative committee. They would investigate the case and interview her. The entire procedure would take at least four or five months.

The situation came to an unexpected crisis within a month. A local newspaper reporter, a new Christian in the G.M.S. church, heard of the love story through the grapevine and reported in the paper that Greg and Ling would soon be married. Immediately, this "international marriage" became the central point of discussion in Yu-Li.

Unable to stand the curious questions and various opinions from relatives, neighbors, friends, and strangers, Ling Tsai's father, an elder of the church, asked Dr. and Mrs. Meyer to urge Greg to marry his daughter as soon as possible. According to tradition, she was forbidden to see Greg until the answer was returned. Greg replied that he had to await the decision of the mission administrative committee. Elder Tsai thought that Greg was puzzled by the bride-price and the wedding expenses, so he sent Dr. and Mrs. Meyer to assure Greg that he would not have to pay these, even though traditionally they are covered by the groom. Again Greg sent back the message that he would have to await the mission decision.

Elder Tsai was furious. He could not imagine that an organization could control Greg's marriage. Neither could the whole Yu-Li community. "That's an unbelievable and unacceptable excuse," Elder Tsai told Dr. Meyer. "This man is attempting to avoid his responsibility, just like those American soldiers did when they were in Taiwan in the past."

Dr. Meyer had called Reverend Anderson and said, "If Greg fails to marry Miss Tsai within two or three weeks, the witness of the mission in this field will be badly damaged."

It was then that Greg found out that Ling was under a five-year teaching obligation to the town of Yu-Li. The town had paid her tuition and supported her through the National Taiwan Normal University, for which assistance she was obliged to teach at Yu-Li Junior High School for five years. She had just begun her third year. If Greg married her, he would have to remain at Yu-Li for three more years. But the Gospel Mission Society transferred its staff regularly from one place to another, according to the needs of the work. With the success of Greg's work, Reverend Anderson would have no reason to keep him and Ling in Yu-Li more than one year. Moreover, since she still had to teach for those three years, she could not become a member of the G.M.S. staff.

Greg had given Reverend Anderson this information as they drove to Elder Tsai's house. Now they were seated in the living room awaiting Anderson's answer. As he looked at the lovely young lady seated across from him, and at Greg, Reverend Anderson again asked himself, "How can I hurt these enthusiastic young Christian workers? On the other hand, how can I go against mission policy?" During the thirty years he had been in the field, even when he faced the threat of the Communists in Mainland China, he had never struggled so hard to come up with an answer.

58

Trouble with Servants
Matt Howell

"Mark, what are we going to do with Nadine?" Linda was at her wit's end. Her husband gave a sigh. Nadine, their maid in Haiti for over two years, had refused to do her full job the last few weeks. Mark knew they could hardly let her go. She seemed like family now and she would have no place to go and no means of support if she were fired.

When Mark and Linda first came to Haiti, they both planned to work full-time. Mark was a hospital administrator, and Linda taught high-school English at the local missionary school. The found out when they arrived that just keeping house in that subtropical country was a full-time job in itself. Occupied fully with their jobs, neither one had time to go to the market and bargain for the food that had to be bought daily to ensure its freshness. Nor had they the time to soak the fruits and vegetables in permanganate solution to kill bacteria, to boil all the water needed for drinking and cooking, or to kill and clean the chickens, which were still running around when they got them in the market. Around the house, the garbage had to be burned, food protected from insects, floors mopped, laundry hung and rehung to dry, and a daily ritual performed of wiping the dust that came in freely off the unpaved roads. They soon found themselves overwhelmed with domestic duties that kept them from fulfilling the tasks of their mission. Their colleagues encouraged them to hire a Haitian maid.

The idea of having a maid did not sit well with Mark and Linda at first. The last thing they wanted to do was help perpetuate white supremacy in an already oppressed society. But they began to realize that besides freeing themselves from household chores so that they could use their abilities in ministry, they could also provide adequate housing, a balanced diet, and a Christian witness to a Haitian that had known none of these before.

Through the recommendation of a friend, they hired Nadine to help them around the house. They knew at once they had made the right decision. Nadine worked hard and did everything she was instructed to do, even though she had to be reminded at times. Between her broken English and Mark's and Linda's limited Creole, they were able to communicate adequately enough to get the job done. Nadine was also able to get better bargains at the market than her employers, because she knew the barter-trade system inside out. Mark and Linda and Nadine soon became good friends.

From a Haitian perspective, Nadine now had a high-paying job with room and board in a "blanc's big house," and she was therefore looked on with envy by her Haitian friends. At first she enjoyed the prestige, but then it began to go to her head. Her old friends saw less of her, as Nadine began to associate with other Haitians who were better off.

After a while Mark and Linda began to notice that Nadine had become a bit more lax in her responsibilities, but they brushed it aside as nothing important. Nadine had become like family to them, and they were enjoying the little community that had formed. Soon after Nadine was hired, her husband, an older man who could not work because he lacked skills, had moved in with her in the basement apartment. Not long after that, she became pregnant, and Linda was given the opportunity to become a midwife. With the birth of her baby girl, Nadine's young niece moved in from the country to help around the house until Nadine could get back on her feet. Mark and Linda were glad they could help these Haitian people and were especially pleased when the family started attending a local Haitian church.

Then Linda realized that again the house was not being kept very well. She had to remind Nadine to do her regular chores more often. She spoke to Mark about this, and he in turn talked to Nadine, who simply smiled and explained that as a new mother she had many responsibilities, but she would see that the chores got done.

Mark and Linda began to see less and less of Nadine. Her niece was sent in to help, but she did not do a good job. It was finally obvious that Nadine did only the essentials of her duties and made her family members cover the rest of her work load, which was poorly done.

Mark could no longer stand the way things were going. Now Linda was pregnant and had to do more and more around the house with the result that her strength and patience were decreasing daily. Finally Mark confronted Nadine. Lovingly, yet firmly, he demanded to know why she had ceased doing some of her chores. She replied that she had been freed from lower Haitian work. She was now beyond those duties because she had been "raised up" by the good treatment of her missionary friends. Mark and Linda were now her friends; and she would help share the chores but could never again work like a lower Haitian for them as before.

Mark now realized their innocent mistake. In befriending Nadine, they had raised her social status to a point where she no longer considered herself to be of the lower working class. In her mind, Nadine had been liberated from mopping floors by the friendship of her white saviors and the money she had collected and saved for her family from her generous wages.

Mark and Linda discussed what they should do. Nadine could not be shaken from her attitude, even though they threatened to fire her. They could barely afford Nadine, much less hire additional help. If they fired her, she could not get another job without a good recommendation. Moreover, Nadine said that now she would only work for "good white people" like Linda and Mark, but such jobs were almost nonexistent. Unemployed and homeless, Nadine would face a cruel world with a baby and two other dependents to feed. When they asked their Haitian friends for advice, they told the missionaries to beat her at once and put her in her place.

When Mark and Linda's baby was due, and good help around the house became even more a necessity, they knew they would have to do something about Nadine. It was a tough decision for Mark and Linda to make, because they felt responsible for creating the dilemma in the first place. Finally, after much discussion and prayer, they decided what they had to do and called Nadine into the house . . . .

59

Pastor Gopalan and His Hindu Parents
Vihari Hivale

Honey, my parents are coming from India to visit us!"
Girish shouted to his wife, Shalini, who was tidying up the children's
bedroom upstairs. The postman had just delivered the mail to their
home in Canada, and Girish was excited by this news from his parents.
Then, as Shalini hurried down the steps, the problems of the visit
began to dawn on him. "What are we going to do about their idols and
rituals, and what will we say to the children?" he asked, more to himself than to his wife. Both looked forward to the visit, for Girish had not
seen his parents for eight years, but they knew that it would not be an
easy time, because their parents still clung to their traditional Hindu
customs.

Girish had come to accept Jesus as his Savior while attending Youth
for Christ meetings during his college years in Bombay. His parents
belonged to a high-caste Brahmin community in South India, but for a
number of years had lived in Bombay, where Girish's father worked as
an auditor for the State Bank.

Although Mr. and Mrs. Gopalan were shocked when their son became a Christian, in time they came to accept it. They were pleased to
see his joy and his affection for them, but they remained orthodox
Hindus and faithfully made offerings to their gods each day.

In college Girish fell in love with Shalini, a South Indian woman
from a Christian home, and soon after graduation they were married.
Because Shalini's father and Girish's father were good friends and
worked in the same office, it was not too difficult for the Gopalans to
accept the marriage.

Two years after their marriage, Girish and Shalini moved to Canada for higher studies. Girish graduated with honors in chemical engineering and was employed by a large international chemical company. Within a few years the young couple had their own home, a new car, a color TV, and all the comforts of modern life.

Girish and Shalini attended the Riverside Missionary Church regularly and took part in Bible-study classes, visitation, choir, and other church activities. After hearing several of the missionaries his church supported, Girish felt that he, too, should serve in the church. He was an articulate speaker and had won several debate competitions during his college years. When he shared his sense of call with Shalini, she was very happy. They prayed about the matter for some time and then shared it with their senior pastor, who strongly affirmed their decision. The pastor discussed the young couple's call with the church board, and it agreed unanimously to appoint Girish to their staff as a preaching pastor.

Girish resigned his job, and the couple sold their house and moved with their two young children into the house beside the church. All of them were well adapted to the Canadian lifestyle. Girish preached eloquently without any trace of his Indian accent, and Shalini sang in the choir as a soloist. But, as a good Indian, Girish loved and respected his parents very much, even though they were not Christians. He had not seen them since he left India, but he continued to pray that one day they would find the true Savior.

Then Girish and Shalini received the letter saying that Girish's parents would come to Canada in a few weeks to visit them for six months. Without question, they would host his parents in their home; Indian rules of hospitality would not allow otherwise. But this did raise some difficult problems. Girish's father was an orthodox Brahmin who never forgot to place a *pottu* (white U-shaped mark) on his forehead and always wore a white wraparound loincloth. His mother always put the large red *kunkum* spot on her forehead and wore nine-yard saris. Girish knew that they would bring their idols and all their ritual paraphernalia so they could continue their daily worship ceremonies in Canada. He could already imagine that they would arrange an altar in their bedroom, light oil lamps, burn incense, tinkle bells, and ask for flowers and coconut for their worship *puja*.

As they discussed the visit, Shalini and Girish realized they had several important questions to answer. What would their children think of their grandparents when they saw them worship idols in such strange ways? Their five-year-old daughter, Sangeeta, had recently asked if her grandpa in India would go to heaven. Would the congregation accept Girish's parents in their strange attire and the conducting of Hindu rituals in the pastor's residence? After all, their house was church property. Would the worship of idols affect the sanctity of the pastor's house? And what about the parents? Would they attend the worship services next door, and what would they feel when they saw their own son preaching in a Christian church? Perhaps they would be more receptive to the gospel in a predominantly Christian environment. But how would they respond if the congregation took issue with their Hindu worship ceremonies? Girish and Shalini looked at each other. They knew that they had less than a month to deal with these questions.

60

Where Should Kathy Go to School?
Frances F. Hiebert

Brenda Jackson was maneuvering her car through a crowded Madras street one hot and humid afternoon in early August. She dodged people, oxcarts, trucks, and other cars with the constant help of her horn. Driving in Madras was always enough to try the patience of a saint which, she told herself, she certainly was not. Kathy would be late for her piano lesson again unless the car could sprout wings.

Every morning and afternoon, five days a week, Brenda drove across town to take Kathy to and from school. On Fridays, the afternoon trip included a long detour past the piano teacher's home.

Today, as often happened because of the Jacksons' strategic location in the city, guests would join them for dinner and stay the night. Brenda felt quite ambivalent about this steady stream of visitors. It was nice to see Westerners occasionally, but entertaining them did put a heavy demand on her and their family life. She also had duties as an accountant for the seminary where her husband was the principal. Sometimes she wished for a formal job description to limit the demands made on her. Yet there were other times when the guests proved to be blessings in disguise who ministered to the Jacksons' own needs.

In addition to the turmoil on the road and the waiting dinner guests, an even larger problem occupied Brenda's mind. She and her husband, Grant, had to decide about Kathy's future education. For more than a year, they had discussed their options without coming to a definite conclusion. Now time was running out; they had to decide by the first of September.

Grant and Brenda Jackson were missionaries in India. Brenda also had grown up in India because her parents were American missionaries, although they had worked in the North rather than the South where the Jacksons now lived. Grant had come to India as a young missionary from Australia to work in the same mission. In good Indian fashion, Brenda's father had arranged their marriage—with their consent, of course. Grant was eleven years older than Brenda, and Kathy was their only child. She would remain their "only child" because Brenda was unable to have more children. Kathy was now nine years old and would be entering the fourth grade.

Kathy attended a school in Madras where the medium of instruction was English. It was a secular school patterned after the British system of education rather than the American and drew students from the sector of society that could afford private education for their children. There were only three other non-Indian children in the school. While the instruction had been fairly adequate until now, both Grant and Brenda felt Kathy was not being challenged academically to the extent of her abilities. They believed that if Kathy stayed in school in Madras, the quality of her education would decrease as she moved into the higher grades.

When Brenda finally drove into the schoolyard, Kathy skipped out to the car, holding the hand of one of her Indian schoolmates. She said good-bye to the girl, jumped into the car, gave her mother a hug, and began to chatter animatedly about the events of the day.

Brenda and Kathy arrived home after the piano lesson in reasonably good time, after all. Grant was just walking across the compound from his office in the seminary when they drove up. Kathy jumped out of the car and was immediately swept up into his arms, giggling with pleasure as his substantial handlebar moustache tickled her face. Brenda felt the tension drain out of her as early dusk settled with the twittering birds on the pagoda trees around the house and she got her own loving welcome from her husband.

Later in the evening, after a pleasant dinner, the Jacksons and their visitors got up from the table and settled comfortably in the living room. Brenda breathed a little prayer of thanks for her dependable cook and her helper. A simple but tasty meal had been ready and waiting for them. Now Brenda was free from any cleanup chores and could join in the conversation. Many American women were not so privileged, she reminded herself.

The guests turned out to be more compatible than some who accepted the Jacksons' hospitality. In fact, not far into the conversation, they discovered they were "kindred spirits," although the Bennets were a few years older than their hosts. In addition to a strong commitment to the gospel, they shared common perspectives on how to carry out the missionary mandate and the problems of cross-cultural living.

The Bennets had been missionaries in Africa. Now Jeff Bennet had been appointed to an administrative position in their mission society, which was why he and Anne were traveling to visit the work in various parts of the world. Like Brenda, Jeff was a second-generation missionary. His parents had also been missionaries, but in Africa. He and Anne had two children who were now in college in America.

The conversation was cheerful and lively—and in their own language and thought patterns. After a day of cross-cultural communication, they all enjoyed that. But when Kathy said good-night and scampered up the steps to bed, a serious look came over Grant's face. It was he who opened the subject of Kathy's further education.

"We're going to have to make a decision very soon," Grant said. "We are praying hard that it will be the right one for Kathy. It will be painful for all of us if she goes away to school. And yet we have to consider what is best for her in the long run."

Brenda joined Grant in describing the options open to them. There were two major schools for missionary children in India. One was Kodaikanal in the mountains at the southern tip of India and the other was Woodstock in the North. Both schools operated on the North American system of education and had excellent academic ratings. Their graduates could easily compete with those of the best college-prep schools in the States.

Another advantage of sending Kathy to either of the boarding schools was that they both offered private tutoring in art and vocal or instrumental music. There also would be opportunities to participate in drama and sports events.

As a rule, missionaries in South India sent their children to "Kodai," as it was usually called, and people in the North sent their children to Woodstock. There was a fair amount of rivalry between the two schools. Long after their high-school years and in other countries where they settled, missionary children always identified themselves as graduates of whichever school they had attended. Brenda, who had grown up in North India, was a graduate of Woodstock.

Now that they lived in Madras, Kodai was much closer to the Jacksons' home than was Woodstock. It took only seven or eight hours by train and about two hours by bus up the mountain to get there. Their mission society had its own boarding home for missionary children at Kodai, and the houseparents were placed by the mission.

The Jacksons were concerned about what they had heard from some missionary parents whose children were at Kodai. The school seemed vulnerable to whatever fad was passing through American schools.

Because of their isolation in a different culture, the students seemed to take these fads even more seriously. The administration tended to ride out the fashions as tolerantly as possible and used discipline only as a last resort, when a student's well-being or that of others was threatened.

Although the school had been started for missionary children, there had always been a small group of students from families of the Western business and diplomatic communities. And, of course, many different Christian denominations and mission societies were represented there. The school had recently been "internationalized" and was working hard to encourage Indian students to matriculate. Some parents felt that this diversity was becoming a threat, while others welcomed the cross-cultural opportunities it provided their children.

Woodstock, on the other hand, remained a more homogeneous school. The administration still considered the education of missionary children as their primary *raison d'être*. Although it was an American school, it was more structured in what it required of the students both in the way of behavior and academic achievement. Some parents felt that the requirements were too stern, especially for the younger students.

Brenda noted ruefully that while Woodstock was her own alma mater, it was now two hard days' travel away by train. Kathy would be separated from them for at least two three-month periods a year. Their mission did not have its own boarding facility at Woodstock, and there was only one dormitory for boys and one for girls for the whole school. One advantage, however, was that Brenda had a second cousin who was teaching in the school.

Grant and Brenda did not try to hide their strong affection for their daughter. Kathy was very small, but she was quite mature for her age, they told the Bennets. Perhaps this was because she was an only child and often thrown together with adults. Also, she was not too robust physically and had been forced to endure some rather serious illness.

Anne Bennet smiled when she heard this explanation and thought to herself that there might be another reason for Kathy's maturity. Her Australian father, to whom she was the apple of his eye, probably required more maturity from his daughter than an American father might. That had become apparent in the way they related at the table earlier in the evening.

At that point in the conversation, Anne related their experience with their own children's education. She had been trained as a teacher, so the Bennets had decided to teach their children at home. In the early grades, Anne used her own teaching materials but later ordered courses from an American correspondence school for her children. Jeff concurred with her that both children were now doing well in college.

Anne pointed out the obvious advantages to teaching children at home. There can be no real substitute for parental care, she said. Parents then have the opportunity to be the main influence on their children's values and religious commitment. In her opinion, the quality of home education was at least equal to that of any school, if the parents applied themselves to it.

Brenda expressed her admiration for the Bennets' commitment but pointed out that neither she nor Grant had primary-school teaching experience. Anne immediately assured Brenda that anyone who was educated through high school could give his or her children a first-rate education because of the specific and adequate nature of the correspondence materials.

The Bennets agreed with the Jacksons that socialization with peers was no small consideration and on that point, they all recognized the age-old missionary dilemma. When their children grow up as bi-cultural people, should they be socialized more along the lines of the parents' culture or the culture in which they were living and working? Which culture would bi-cultural children finally choose to be their cultural "home"? Or, as Jeff put it, tongue in cheek, would they be forever doomed to feel most comfortable on the plane flying between the two cultures?

Here there would be some difference between the two boarding schools. Woodstock was a more homogeneous school with a decidedly Western orientation. Kodai, having become an international school, was attracting students from all over Asia as well as American and other Western expatriates.

The earnest conversation between the Jacksons and the Bennets came to an abrupt end when a small shadow in a white nightie detached herself from the stairwell and slipped into the living room. Kathy snuggled into her mother's lap with a little sigh and said, "I couldn't sleep, Mummy."

Grant looked over at his wife and daughter. "Oh, God," he prayed silently, "help us make the right choice!"

61

Sex and the Missionary Kid
Dexter Teruya

There had been a long silence at the breakfast table. "Jim," said Mary finally, "I really don't think we should come back for another term."

Jim remained silent. He had tossed and turned in his bed most of the previous night, debating the issue in his mind. They had to make their decision within the next three days because Keaka, the chairman, and other members of the school board were coming on the weekend to get an answer from them. Would staying here be fair to their children?

Jim and Mary had come to Unika village on the island of Bolao three years before. Jim had completed his Ph.D. in theology and was assigned to teach in a school for church leaders. Mary's doctorate was in anthropology. The couple had delayed beginning their family long enough, so Mary was not given a teaching assignment. Instead, she kept busy at home with their son, Sam, who had been born six months after they arrived. She was now pregnant with their second child.

Jim and Keaka had become good friends almost immediately. Keaka was not one who felt that the contribution of Western missionaries was no longer needed. "We need missionaries to come and help us grow in our understanding of Christian faith," he told Jim soon after they arrived. For his part, Jim pledged to Keaka that he and Mary would stay as long as they were needed. They were also looking forward to raising their family on this beautiful island, away from the rampant materialism of the Western world.

When they first came to this island paradise, Jim and Mary had no idea that the sexual mores involving children would become almost as much a threat to them as Western materialism. But that is exactly what had happened, and why they now were on the horns of a dilemma over their return for a second term.

The previous night, the new missionary couple, Liesl and Micah, who had been on the island only three months, came to Mary and Jim's home for dinner. The two couples enjoyed each other's company greatly, so the evening had begun in high spirits. Later, however, a more serious atmosphere settled over them as Jim and Mary shared their concerns with the younger couple. Could they raise their children in this culture and somehow keep them free from unacceptable sexual practices?

"Keeping our own children segregated is out of the question," said Jim. "In the first place, it would be an affront to the nature of the gospel. And anyway, it would be impossible to enforce—there are no other missionary children on the island for them to play with."

Liesl and Micah had no children, but since they planned to have a family, the question was just as important for them. Like Jim and Mary before they came to Bolao, they had not anticipated this kind of a problem.

Liesl and Micah were always eager to learn from Jim and Mary because of their training and experience. But, until now, they had never discussed the sexual practices of the islanders. As they listened to the other couple, Liesl and Micah sat with eyes and mouths wide open in disbelief.

Mary was explaining that here mothers often pacify their crying children by rubbing or sucking their genitals. Older children copy this adult behavior and also indulge in games that satisfy their curiosity about sexual functions and differences.

Sometimes the play turns rough. Mary related an incident that had confirmed what she had not wanted to believe about the people's practices. One day a young woman came to the dispensary with her two children and a baby. Although Mary did not work there, she went over to talk with this woman because she had recently become acquainted with her.

"How are you all?" Mary asked. "Is someone sick?"

Casting an angry glance at one of the children, the woman removed the cloth that diapered the baby boy. She explained that the older child had bitten him. Mary could see the evidence of blood.

Jim reasoned that the children's freedom in sexual matters was a carry-over from the general lack of adult supervision and control. "Besides, they're just imitating what they all observe in their one-room homes," he said.

"Allowing children to run about naked until they're eight or ten years old doesn't help matters," Mary commented. "Another practice that probably will shock you is that mothers often manipulate a baby girl's genitals so as to enlarge them. It is believed that this early manipulation will increase sexual gratification for her as well as for her partner after she becomes a woman."

"Liesl, you know Lora, don't you?" Mary glanced over at the younger woman, whose face reflected the shock that Mary had predicted. "Well, Lora came to me about a year ago because she was worried about a friend. I won't name the friend because Lora wanted it to be strictly confidential. The problem was that her friend had very heavy vaginal discharges that Lora blamed on the practice that I have just described. It was the first time I had ever heard of this, so I asked Lora if it had been done to her and if it was still being done."

"Lora told me that her mother had done this to her, but when Lora got older, it made her angry and she had insisted that her mother not do it to her younger sisters. She told me that it was still widely practiced. But she also said that she didn't think these days Christian guys like it."

Mary paused for a moment and added, "I'm afraid now that Lora's friend may have vaginal cancer. She has had the discharge for a long time, but it has become worse, which is why Lora came to ask my advice. I told her that her friend must come for an examination, but Lora was afraid she would be too embarrassed to do it. I really can't say anything to her myself without breaking Lora's confidence."

Micah, who had said almost nothing since the conversation had turned to sexual practices, finally found his voice. "Are you sure these things are still happening?" he asked. "Maybe in the old days the villagers did those things, but surely not now since they've learned Christian principles. After all, women in our culture have vaginal diseases, too. And we haven't observed any of the kinds of behavior you've described since we've been here."

"Well," Jim replied, "missionaries have taught against these practices, so the people are likely to cover them up when we're around. But I'm afraid the people haven't understood why such things are wrong, which has only driven them underground."

"We're really worried about the kinds of habits our own children will develop if we come back for a second term," Mary added, coming back to their immediate problem. "Just the other day I caught Sam urinating with the other village boys in the bushes behind our garden. I'm afraid that if we don't watch him every minute, he'll soon join the other children in their sexual antics.

"It's not that we didn't count the cost before we decide to commit ourselves to serve the Lord on this island. We knew that there would be hardships and a different lifestyle, and we were ready for that. But risking our children's moral welfare is more than we bargained for. Surely God expects us first to be sure that our own children are not lost," Mary concluded.

"I'm sure that if we have children, we will be just as concerned as you are," said Micah slowly. "But aren't you forgetting something? Our own culture isn't such a paradigm of virtue these days either. Yesterday, a man from the village came into our house and picked up my new sports magazine. There was a girl in a bikini in an outboard-motor advertisement on the back cover. He looked shocked, and I was very embarrassed.

"American kids are bombarded with fairly explicit sexual imagery every day of their lives," Micah went on. "Advertising and all the media are full of it. Add to that the problem of drugs and violence in the schools, and you don't have a very pretty picture at home either."

Liesl murmured agreement with her husband and then added, "Maybe we must put the call of God first in our lives and trust that 'all these things shall be added unto us,' as God has promised."

The conversation turned back to lighter matters after that. Micah mentioned that he had visited the community cookhouse with some men from the village. They gave him his first taste of steaming breadfruit wrapped in taro leaves, which he described to the others as "delicious!"

The evening had ended on that happy note, but not before Micah and Liesl promised to pray for Jim and Mary and the decision they had to make.

As Jim and Mary prepared for bed, Jim stepped out onto the veranda to drink in the cool, clean evening air. A myriad of stars with no competition from city lights sparkled in the black velvet sky. The symphony of silence was the most beautiful he had ever heard. If only the turmoil in his heart and mind could be carried away by the breeze that gently touched his cheek!

As he lay down beside Mary, she said softly, "Jim, we have gotten very close to Liesl and Micah in these last few months. I know they are young and full of zeal for the work of the Lord. And, of course, we can't expect them to understand our concern completely because they don't have any children of their own. But it did hurt me a little when Micah said what he did. It almost seemed as if he was questioning the strength of our commitment. And I'm not sure they quite believe people still do the things we were talking about."

Jim's only answer to his wife was to kiss her tenderly and rub her back for a few minutes before he turned on his side to try to fall asleep. It had not been an altogether peaceful evening.

Now, the next morning, after the family had eaten breakfast and Sam had been released from his chair to watch a caterpillar make its way across the veranda, Jim asked Mary to read their daily portion of Scripture. Then they both prayed fervently that God would show them what to do.

"Well, darling," said Jim as he stood and began to clear away the breakfast dishes, "we are one day closer to the weekend than we were yesterday. I can't forget that I promised Keaka we would stay as long as we were needed. What will he think if we decide not to come back?"

62

Costly Compassion
Gary A. Glassco

In an instant of time, I had to make one of the most difficult decisions of my life. I had to choose whether or not to try to save the life of the person I had just hit with my car. But by choosing to help the injured person, I would jeopardize my own life and the lives of my family who were in the car with me.

We were missionaries in Papua New Guinea. Our family had been looking forward eagerly to a short holiday in Goroka, which was a three-and-a-half-hour drive from where we lived. The five of us piled into the mission bus. It was made to carry nine passengers, so we were quite comfortable.

We made a brief stop at our Bible College and our hospital and then headed towards Goroka. Our holiday had begun, and we were all having a good time. Everyone was relaxed and filled with anticipation.

The paved road gave way to gravel for a short stretch where the Highlands Highway was still incomplete. We were soon past it. Just after we came back on the pavement, I slowed to a cautious speed because we had entered a road bung. A bung is an open-air market held along the roadside where two roads intersect. Many people were milling around, buying and selling just off the pavement of the highway.

Suddenly, in a split second, an elderly man stepped out in front of our bus. There was no time to brake or swerve or even register it in my mind before it was over. I had hit the man with the right front of the bus just above the turn signal. The impact threw him over onto the side of the road. I slammed on the brakes and the bus came almost to a complete stop. My first thought was to stop and see if I could move the injured man to a nearby medical clinic or, if not, to go there and bring back help.

Then, feeling like a criminal, I stepped on the accelerator because I remembered what our mission doctor had told us to do in a case like this. "Don't stop, whatever you do," he had advised us after an experience like this of his own. Amid the screams of our children and the yells of the people churning around the car outside, the doctor's voice prevailed, and I kept the car in motion. I suspected that the man had been killed on impact, and as I drove on I wondered how many of his tribesmen had witnessed the accident.

To even begin to understand why a Christian missionary would do such a thing, you need to know about the "payback system" in the highlands culture of Papua New Guinea. You see, the people there are even more capitalistic than the West, in some ways at least. Every person—man, woman, or child—has a price on his or her head in a very real sense. Each individual is seen by the tribe to be a material asset to them. Therefore, the loss of a person to the tribal line is seen in terms of material worth. When a loss has been incurred, the person responsible is required to pay back to the tribe something of comparable worth.

The payback system has survived in this culture even after its explosive propulsion into modernity through Westernization. The system is based on the instinct to get even and is meant to be carried out swiftly and accurately. Fear strikes the hearts of nationals as well as expatriate Westerners because of this age-old cultural institution.

As I drove on down the highway, there was now a heavy silence in our bus, but turmoil and anxiety swirled through my head. I had done what I felt I had to do for the sake of my family, and yet I had possibly sacrificed another human life.

I stopped at the next police station, which was about one hour down the road, and reported the accident. There we were held in custody until word came that the man had died. My driver's license and passport were taken from me, and I was arrested for dangerous driving. Bail was set at K 500.00, and a court date was arranged for three months from that day. Then we were escorted to our home by armed policemen, who told us that there we would be safe from the tribe. Our holiday had turned into a nightmare.

In the days between the accident and trial, I never stopped asking myself if I had done the right thing. Friends and other missionaries tried to justify my decision by reminding me of the many stories of people who had been brutally beaten or even axed to death when they stopped at the scene of an accident. But I still see a dying man lying beside the road. I wonder if I will ever know whether what I did was right or wrong . . . .

Postscript

The tribal village court fined the author of this case K 10,000 (U.S. $12,000) and 40 pigs, worth about K 400.00 each. This "sorry" money was to be paid in addition to any insurance coverage.

Mission leaders contested this judgment, and the final settlement reached was K 2,000 ($2,500). This was then considered by the tribe as payment in full for the loss of their tribesman.

Teaching Case Studies

Case studies such as those in this book help us understand the problems missionaries face in their everyday lives. They may be used in churches to help people think more deeply about missionary concerns. They are also valuable as supplemental material in the classroom to help students face real mission situations and think through their responses. In such settings, case studies can amplify the major thrust of a course in addition to lectures, reading, and audiovisual aids.

Teaching a case is different from giving a lecture, because the case-study teacher is not a dispenser of knowledge, but a learner along with the students. The teacher must encourage a meaningful dialogue among the students and seek to bring this to closure at the end of the discussion.

Roles of the Teacher

As Ann Meyers and Louis Weeks point out, the teacher plays three key roles in facilitating case discussions.

First, she or he must probe the students' insights into the case by asking such questions as: What really is the dilemma? Who are the persons involved; where do they come from; and how are they affected by various outcomes? What issues are involved in the case? What are the possible solutions?

Second, the teacher is a referee, allowing disagreements and conflicts to arise, but making certain that they do not damage anyone. At times it is useful to encourage debates to stimulate the participants to think.

Third, the teacher is an overseer who makes sure that the discussion of the case proceeds towards some resolution. Participants must be encouraged to hold their own positions, and ample time should be given to air the issues as fully as possible. In the end, it is the teacher who must manage relationships between the students and make certain that group dynamics such as leadership, internal controls, cooperation, and conflict are constructive.

Development of the Case

In teaching a case, it is important to have in mind a clear progression for the discussion. In general, an analysis of the facts should be made before solutions are proposed. One common procedure is as follows:

1. *Establishing a time line.* In complex cases, make certain at the outset that everyone has a clear understanding of the sequence of events. This can be done by constructing a "time line"—by drawing a line along which the events are placed in chronological order. This is normally constructed by eliciting information regarding events from the participants. If time is short, the sequence can be outlined by the teacher.

2. *Discussion of characters.* Each character in the case should be discussed at some length by eliciting facts about them from the participants. This enables participants to look at the case through the eyes of each of the characters involved. Care should be taken here to differentiate between the *facts* known about a character and the inferences participants might make about how they view the situation.

3. *Discussion of issues.* After the characters are examined, the teacher should elicit from the participants what they believe to be the key issues that must be taken into account in seeking a solution to the case. These may include such issues as cultural practices and cultural differences, ethical norms, and implications for evangelism and the maturation of the church.

4. *Discussion of possible solutions.* After discussing the issues involved, the teacher can ask for possible solutions to the case. The implications of each solution *vis-à-vis* the issues involved should be examined. Several proposed solutions may be combined in seeking a final resolution to the case.

5. *Closure.* Near the end of the session, the teacher should seek to bring the discussion to a definite resolution. This may be done by seeking a consensus, by majority vote, or by asking each participant to decide on a specific solution. In reaching a solution, the teacher must be particularly sensitive to the feelings of those who disagree with the general consensus.

6. *Debriefing.* The teacher should make it clear when the case discussion is over and the class has returned to the present. In debriefing,

participants should be encouraged to examine the case-study process itself in order to analyze the benefits and limitations of the method. Participants should also be encouraged to express hard feelings, such as anger and alienation, that may have occurred in the process. These must be dealt with so that they do not continue on into real life.

Teaching Suggestions

Ann Meyers and Louis Weeks suggest some practical aids in the teaching of cases:

Role play. The teacher may assign parts to individuals or groups within the class. For example, in the case "Unity and Diversity," one group might play the part of the "untouchables," a second group the part of the high-caste converts, and a third the role of the missionary.

Votes. At some point the teacher may ask the class if it is ready to vote on the matter or to test the consensus by taking a "straw vote."

Honesty. The teacher should share his or her own honest feelings and encourage the students to do the same. They must know that they will not be attacked personally, even if their responses meet disapproval by others. On the other hand, the teacher should express his or her opinion frankly if a solution is presented that sounds unbelievable or has been disproven in practice.

Call on participants. Frequently the quiet person can use a nudge. If the person is not unduly threatened, it is easy to ask, "George, you have been pretty quiet. How does that last suggestion sound to you?"

Call for evidence. Sometimes the teacher may call for a clarification of a statement or for evidence in support of a position.

Time limits. The teacher may need to gently interrupt a long-winded person so that others have an opportunity to speak. Those who have not spoken recently (or at all) should be given an opportunity to express themselves before others who speak out frequently. A warning of the time remaining often helps at the end to bring the discussion to some resolution.

Observe the "little thing." The teacher must be attentive to eye contact, body postures, gestures, and other media by which students express their attitudes, It is important to make certain that no one is emotionally destroyed during the course of the discussion.

Record and relate contributions. The teacher should record participants' contributions on the board, possibly linking them to each
other in order to show the development of the discussion.

Closure. The teacher should not impose his or her own solution on
the case, but should lead the class to some kind of resolution. This
may be done by voting, by articulating a consensus, or by agreeing to disagree on some of the solutions.

Appendix B

Writing Case Studies

Writing a case study may not be as simple as it first appears. It is important to choose an actual event that has at least one major issue to be resolved. The writer must also be able to get enough information about the case so as to present the issues clearly. The case may come from the writer's own experience, or it may come from information available to the writer from other sources. It is important to remember, however, that the case or event must be essentially factual. Hypothetical and contrived cases have been shown to be almost completely unsuccessful as a teaching device. Perhaps this is because just as "truth is stranger than fiction," reality is also more complex than fiction.

Normally a case is written in the third person. The case writer is more like a reporter than an artist, because the success of the case depends to a large measure on the degree of objectivity achieved by the writer. In other words, the writer must be completely impartial in presenting the facts of the case, thus encouraging the reader to make his or her own decisions about the issues. It is especially important that the writer avoid value judgments in describing the case. For example:

WRONG: Gopal was a good teacher.

RIGHT: Gopal's students said he was a good teacher.

Just as a good reporter has to "dig for the facts," a case writer must do careful research that may require reading, personal interviews, and writing letters to get information. In some cases, the issues being discussed are of a highly sensitive nature, and the writer must take care not to insult or antagonize any of the parties involved. One way to avoid trouble is to change all the names and places described. This is best done after the writer has first written the case with the real names, so that the writing does not become stilted or sound artificial.

266.0092

H6 33 264

LINCOLN CHRISTIAN COLLEGE AND SEMINARY

77856

Whenever possible, permission should be secured from the major people involved in the case. Of course, if the facts of the case are common knowledge, there is less need for such protection than if the information was gained from a private source.

The writer should begin the case by clearly describing the setting. This would include the date, time, and place of the events in the story. Very near the beginning, the writer should allow the reader to see the major question to be resolved. This may be done through a direct statement of the dilemma by the writer, or by having the character involved make the statement. After this initial statement of the crisis, the writer should go back to the beginning to show how the problem originated and what events led up to the present critical situation. This is called the development of the case. Finally, there should be a restatement of the problem. In summary, the three main parts of a written case are:

1. The statement of the dilemma and its setting
2. The development of the case
3. A restatement of the problem

The end of the written case will depend upon the circumstances. Sometimes, if the writer knows how the issue was resolved, she or he may wish to include this at the end of the account. Usually, it is best to end the case at the point of the high tension of decision, for this will encourage more discussion and debate when the case is taught.

Bibliography

Case Study Institute, and Association of Theological Schools. 1981. *Cases in theological education.* Compiled by Garth Rosell.

Evans, Robert A., and Parker, Thomas D., eds. 1976. *Christian theology: A case method approach.* New York: Harper & Row.

Evans, Robert and Alice, and Weeks, Louis and Carolyn. 1977. *Casebook for Christian living.* John Knox Press.

Glasse, James D. 1972. *Putting it together in the parish.* Nashville: Abingdon.

Rogers, Jack, et al. 1977. *Case studies in Christ and salvation.* Philadelphia: Westminster Press.

Williams, Oliver, and Houch, John. 1978. Cases in Christian business ethics. New York: Harper & Row.

Information on the case-study method and examples of cases involving a wide range of topics can be obtained from the Case Study Institute, Intercollegiate Case Clearing House, Soldiers Field, Boston, MA 02163.